Toni Morrison's

Beloved

MODERN CRITICAL INTERPRETATIONS

Toni Morrison's

Beloved

Edited and with an Introduction by

Harold Bloom

Viva Books

New Delhi | Mumbai | Chennai | Kolkata | Bengaluru | Hyderabad | Kochi | Guwahati

First Indian Edition 2007
Reprinted 2011

VIVA BOOKS PRIVATE LIMITED

- 4737/23 Ansari Road, Daryaganj, New Delhi 110 002
  E-mail: vivadelhi@vivagroupindia.net, Tel. 42242200
- 76, Service Industries, Shirvane, Sector 1, Nerul, Navi Mumbai 400 706
  E-mail: vivamumbai@vivagroupindia.net, Tel. 27721273, 27721274
- Jamals Fazal Chambers, 26 Greams Road, Chennai 600 006
  E-mail: vivachennai@vivagroupindia.net, Tel. 28290304, 28294241
- B-103, Jindal Towers, 21/1A/3 Darga Road, Kolkata 700 017
  E-mail: vivakolkata@vivagroupindia.net, Tel. 22836381, 22816713
- 7, Sovereign Park Apartments, 56-58, K. R. Road, Basavanagudi, Bengaluru 560 004
  E-mail: vivabangalore@vivagroupindia.net, Tel. 26607409, 26607410
- 101-102 Mughal Marc Aptt., 3-4-637 to 641, Narayanguda, Hyderabad 500 029
  E-mail: vivahyderabad@vivagroupindia.net, Tel. 27564481, 27564482
- First Floor, Beevi Towers, SRM Road, Kaloor, Kochi 682 018, Kerala
  E-mail: vivakochi@vivagroupindia.net, Tel: 0484-2403055, 2403056
- 232, GNB Road, Beside UCO Bank, Silpukhuri, Guwahati 781 003
  E-mail: vivaguwahati@vivagroupindia.net, Tel: 0361-2666386

Published by arrangement with:

Facts on File, Inc.
132 West 31st Street
New York NY 10001
USA

ISBN : 978-81-309-1888-4

Published by Vinod Vasishtha for Viva Books Private Limited, 4737/23, Ansari Road, Daryaganj New Delhi - 110 002. Printed and bound by Anand Sons, Delhi - 110 092.

Contents

Editor's Note

This volume gathers together a representative selection of essays on Toni Morrison's most celebrated volume, *Beloved*. The editor's "Introduction" is rather at variance with the essays, since I express some reservations as to the lasting aesthetic value of *Beloved*.

Two book reviews, by Margaret Atwood and Roger Sale, express judgments of *Beloved* different from my own. Marilyn Sanders Mobley begins the sequence of ideological essays by insisting that traditional views of canonical literary value have no relevance to *Beloved*. For Susan Bowers, Morrison's novel belongs to a new apocalyptic genre, while David Lawrence considers the ghostly aspects of Morrison's tale.

Bernard W. Bell invokes the genre of slave narratives, after which Stephanie A. Demetrakopoulos sees *Beloved* as a critique of maternal bonds.

Three essays regard *Beloved* as a triumphant historical recovery of the realities of slavery in America: Linda Krumholz, Elizabeth Fox-Genovese, and Ashraf H.A. Rushdy.

The supposed genre of the post-apocalyptic is invoked by Josef Pesch, while Caroline Rody joins the other essayists in praising Morrison's historical vision.

For James Berger, *Beloved* marks the obsolescence of liberal views of race relations, after which Pamela E. Barnett concludes this volume of ideological critiques by lauding Morrison's fusion of the images of rape and of ghosts.

Introduction

The cultural importance of Toni Morrison's most popular novel, *Beloved* (1987) hardly can be overstressed. I have just reread it, after a decade, in a paperback printing numbered 41, and in time doubtless there will be hundreds of reprintings. Of all Morrison's novels, it puzzles me most: the style is remarkably adroit, baroque in its splendor, and the authority of the narrative is firmly established. The characters are problematic, for me; unlike the protagonists of Morrison's earlier novels, they suggest ideograms. I think that is because *Beloved* is a powerfully tendentious romance; it has too clear a design upon its readers, of whatever race and gender. The storyteller of *Sula* (1975) and of *Song of Solomon* (1977) has been replaced by a formidable ideologue, who perhaps knows too well what she wishes her book to accomplish.

Morrison strongly insists that her literary context is essentially African American, and *Beloved* overtly invokes slave narratives as its precursors. I hardly doubt that the novel's stance is African-American feminist Marxist, as most of the exegetes reprinted in this volume proclaim. And yet the style and narrative procedures have more of a literary relationship to William Faulkner and Virginia Woolf, than to any African-American writers. I am aware that such an assertion risks going against Morrison's own warning "that finding or imposing Western influences in/on Afro-American literature had value provided the valued process does not become self-anointing." I mildly observe (since both my personal and critical esteem for Morrison is enormous) that "finding *or* imposing" (italics of course mine) is a very shrewd equivocation. Morrison, both in prose style and in narrative mode, has a complex and permanent relationship to Faulkner and to Woolf. *Beloved*, in a long perspective, is a child of Faulkner's masterpiece, *As I Lay Dying*, while the heroine, Sethe, has more in common with Lena Grove of *Light in August* than with any female character of African-American fiction. This is anything but a limitation, aesthetically considered, but is rejected by Morrison and her critical disciples alike. Ideology aside, Morrison's fierce assertion of independence is the norm for any strong writer, but I do not think that this denial of a swerve from indubitable literary origins can be a critical value in itself.

None of this would matter if the ideologies of political correctness were not so deeply embedded in *Beloved* as to make Sethe a less persuasive representation of a possible human being than she might have been. Trauma has much less to do with Sethe's more-than-Faulknerian sense of guilt than the novel's exegetes have argued. The guilt of being a survivor is not unique to any oppressed people; programs in guilt are an almost universal temptation. *Beloved* is a calculated series of shocks; whether the memory of shock is aesthetically persuasive has to seem secondary in a novel dedicated to the innumerable victims of American slavery. One steps very warily in raising the aesthetic issue in regard to a book whose moral and social value is beyond dissent. Still, Sethe is a character in a visionary romance that also insists upon its realistic and historical veracity. A literary character has to be judged finally upon the basis of literary criteria, which simply are not "patriarchal" or "capitalistic" or "Western imperialist." Morrison, whose earlier novels were not as over-determined by ideological considerations as *Beloved* is, may have sacrificed much of her art upon the altar of a politics perhaps admirable in itself, but not necessarily in the service of high literature (if one is willing to grant that such an entity still exists.)

The terrors depicted in *Beloved* may be beyond the capacity of literary representation itself, which is an enigma that has crippled every attempt to portray the Nazi slaughter of European Jewry. The African-American critic Stanley Crouch has been much condemned for expressing his disdain in regard to *Beloved*. Crouch, I think, underestimated the book's stylistic achievement, but his healthy distrust of ideologies is alas germane to aspects of *Beloved*. Sentimentalism is not in one sense relevant to *Beloved*: how can any emotion be in excess of its object, when slavery is the object? And yet the novel's final passage about Sethe could prove, some day, to be a kind of period piece:

> He is staring at the quilt but he is thinking about her wrought-iron back; the delicious mouth still puffy at the corner from Ella's fist. The mean black eyes. The wet dress steaming before the fire. Her tenderness about his neck jewelry—its three wands, like attentive baby rattlers, curving two feet into the air. How she never mentioned or looked at it, so he did not have to feel the shame of being collared like a beast. Only this woman Sethe

> could have left him his manhood like that. He wants to put his story next to hers.
>
> "Sethe," he says, "me and you, we got more yesterday than anybody. We need some kind of tomorrow."
>
> He leans over and takes her hand. With the other he touches her face. "You your best thing, Sethe. You are." His holding fingers are holding hers.
>
> "Me? Me?"

The pathos is admirable, rather too much so. Sethe is given the explicit tribute that the entire book has sought to constitute. She is the heroic African-American mother, who has survived terrors both natural and supernatural, and has maintained her integrity and her humanity. Morrison's design has been fulfilled, but is Sethe a person or an abstraction? Time will sift this matter out; cultural politics do not answer such a question. Morrison must be judged finally, in *Beloved*, against *As I Lay Dying* and *Mrs. Dalloway*, rather than against Harriet Jacobs's *Incidents in the Life of a Slave Girl* (1861). The canonical novelist of *Song of Solomon* deserves no less.

MARGARET ATWOOD

Haunted by Their Nightmares

Beloved is Toni Morrison's fifth novel, and another triumph. Indeed, Ms. Morrison's versatility and technical and emotional range appear to know no bounds. If there were any doubts about her stature as a pre-eminent American novelist, of her own or any other generation, *Beloved* will put them to rest. In three words or less, it's a hair-raiser.

In *Beloved*, Ms. Morrison turns away from the contemporary scene that has been her concern of late. This new novel is set after the end of the Civil War, during the period of so-called Reconstruction, when a great deal of random violence was let loose upon blacks, both the slaves freed by Emancipation and others who had been given or had bought their freedom earlier. But there are flashbacks to a more distant period, when slavery was still a going concern in the South and the seeds for the bizarre and calamitous events of the novel were sown. The setting is similarly divided: the countryside near Cincinnati, where the central characters have ended up, and a slaveholding plantation in Kentucky, ironically named Sweet Home, from which they fled 18 years before the novel opens.

There are many stories and voices in this novel, but the central one belongs to Sethe, a woman in her mid-30's, who is living in an Ohio farmhouse with her daughter, Denver, and her mother-in-law Baby Suggs. *Beloved* is such a unified novel that it's difficult to discuss it without giving away the

---

plot, but it must be said at the outset that it is, among other things, a ghost story, for the farmhouse is also home to a sad, malicious and angry ghost, the spirit of Sethe's baby daughter. who had her throat cut under appalling circumstances eighteen years before, when she was two. We never know this child's full name, but we—and Sethe—think of her as Beloved, because that is what is on her tombstone. Sethe wanted "Dearly Beloved," from the funeral service, but had only enough strength to pay for one word. Payment was ten minutes of sex with the tombstone engraver. This act, which is recounted early in the novel, is a keynote for the whole book: in the world of slavery and poverty, where human beings are merchandise, everything has its price and price is tyrannical.

"Who would have thought that a little old baby could harbor so much rage?" Sethe thinks, but it does; breaking mirrors, making tiny handprints in cake icing, smashing dishes and manifesting itself in pools of blood-red light. As the novel opens, the ghost is in full possession of the house, having driven away Sethe's two young sons. Old Baby Suggs, after a lifetime of slavery and a brief respite of freedom—purchased for her by the Sunday labor of her son Halle, Sethe's husband—has given up and died. Sethe lives with her memories, almost all of them bad. Denver, her teen-age daughter, courts the baby ghost because, since her family has been ostracized by the neighbors, she doesn't have anyone else to play with.

The supernatural element is treated, not in an "Amityville Horror," watch-me-make-your-flesh-creep mode, but with magnificent practicality, like the ghost of Catherine Earnshaw in *Wuthering Heights*. All the main characters in the book believe in ghosts, so it's merely natural for this one to be there. As Baby Suggs says, "Not a house in the country ain't packed to its rafters with some dead Negro's grief. We lucky this ghost is a baby. My husband's spirit was to come back in here? or yours? Don't talk to me. You lucky." In fact, Sethe would rather have the ghost there than not there. It is, after all, her adored child, and any sign of it is better, for her, than nothing.

This grotesque domestic equilibrium is disturbed by the arrival of Paul D., one of the "Sweet Home men" from Sethe's past. The Sweet Home men were the male slaves of the establishment. Their owner, Mr. Garner, is no Simon Legree; instead he's a best-case slave-holder, creating his "property" well, trusting them, allowing them choice in the running of his small plantation, and calling them "men" in defiance of the neighbors, who want all male blacks to be called "boys." But Mr. Garner dies, and weak, sickly Mrs. Garner brings in her handiest male relative, who is known as "the schoolteacher." This Goebbels-like paragon combines viciousness with intellectual pretensions; he's a sort of master-race proponent who measures the heads of the slaves and tabulates the results to demonstrate that they are more like animals than people. Accompanying him are his two sadistic and repulsive nephews. From there it's all downhill at Sweet Home, as the slaves try to escape, go crazy or are murdered. Sethe, in a trek that makes the icefloe scene in *Uncle Tom's Cabin* look like a stroll around the block, gets out, just barely; her husband, Halle, doesn't. Paul D. does, but has some very unpleasant adventures along the way, including a literally nauseating sojourn in a nineteenth-century Georgia chain gang.

Through the different voices and memories of the book, including that of Sethe's mother, a survivor of the infamous slave-ship crossing, we experience American slavery as it was lived by those who were its objects of exchange, both at its best—which wasn't very good—and at its worst, which was as bad as can be imagined. Above all, it is seen as one of the most viciously antifamily institutions human beings have ever devised. The slaves are motherless, fatherless, deprived of their mates, their children, their kin. It is a world in which people suddenly vanish and are never seen again, not through accident or covert operation or terrorism, but as a matter of everyday legal policy.

Slavery is also presented to us as a paradigm of how most people behave when they are given absolute power over other people. The first effect, of course, is that they start believing in their own superiority and justifying their actions by it. The second effect is that they make a cult of the inferiority of those they subjugate. It's no coincidence that the first of the deadly sins, from which all the others were supposed to stem, is Pride, a sin of which Sethe is, incidentally, also accused.

In a novel that abounds in black bodies—headless, hanging from trees, frying to a crisp, locked in woodsheds for purposes of rape, or floating downstream drowned—it isn't surprising that the "whitepeople," especially the men, don't come off too well. Horrified black children see whites as men "without skin." Sethe thinks of them as having "mossy teeth" and is ready, if necessary, to bite off their faces, and worse, to avoid further mossytoothed outrages. There are a few whites who behave with something approaching decency. There's Amy, the young runaway indentured servant who helps Sethe in childbirth during her flight to freedom, and incidentally reminds the reader that the nineteenth century, with its child labor, wage slavery and widespread and accepted domestic violence, wasn't tough only for blacks, but for all but the most privileged whites as well. There are also the abolitionists who help Baby Suggs find a house and a job after she is freed. But even the decency of these "good" whitepeople has a grudging side to it, and even they have trouble seeing the people they are helping as full-fledged people, though to show them as totally free of their xenophobia and sense of superiority might well have been anachronistic.

Toni Morrison is careful nor to make all the whites awful and all the blacks wonderful. Sethe's black neighbors, for instance, have their own envy and scapegoating tendencies to answer for, and Paul D., though much kinder than, for instance, the woman-bashers of Alice Walker's novel *The Color Purple*, has his own limitations and flaws. But then, considering what he's been through, it's a wonder he isn't a mass murderer. If anything, he's a little too huggable, under the circumstances.

Back in the present tense, in chapter one, Paul D. and Sethe make an attempt to establish a "real" family, whereupon the baby ghost, feeling excluded, goes berserk, but is driven out by Paul D.'s stronger will. So it appears. But then, along comes a strange, beautiful, real flesh-and-blood young woman, about twenty years old, who can't seem to remember where she comes from, who talks like a young child, who has an odd, raspy voice and no lines on her hands, who takes an intense, devouring interest in Sethe, and who says her name is Beloved.

Students of the supernatural will admire the way this twist is handled. Ms. Morrison blends a knowledge of folklore—for instance, in many traditions, the dead cannot return from the grave unless called, and it's the passions of the living that keep them alive—with a highly original treatment. The reader is kept guessing; there's a lot more to Beloved than any one character can see, and she manages to be many things to several people. She is a catalyst for revelations as well as self-revelations; through her we come to know not only how, but why, the original child Beloved was killed. And through her also Sethe achieves, finally, her own form of self-exorcism, her own self-accepting peace.

Beloved is written in an antiminimalist prose that is by turns rich, graceful, eccentric, rough, lyrical, sinuous, colloquial and very much to the point. Here, for instance, is Sethe remembering Sweet Home:

> . . . suddenly there was Sweet Home rolling, rolling, rolling out before her eyes, and although there was not a leaf on that farm that did not want to make her scream, it rolled itself out before her in shameless beauty. It never looked as terrible as it was and it made her wonder if hell was a pretty place too. Fire and brimstone all right, but hidden in lacy groves. Boys hanging from the most beautiful sycamores in the world. It shamed her—remembering the wonderful soughing trees rather than the boys. Try as she might to make it otherwise, the sycamores beat out the children every time and she could not forgive her memory for that.

In this book, the other world exists and magic works, and the prose is up to it. If you can believe page one—and Ms. Morrison's verbal authority compels belief—you're hooked on the rest of the book.

The epigraph to *Beloved* is from the Bible, Romans 9:25: "I will call them my people, which were not my people; and her beloved, which was not beloved." Taken by itself, this might seem to favor doubt about, for instance, the extent to which Beloved was really loved, or the extent to which Sethe herself was rejected by her own community. But there is more to it than that. The passage is from a chapter in which the Apostle Paul ponders, Job-like, the ways of God toward humanity, in particular the evils and inequities visible everywhere on the earth. Paul goes on to talk about the fact that the Gentiles, hitherto despised and outcast, have now been redefined as acceptable. The passage proclaims, not rejection, but reconciliation and hope. It continues: "And it shall come to pass, that in the place where it was said unto them, Ye are not my people; there shall they be called the children of the living God."

Toni Morrison is too smart, and too much of a writer, not to have intended this context. Here, if anywhere, is her own comment on the goings-on in her novel, her final response to the measuring and dividing and excluding "schoolteachers" of this world. An epigraph to a book is like a key signature in music, and *Beloved* is written in major.

ROGER SALE

Morrison's Beloved

Among the score of American novels of last year that I read, *the* book is Toni Morrison's *Beloved.* Not without hue and cry: there was Stanley Crouch's very sour review in *The New Republic*, which itself caused a storm, and I have had some heated conversations about it with my colleague, Charles Johnson, whose *Being and Race: Black Writing since 1970* reveals a fine shrewd mind on every page. Not without reservation either. *Beloved* was written in the palace of Art, its ways with history are like those of *Nostromo* or Ford's *Fifth Queen* series, its verbal texture is as rich as that of *Mrs. Dalloway*, and Morrison is thereby heir to more problems than she perhaps knows. No matter. This is a major book.

Here are the opening sentences:

> 124 was spiteful. Full of a baby's venom. The women in the house knew it and so did the children. For years each put up with the spite in his own way, but by 1873 Sethe and her daughter Denver were its only victims. The grandmother, Baby Suggs, was dead, and the sons, Howard and Buglar, had run away by the time they were thirteen years old—as soon as merely looking in a mirror shattered it (that was the signal for Buglar); as soon as two tiny hand prints appeared in the cake (that was it for Howard).

From *Massachusetts Review* 29:1 (Spring 1988).

Finish the book and reread this and you know that 124 is a house, Sethe and Denver are the central characters, Baby Suggs is the most memorable minor character since one of Faulkner's, Howard and Buglar never reappear, and the baby with the venom "is" the "almost crawling? baby" *and* the Beloved of the title.

But the art is right there for the first-time readers. Morrison tosses many balls in the air in these five sentences without telling us which ones to make sure to watch. She gives us many different ways of dealing with time—"for years," "by 1873," "thirteen years old," without telling us how, or how soon, each might matter. By the time we have gotten to Howard and the hand prints, Morrison has so enmeshed us in verbal machinery that it is not easy to remember, let alone feel any impact from "spiteful" in the first sentence or "venom" in the second. What did Howard see in the hand prints, or Buglar in the mirror? How many years had these boys put up with the spite of the baby's venom? Everything in Morrison's way of rendering creates distance, a sense that she will in her own sweet time tell us all she thinks we need to know and no more. And, by the end of the novel the hand prints and the face are still unclear to me, and I've read *Beloved* twice, once aloud.

So Stanley Crouch is out of court when he calls the novel a soap opera. In a soap we are supposed to respond, fully, directly, and right now, to each scene put in front of us, while for long stretches of *Beloved* we simply don't know how to do this, because we don't know yet what we're seeing. Crouch is just finding an easy way to put the book down. For the same reason, he is quite mistaken when he suggests this is like a Holocaust novel (for Concentration Camps read Slavery). There are horrible images of things that happened to slaves here, no question. Sethe is held down and milked by some young men, one of her companions is bridled and bitted like a mule and spends a horrible stretch in a chain gang, another is burned alive after being caught trying to escape. But Morrison's art makes us gasp at these moments, then insists we not organize our feeling as if for protest or other action, but instead move back into the heavy verbal texture of her fiction.

There is a fundamental objection to writers and books where the author is so openly and powerfully in control; it is the one made by Lawrence to Mann and Flaubert about the will of the artist to be superior to the materials being created and worked with. In this respect, I felt no difficulty with *Beloved*, no sense that it is the intent of Morrison's art to show off its own ability and power. She works very much, though in her own way, in the service of person, scene, situation, life; it's just that her way is not that of dramatic realism.

I can, however, state a similar objection that may prove more germane. Morrison is so constantly telling you and not telling you, telling you a bit more but leaving you wondering if you've missed something, that she encourages, almost forces, readers to read too fast, to rush ahead to the clarifying moments. The book became a page turner for me the first time through. My guess is that the result will be some enthralled readers who will end up unsure what they have read, and perhaps a smaller number—and my money is on their being mostly men—of unenchanted ones who end up praising Morrison's lyric gifts and claiming that as a novel it is mostly a trick. So some of the hue and cry may be built into the nature of Morrison's art and its relation to its readers. Not everyone is going to find out how beautifully this book reads when read slowly, and in small doses.

That said, let the rest be praise:

> "Where I was before I came here, that place is real. It's never going away. Even if the whole farm—every tree and grass blade of it dies . . . if you go there—you who never was there—if you go there and stand in the place where it was, it will happen again; it will be there for you, waiting for you. So, Denver, you can't ever go there. Never. Because even though it's all over—over and done with—it's going to always be there waiting for you. That's how come I had to get all my children out. No matter what."

And that's how come Sethe is willing to murder her children rather than have them taken back when a slavecatcher comes after they've escaped and are living at 124, in a house not far from Cincinnati.

Not since time past, present, and future in "Burnt Norton," maybe, has someone played such games for us about time. But Eliot offers us propositions, and Sethe gives us, at once, insistent perplexity and insistent assurance. The farm is Sweet Home, Kentucky, where Sethe was a slave; she is speaking to Denver, who was born after Sethe escaped. That Sweet Home lives for Sethe, and would even if it were in fact destroyed, we understand as memory. But Sethe has another word, "rememory," that seems at times just another word like "remember," but here it is Seth's memory as it would happen to Denver if she went to Sweet Home. "It will be . . . waiting for you," so "You can't never go there" or else you will know what happened to me there.

As a proposition I'm not sure what to make of it, what I "believe." But *Beloved* is not concerned with propositions but with experience, and at this point (we are on p. 37) we have two propositions that for Sethe are experiences: "124 was spiteful. Full of a baby's venom," and "That's how come I had to get all my children out" of Sweet Home and of my memory of my life as a slave. She is saying, in effect, though I doubt if even the shrewdest reader can take it in, "You are living in this spiteful house, full of a baby's venom, because *that* rememory is preferable to the one you would, or will, face the moment you see Sweet Home and my rememory of it." There seems something a little crazy here, though we are far from knowing if that is an appropriate word. But if we cannot take it in, we can engage in the story, in our finding out.

Now let me add Paul D, who has been engaged in a counter activity, the keeping dead of memory as much as Sethe is keeping memory alive. Paul D was a slave at Sweet Home, he is the one who is bitted like a mule, who endures the chain gang, who escapes and is told, since it is February, "follow the tree flowers" that will keep telling him where north is. He spends eighteen years wandering, all the time learning to forget, and not to know what he once felt:

> It was some time before he could put Alfred, Georgia, Sixo, schoolteacher, Halle, his brothers, Sethe, Mister, the taste of iron, the sight of butter, the smell of hickory, notebook paper, one by one, into the tobacco tin lodged in his chest. By the time he got to 124 nothing in this world could pry it open.

It would be fun to show how all the items on that list come into the novel even as Paul D is trying to lock them away into the tobacco tin in his chest. But that would take too long, and I must settle for saying that when Paul D comes to 124, he senses immediately that the house is spiteful, haunted with rememory, though he is told little about the baby's venom. Dedicated to killing the past, he exorcises the ghost of the house: "Holding the table by two legs, he bashed it about, wrecking everything, screaming back at the screaming house. 'You want to fight, come on! God damn it! She got enough without you. She got enough!'" Then "it was gone," Paul D takes Sethe up to her bed, and the next day Sethe begins to think she might be able to plan her days, her life, ahead a little. But shortly thereafter the mysterious Beloved appears, an intent young woman who is just the age the baby with the venom would have been had Sethe not murdered her to keep her from the slave-catcher. So the house is once again haunted.

The rest of the novel shows the struggle of Beloved and Paul D for Sethe, who loves Paul D but who is so ravaged by guilt and her rememory, that for a long stretch Paul D must leave 124 and let Beloved reign there, so it is not Paul D but Denver who finally sets in motion the events that bring the story to its climax. When Stanley Crouch comes to his senses, he will have to examine his motives in linking Morrison and *Beloved* with Alice Walker and *The Color Purple* concerning their treatment of black men. Since Morrison not only treats Paul D with admiration and respect—at a number of points one is grateful indeed for his presence among a group of women who seem almost lunatic—but reserves for him some of her most lavish and loving prose. My guess is that Crouch's feelings follow a logic similar to this: *The Color Purple* is a not very good novel that was adored by black women and white folks; it looks as though the same thing will happen with *Beloved*; if I can suggest that Morrison is "not good about" black men too, maybe I can get away with calling *Beloved* trite and sentimental; Morrison has a lot more talent than Walker, and I need to stop this stampede—call them "feminists" as if that *were* a dirty word—soon. Crouch got one thing right: *The Color Purple* is not a very good novel, though I see no reason to call it a bad novel, and in any event, it is irrelevant to consideration of *Beloved*. And among the things Crouch could not dare do in his review is quote from the scenes between Paul D and the Underground Railroad worker with the wonderful name of Stamp Paid.

It is Toni Morrison's ambition to create a form, and a storytelling, that keeps alive the struggle to remember, the need to forget, and the inability to forget. Something terrible happened, and keeps happening, and it is not entirely clear what, or even when. Though the events of *Beloved* could be arranged to make a drama, though there is a grand climatic scene, the book is elegy, pastoral, sad, sweet, mysterious.

I trace part of a thread: way back, about as far back as the novel's memory goes, a slave named Halle got permission from his owner to work for pay on Sundays so that, years later, after Halle had married Sethe, he could buy freedom for his mother, Baby Suggs. With the help of the whites who own the house, Baby Suggs had come to live at 124—so that 124 is where Halle and Sethe will come after they escape, except they are separated and Sethe arrives alone. Baby Suggs had "decided that, because slave life had 'busted her legs, back, head, eyes, hands, kidneys, womb and tongue,' she had nothing left to make a living with but her heart," and she becomes a preacher:

> The company watched her from the trees. They knew she was ready when she put her stick down. Then she shouted, "Let the children come!" and they ran from the trees toward her.
>
> "Let your mothers hear you laugh," she told them, and the woods rang. The adults looked on and could not help smiling.
>
> Then "Let grown men come," she shouted. They stepped out one by one from among the ringing trees.
>
> "Let your wives and children see you dance," she told them, and groundlife shuddered under their feet.
>
> Finally, she called the women to her. "Cry," she told them.

> "For the living and the dead. Just cry." And without covering their eyes the women let loose.
>
> It started that way: laughing children, dancing men, crying women and then it got mixed up. Women stopped crying and danced; men sat down and cried; children danced, women laughed, children cried until, exhausted and riven, all and each lay about the Clearing damp and gasping for breath. In the silence that followed, Baby Suggs, holy, offered up to them her great big heart.

But this rememory, called up because Paul D's arrival, which killed the ghost, forced Sethe to tell herself she would never see Halle again: "Why now, with Paul D instead of the ghost, was she breaking up? getting scared? needing Baby? The worst was over, wasn't it?"

No, because other parts of the past can reach out and clutch like the tentacles of an octopus, because Beloved is there to cast a spell over Sethe, because Denver must finally seize the day, because Paul D, who had locked the tobacco tin of his past in his chest, must come to remember. Yet there does come a time when the worst indeed is over:

> "Sethe," Paul D says, "me and you, we got more yesterday than anybody. We need some kind of tomorrow."
>
> He leans over and takes her hand. With the other he touches her face. "You your best thing, Sethe. You are." His holding fingers are holding hers.
>
> "Me? Me?"

Paul D is strong here because he has remembered what another slave had said, twenty years ago, about his woman, "She is a friend of my mind," and so Paul D can know what Sethe is for him. And she, bewildered, loved, can now forget. It's a long and beautiful tale.

MARILYN SANDERS MOBLEY

A Different Remembering: Memory, History and Meaning in Toni Morrison's Beloved

> ***The slave woman ought not to be judged by the same standards as others.***
> —HARRIET JACOBS, *Incidents in the Life of a Slave Girl*

> ***. . . when we get a little farther away from the conflict, some brave and truth-loving man, with all the facts before him . . . will gather . . . the scattered fragments . . . and give to those who shall come after us an impartial history of this the grandest moral conflict of the century. {For} Truth is patient and time is just.***
> —FREDERICK DOUGLASS

> ***Every age re-accentuates in its own way the works of its most immediate past.***
> —MIKHAIL BAKHTIN, "Discourse in the Novel"

In 1974 Toni Morrison edited an often overlooked publication called *The Black Book.* This collection of memorabilia represents 300 years of black history, and not only records the material conditions of black life from slavery to freedom, but also exhibits the black cultural production that grew out of and in spite of these conditions. Compiled in scrapbook fashion, it contains everything from bills of sale for slaves to jazz and poetry. Through diverse images of black life presented in such items as photos of lynchings, sharecropping families and slave-made quilts, and encoded in excerpts from such sources as slave narratives, folk sayings and black newspapers, *The Black Book* tells a complex story of oppression, resistance and survival. More importantly, it was published at a moment in American history when many feared that the Black Power movement of the 1960s and early 1970s would be reduced to faddish rhetoric and mere image rather than understood for its cultural and political implications. Morrison herself feared the movement propounded a kind of historical erasure or denial of those aspects of the past which could not be easily assimilated into its rhetorical discourse or into the collective consciousness of black people as a group. She feared, for example, that the rhetoric of the movement, in its desire to create a new version of history that would affirm the African past and the heroic deeds of a few great men, had inadvertently bypassed the equally heroic deeds of ordinary African-Americans who had resisted and survived the painful traumas of slavery. In other words, she questioned what she perceived to be a romanticization of both the African past and the American past that threatened to devalue 300 years of black life on American soil before it was fully recorded, examined or understood for its complexity and significance. Thus, *The Black Book* was a literary intervention in the historical dialogue of the period to attest to "Black life as lived" experience.

What is particularly pertinent, however, is that in the process of editing *The Black Book*, Morrison discovered the story that would become the basis of her fifth novel, *Beloved*. Indeed, on the tenth page of *The Black Book* is a copy of a news article, "A Visit to the Slave Mother Who Killed Her Child," that documents the historical basis for what would later become Morrison's most challenging fictional project. Although the relevance of history informs all her novels from *The Bluest Eye* to *Tar Baby*, it is in *Beloved* that history simultaneously becomes both theme and narrative process. In other words, *Beloved* dramatizes the complex relationship between history and memory by shifting from lived experience as documented in *The Black Book* to remembered experience as represented in the novel.

Yet the intertextual relationship between *The Black Book* and *Beloved* is not the only one that can illuminate the compelling intricacies of this novel. Several reviewers place it in the American literary tradition with intertextual connections to Harriet Beecher Stowe's *Uncle Tom's Cabin* (1852). Others compare Morrison's narrative strategies to those of William Faulkner, who incidentally, along with Virginia Woolf, was the subject of her master's thesis. Certainly, the thematics of guilt and the complex fragmentation of time that shape Morrison's fiction are inherent in Faulkner's writing, as well as in the work of many other white authors of the American literary tradition. Yet Morrison's own expressed suspicions of critical efforts to place her in a white literary tradition are instructive. She explains:

> Most criticism . . . justifies itself by identifying black writers with some already accepted white writer . . . I find such criticism dishonest because it never goes into the work on its own terms. It comes from some other place and finds content outside of the work and wholly irrelevant to it to support the work . . . It's merely trying to place the book into an already established literary tradition.

With Morrison's own comments in mind, I would like to suggest that the intertextual relationship between *Beloved* and the slave narratives—the genre that began the African-American literary tradition in prose—offers significant interpretative possibilities for entering the hermeneutic circle of this novel. More specifically, I would like to argue that Morrison uses the trope of memory to revise the genre of the slave narrative and thereby to make the slave experience it inscribes more accessible to contemporary readers. In other words, she uses memory as the metaphorical sign of the interior life to explore and represent dimensions of slave life that the classic slave narrative omitted. By so doing, she seeks to make slavery accessible to readers for whom slavery is not a memory, but a remote historical fact to be ignored, repressed or forgotten. Thus, just as the slave narratives were a form of narrative intervention designed to disrupt the system of slavery, *Beloved* can be read as a narrative intervention that disrupts the cultural notion that the untold story of the black slave mother is, in the words of the novel, "the past something to leave behind."

One of the first observations often made about the slave narratives is the striking similarities that exist among the hundreds of them that were written. In the "Introduction" to *The Classic Slave Narratives*, Henry Louis Gates, Jr., accounts for this phenomenon by reminding us that

> when the ex-slave author decided to write his or her story, he or she did so only after reading and rereading the telling stories of other slave authors who preceded them.

While we cannot know exactly which narratives Morrison read, it is certain that she read widely in the genre and that she is familiar with the two most popular classics—Frederick Douglass's *Narrative* (1845) and Harriet Jacobs's *Incidents in the Life of a Slave Girl* (1861). As prototypical examples of the genre, they adhere to the narrative conventions carefully delineated and described by James Olney. According to him, the vast majority of narratives begin with the three words "I was born" and proceed to provide information about parents, siblings, the cruelty of masters, mistresses and overseers, barriers to literacy, slave auctions, attempts, failures and successes at escaping, name changes, and general reflections on the peculiar institution of slavery. As Valerie Smith points out, however, the important distinction between the narratives of Douglass and Jacobs is that while his narrative not only concerns "the journey from slavery to freedom but also the journey from slavery to manhood," her narrative describes the sexual exploitation that challenged the womanhood of slave women and tells the story of their resistance to that exploitation. *Beloved* contains all these characteristics with several signifying differences. While the classic slave narrative draws on memory as though it is a monologic, mechanical conduit for facts and incidents, Morrison's text foregrounds the dialogic characteristics of memory along with its imaginative capacity to construct and reconstruct the significance of the past. Thus, while the slave narrative characteristically moves in a chronological, linear narrative fashion, *Beloved* meanders through time, sometimes circling back, other times moving vertically, spirally out of time and down into space. Indeed, Morrison's text challenges the Western notion of linear time that informs American history and the slave narratives. It engages the reader not just with the physical, material consequences of slavery, but with the psychological consequences as well. Through the trope of memory, Morrison moves into the psychic consequences of slavery for women, who, by their very existence, were both the means and the source of production. In the words of the text, the slave woman was "property that reproduced itself without cost." Moreover, by exploring this dimension of slavery, Morrison produces a text that is at once very different from and similar to its literary antecedent with its intervention in the cultural, political and social order of black people in general and of black women in particular. What the reader encounters in this text is Morrison as both writer and reader, for inscribed in her writing of the novel is her own "reading"—a revisionary rereading—of the slave's narrative plot of the journey from bondage to freedom. In the process of entering the old text of slavery from "a new critical direction," Morrison discovers what Adrienne Rich refers to as a "whole new psychic geography to be explored," and what Morrison herself identifies as the "interior life of black people under those circumstances." Ultimately, *Beloved* responds to Fredric Jameson's dictum to "always historicize" by illustrating the dynamics of the act of interpretation that memory performs on a regular basis at any given historical moment.

Unlike the slave narratives which sought to be all-inclusive eyewitness accounts of the material conditions of slavery, Morrison's novel exposes the unsaid of the narratives, the psychic subtexts that lie within and beneath the historical facts. In the author's words, she attempts to leave "spaces so the reader can come into it." Critic Steven Mallioux refers to such hermeneutic gaps as places where the text must be "supplemented by its readers before its meaning can be discovered." By examining the use of memory in *Beloved*, we can not only discover to what extent she revises the slave narrative, but also explore how her narrative poetics operate through memory and history to create meaning.

The actual story upon which the novel is based is an 1855 newspaper account of a runaway slave from Kentucky named Margaret Garner. When she realizes she is about to be recaptured in accordance with the Fugitive Slave Law, she kills her child rather than allow it to return to a "future of servitude." Indeed, the story itself involves a conflation of past, present and future in a single act. In the novel, Margaret Garner becomes Sethe, a fugitive slave whose killing of her two-year-old daughter, Beloved, haunts her first as a ghost and later as a physical reincarnation. But time is not so much conflated as fragmented in the fictional rendering of the tale. Moreover, the text contains not only Sethe's story or version of the past, but those of her friend and eventual lover, Paul D, her mother-in-law, Baby Suggs, her remaining child, a daughter named Denver, and later, Beloved herself. Each of their fragments amplifies or modifies Sethe's narrative for the reader. In that the fragments constitute voices which speak to and comment on one another, the text illustrates the call and response pattern of the African-American oral tradition.

The setting of the novel is 1873 in Cincinnati, Ohio, where Sethe resides in a small house with her daughter, Denver. Her mother-in-law, Baby Suggs, has recently died and her two sons, Howard and Buglar, have left home, unable to live any longer in a ghost-haunted house with a mother who seems oblivious or indifferent to the disturbing, disruptive presence. Sethe seems locked in memories of her escape from slavery, the failure of her husband, Halle, to show up at the planned time of escape, her murder of her child, and the Kentucky plantation referred to by its benevolent white slave owner as Sweet Home. One of the Sweet Home men, Paul D, inadvertently arrives on her porch after years of wandering, locked in his own guilt, alienation and shame from the psychic scars of slavery. They become lovers, but more importantly, his arrival initiates the painful plunge into the past through the sharing of their individual stories, memories and experiences. Unable to tolerate the presence of the ghost, however, he drives it away, only to be driven away himself by his inability to cope with Sethe's obsession with Denver, whom he calls a "room-and-board witch." A bond of affection unites Sethe, Denver and Beloved until Denver realizes that her mother has become oblivious to her and has begun to devote her attention exclusively to Beloved. As she watches her mother deteriorate physically and mentally in the grips of overwhelming guilt and consuming love, Denver realizes she must abandon the security of home to get help for her mother and to rid their lives of Beloved once and for all. With the help of the black community, she eventually rescues her mother and Beloved vanishes.

What this cursory synopsis of the plot cannot account for is the ways in which Sethe modifies, amplifies and subverts her own memory of the murder that serves as the locus of the narrative. In fact, even in freedom she lives in a kind of psychic bondage to the task of "keeping the past at bay." While she had murdered Beloved to save her from the future, she raises Denver by "keeping her from the past." The two different manifestations of maternal love are just one source of the novel's narrative tension that evolves from Sethe's response to slavery. The more compelling source of tension lies in the complexity Morrison brings to the normal property of literature Frank Kermode refers to as the "secrecy of narrative." While all texts develop to a certain extent by secrecy or by what information they withhold and gradually release to the reader, the text of *Beloved* moves through a series of narrative starts and stops that are complicated by Sethe's desire to forget or "disremember" the past. Thus, at the same time that the reader seeks to know "the how and why" of Sethe's infanticide, Sethe seeks to withhold that information not only from everyone else, but even from herself. Thus, the early sections of the novel reveal the complex ways in which memories of the past disrupt Sethe's concerted attempt to forget.

The first sign of this tension between remembering and forgetting occurs on the second page of the text in a scene where Denver and Sethe attempt to call the ghost forth. When Denver grows impatient with the seeming reluctance of the ghost to make its presence felt, Sethe cautions her by saying: "You forgetting how little it is . . . She wasn't even two years old when she died." Denver's expression of surprise that a baby can throw such a "powerful spell" is countered in the following passage:

> 'No more powerful than the way I loved her,' Sethe answered and there it was again. The welcoming cool of unchiseled headstones; the one she selected to lean against on tiptoe, her knees wide open as any grave. Pink as a fingernail it was, and sprinkled with glittering chips . . . Counting on the stillness of her own soul, she had forgotten the other one: the soul of her baby girl.

In this passage we have several things occurring at once. First, Sethe's verbalization of love triggers her memory of selecting a tombstone for the baby she murdered. The phrase "there it was again" signals that this is a memory that recurs and that brings the ambivalent emotions of consolation and anguish. Second, the memory of the tombstone triggers her memory of the shameful circumstances of getting it engraved. In this memory, the reality of gender and oppression converge, for the engraver offers to place seven letters—the name "Beloved"—on the headstone in exchange for sex. She also remembers that for ten more minutes, she could have gotten the word "dearly" added. Thirdly, this memory raises the issue around which the entire novel is constructed and which is the consequence and/or responsibility that she must carry for her actions.

Throughout the novel there are similar passages that signal the narrative tension between remembering and forgetting. At various points in the text, a single phrase, a look or the most trivial incident rivets Sethe's attention to the very details of the past she is least ready to confront. In the words of the text, "she worked hard to remember as close to nothing as was safe." In another place the text refers to the "serious work of beating back the past." Moreover, a mindless task such as folding clothes takes on grave significance, as the following passage suggests: "She had to do something with her hands because she was remembering something she had forgotten she knew. Something privately shameful that had seeped into a slit in her mind." Morrison even includes vernacular versions of words to suggest the slaves' own preoccupation with mnemonic processes. For example, at one point "rememory" is used as a noun, when Sethe refers to what Paul D stirs up with his romantic attention to her. Later, the same word is used as a verb, when Sethe begins to come to terms with the past through her relationship with Beloved. She allows her mind to be "busy with the things she could forget" and thinks to herself: "Thank God I don't have to rememory or say a thing." Even the vernacular word for forgetting, "disremember," calls our attention to its binary opposite of remembering.

When Paul D arrives at Sethe's home on 124 Bluestone, Denver seeks to frighten this unwanted guest away by telling him they have a "lonely and rebuked" ghost on the premises. The obsolete meaning of rebuked—repressed—not only suggests that the ghost represents repressed memory, but that, as with anything that is repressed, it eventually resurfaces or returns in one form or another. Paul D's arrival is a return of sorts in that he is reunited with Sethe, his friend from Mr. Garner's Sweet Home plantation. His presence signals an opportunity to share both the positive and negative memories of life there. On the one hand, he and Sethe talk fondly of the "headless bride back behind Sweet Home" and thus share a harmless ghost story of a haunted house. On the other hand, when they remember Sweet Home as a place, they regard it with ambivalence and admit that "it wasn't sweet and it sure wasn't home." Sethe warns against a total dismissal of it, however, by saying: "But it's where we were [and it] comes back whether we want it to or not."

What also comes back through the stories Paul D shares are fragments of history Sethe is unprepared for such as the fact that years ago her husband had witnessed the white boys forcibly take milk from her breasts, but had been powerless to come to her rescue or stop them. Furthermore, his personal stories of enduring a "bit" in his mouth—the barbaric symbol of silence and oppression that Morrison says created a perfect "labor force"—along with numerous other atrocities, such as working on the chain gang, introduce elements of the classic slave narrative into the text. Perhaps more importantly, these elements comprise the signs of history that punctuate the text and that disrupt the text of the mind which is both historical and ahistorical at the same time.

I believe the meaning of Morrison's complex use of the trope of memory becomes most clear in what many readers regard as the most poetic passages in the text. These passages appear in sections two through five of Part Two, where we have a series of interior monologues that become a dialogue among the three central female characters. The first is Sethe's, the second is Denver's, the third is Beloved's and the last one is a merging of all three. Beloved's is the most intriguing, for the text of her monologue contains no punctuation. Instead, there are literal spaces between groups of words that signal the timelessness of her presence as well as the unlived spaces of her life. Earlier in the novel, Sethe even refers to Beloved as "her daughter [who had] . . . come back home from the timeless place." Samples of phrases from Beloved's monologue reveal the meaning of her presence: "[H]ow can I say things that are pictures   I am not separate from her there is no place where I stop   her face is my own . . . all of it is now it is always now." These words suggest not only the seamlessness of time, but the inextricability of the past and present, of ancestors and their progeny. In the last interior "dialogue," the voices of Sethe, Denver and Beloved blend to suggest not only that it is always now, but to suggest that the past, present and future are all one and the same.

In an article entitled "Rediscovering Black History," written on the occasion of the publication of the *The Black Book*, Toni Morrison speaks of the "complicated psychic power one had to exercise to resist devastation." She was speaking, of course, not just of slavery, but of the Black existence in America after slavery as well. *Beloved* and all her novels, to a certain extent, bear witness to this psychic power. It must be stated as I conclude, however, that my intertextual reading of this novel as a revision of the slave narrative should not be construed as an attempt to diminish the form and content of the slave narratives themselves in any way. It is, instead, a recognition of the truth that Gates offers in the introduction to *The Slave's Narrative*:

> Once slavery was abolished, no need existed for the slave to write himself [or herself] into the human community through the action of first-person narration. As Frederick Douglass in 1855 succinctly put the matter, the free human being "cannot see things in the same light with the slave, because he does not and cannot look from the same point from which the slave does" . . . The nature of the narratives, and their rhetorical strategies and import, changed once slavery no longer existed.

Beloved is a complex, contemporary manifestation of this shift. In a larger sense, however, it is what Mikhail Bakhtin calls a "reaccentuation" of the past (in this case, the past of slavery) to discover newer aspects of meaning embedded in the classic slave narrative. Morrison's purpose is not to convince white readers of the slave's humanity, but to address black readers by inviting us to return to the very part of our past that many have repressed, forgotten or ignored. At the end of the novel, after the community has helped Denver rescue her mother from Beloved's ferocious spell by driving her out of town, Paul D returns to Sethe "to put his story next to hers." Despite the psychic healing that Sethe undergoes, however, the community's response to her healing is encoded in the choruslike declaration on the last two pages of the text, that this was "not a story to pass on." Yet, as readers, if we understand Toni Morrison's ironic and subversive vision at all, we know that our response to the text's apparent final call for silence and forgetting is not that at all. Instead, it is an ironic reminder that the process of consciously remembering not only empowers us to tell the difficult stories that must be passed on, but it also empowers us to make meaning of our individual and collective lives as well.

SUSAN BOWERS

Beloved and the New Apocalypse

Toni Morrison's *Beloved* joins a long tradition of African-American apocalyptic writing. Early African-American writers believed that "America, after periods of overwhelming darkness, would lift the veil and eternal sunshine would prevail" (Gayle xiii). By the Harlem Renaissance, African-American writers had begun to doubt a messianic age, but the middle and late 1960s saw a return to apocalypticism, emphasizing Armageddon. Many of these works by such writers as John Williams and John Oliver Killens conceived "the longed-for racial battle" as "the culmination of history and the revelatory moment of justice and retribution" (Bigsby 149). Morrison's novel maps a new direction for the African-American apocalyptic tradition which is both more instructive and potentially more powerful than the end-of-the-world versions of the sixties. She has relocated the arena of racial battle from the streets to the African-American psyche from where the racial memories of Black people have been taken hostage.

Morrison has remarked on the dearth of any "songs or dances or tales" about those who died in the Middle Passage and on what was left out of slave narratives.

> *People who did dwell on it, it probably killed them, and the people who did not dwell on it probably went forward. They tried to make a life. I*

From *The Journal of Ethnic Studies* 18:1 (Spring 1990). © 1990 by The Journal of Ethnic Studies.

> *think that Afro-Americans in rushing away from slavery, which was important to do—it meant rushing out of bondage into freedom—also rushed away from the slaves because it was painful to dwell there, and they may have abandoned some responsibility in so doing.* (Morrison, "In the Realm," 5).

She believes that her "job as a writer in the last quarter of the 20th century, not much more than a hundred years after Emancipation, becomes how to rip that veil drawn over 'proceedings too terrible to relate'" (Walters 60).

The word "apocalypse" means unveiling, and this novel unveils the angry presence of the "disremembered and unaccounted for" (Morrison, *Beloved* 274), those who died from slavery and on the Middle Passage (at least 50% of all Africans on slave ships died between Africa and the American plantations during the 320 years of the slave trade [Mannix 123]).

Apocalypticism is a form of eschatology. The root meaning of *eschaton* is "furthermost boundary" or "ultimate edge" in time or space. Apocalypses can be read

> *as investigations into the edge, the boundary, the interface between radically different realms. If the apocalypse is an unveiling* (**apo** *[from or away],* **kalupsis** *[covering] from* **kalupto** *[to cover], and* **kalumma***[veil]), then clearly the veil is the* **eschaton**, *that which stands between the familiar and whatever lies beyond. In this sense the apocalypse becomes largely a matter of* **seeing**. (Robinson xii-xiii).

The veil or *eschaton* in *Beloved* is forgetting. The etymological sense of "forget" is to miss or lose one's hold. The characters of *Beloved*—and by implication, contemporary African-Americans—have lost touch with those who have died from slavery and even with their own pasts. As a result they have lost part of themselves, their own interior lives. Their struggle is to lift the veil of Lethe to reveal the truth of their personal and collective histories. Morrison fuses Christian notions of apocalypse with West African beliefs to create a revised apocalyptic which principally looks backward, not forward in time, and concentrates on the psychological devastation which began with the horrors of slavery and continued when African-Americans had to let the horrors of the Middle Passage and slavery disappear into the black hole of Lethe, that vortex of forgetting. Working from the foundation of West African philosophy, at the heart of which is communion with ancestors (Campbell 145), Morrison presents an apocalyptic demolition of the boundaries between the earthly and spiritual realms, an invasion of the world of the living by the world beyond the veil. The narrative does not drive toward its apocalyptic moment, but recounts the struggle of living through and beyond the reign of the Anti-Christ and of surviving the "mumbling of the black and angry dead" (*Beloved* 198).

Beloved's focus on the past may seem contrary to the forward-looking spirit of apocalypse, especially in American literature, where the apocalyptic is considered fundamental (Robinson xi). However, African-American apocalypse must be clearly differentiated from White American apocalypse. The fact is that "American apocalypse" is founded on a premise which necessarily excludes African-American writing: that America is the New World, land of rebirth and new life, as opposed to Europe, the Old World of decadence, decay and death. When Europeans discovered America in the sixteenth century, "America was conceived as mankind's last great hope, the Western site of the millenium," and "its future destiny was firmly and prophetically linked with God's plan for the world" (Robinson xi). As a result, most White American apocalyptic literature has been based on the optimistic expectation of historical, material change. The reverse experience, of course, is true for African-Americans. They did not leave an Old World of death and decadence for a New World of hope and rebirth, but were torn from the world of their families, communities, their own spiritual traditions and languages, to be taken to a world of suffering, death, and alienation. The good life lay not before them, but behind them; yet, every attempt was made to crush their memories of the past. Slaves were isolated from other members of their tribes to keep them from communicating in their own languages and maintaining their own traditions. In *Beloved*, only when characters can recover the past do they begin to imagine a future.

One way Morrison avoids the end-of-the-world perspective of most apocalyptic fiction is by basing her novel, like Ralph Ellison's *Invisible Man* (Lewicki 48), on West African philosophy, including the notion of cyclical time. The West African sense of time is part of an organic philosophy that views the world as living—"subject to the law of becoming, of old age and death" (Eliade 45). For such a culture, apocalypse is repeatable and survivable. On the other hand, there can be only one apocalypse if time is conceived of as linear and irreversible as it is in the Judeo-Christian tradition (Zamora 3). The constant circling of the narrative in *Beloved* from present to past and back again enacts the West African perspective and reinforces the importance of the past for both the individual and collective psyche.

Morrison shares with post-Holocaust Jewish artists the monumental difficulties attendant of depicting the victims of racial genocide. What Elie Weisel has stated about the Holocaust applies to the slaughter of ten times as many Africans and African-Americans as the six million Jews killed by Hitler (Morrison has said that 60 million is the smallest figure she had gotten from anyone for the number of slaves who died as a result of slavery [Angelo 120]).

> *The Holocaust is not a subject like all the others. It imposes certain limits. . . . In order not to betray the dead and humiliate the living, this particular subject demands a special sensibility, a different approach, a rigor strengthened by respect and reverence and, above all, faithfulness to memory.* (Wiesel 38)

Betrayal would include sentimentalizing and thus trivializing the victims of slavery, rendering them merely pathetic and pitiable. Morrison does not do that. She dedicated *Beloved* to the "Sixty Million and More," and her novel conjures slaves back to life in many-dimensional characters with a full range of human emotions. They love and hate, sin and forgive, are heroic and mean, self-sacrificing and demanding. They endure incredible hardships to sustain relationships, but the inconceivable brutality and degradation which they experience fractures their communities and inflicts both physical and perhaps irreparable psychological damage on individuals.

One of the questions which *Beloved* asks is whether it is possible to transform unspeakably horrific experiences into knowledge. Is the magnitude of their horror too great to assimilate? Perhaps because the novel asks its readers, especially African-Americans, to "dwell on the horror" which those rushing away from slavery could not, it addresses what happens when the magnitude of that horror is acknowledged, even suggesting how to survive the bringing into consciousness of what has lain hidden for so long. The struggle of *Beloved*'s characters to confront the effects of the brutality and to recover their human dignity, their selves "dirtied" by White oppression—to transform their experiences into knowledge—is presented in the form of a slave narrative that can be read as a model for contemporary readers attempting to engage these brutal realities. Slave narratives emphasize personal quest as a means of "wrest[ing] the black subject out of anonymity, inferiority and brutal disdain" (Willis 213). *Beloved* combines the personal quest theme with the collective memory of racial brutality, for although apocalyptic literature features the destiny of the individual and personal salvation, its "overall perspective is still that of the community" (Russell 27).

It is important to note that *Beloved* is more explicit than most early slave narratives which could not reveal fully the horror of slave experience, either because their authors dared not offend their White abolitionist audiences or because they too could not bear to dwell on the horror. *Beloved* does not subordinate the stories of slave life to abstract ideas, unlike the slave narratives which were usually "sandwiched between white abolitionist documents, suggesting that the slave has precious little control over his or her life—even to its writing" (Sekora 109). Moreover, Morrison's modeling of her novel on the slave narrative is one way of giving African-Americans back their voices. The slave narrative was an extremely popular form of literature until the Civil War. But after the war, the narratives were "expelled from the center of our literary history.

While an editor at Random House, Morrison worked for 18 months in the early 1970s on a project to unveil the reality of African-American life, *The Black Book*, which she called "a genuine Black history book—one that simply recollected Black life as lived" (Morrison, "Behind the Making . . . 89). *The Black Book*, contains what became the germ of *Beloved*: the story of a slave woman in Cincinnati who killed one child and tried to kill the other three, to, in her words, "end their sufferings, [rather] than have them taken back to slavery, and murdered by piecemeal" ("A Visit to the Slave Mother" 10). But this "folk journey of Black America" (Cosby iii) had a far more profound impact upon Morrison than providing her with an initial spark, because it was a model of attempting to tell the truth about a part of African-American life that has been either whitewashed or forgotten, a truth so horrible that it could make a mother see death as desirable for her child.

What *The Black Book* models is an uncensored exposure of brutality through newspaper clippings and photographs of lynchings and burnings of Black people, for instance, juxtaposed with the celebration of African-American strengths and achievements and folkways. Essentially, *The Black Book* models the remembering of African-American experience.

"Rememorying" is what Morrison's characters call it, and it is the central activity in *Beloved*. Because of it the narrative moves constantly back and forth between past and present, mixing time inextricably, as memory escalates its battle against amnesia. The voice of the former slave "above all *remembering* his ordeal in bondage" can be "the single most impressive feature of a slave narrative" (Stepto 1). The characters' rememorying in *Beloved* epitomizes the novel's purpose of conjuring up the spirits and experiences of the past and thus ultimately empowering both characters and readers. *Beloved* pairs the stories of a woman and a man, Sethe and Paul D. Sethe's name may be an allusion to Lethe, the spring of forgetfulness in Greek myth. The past that was too painful for either to remember alone can be recovered together: "Her story was bearable because it was his as well" (*Beloved* 99). Their stories reveal that the worst brutality they have suffered "is less a single act than the systematic denial of the reality of black lives" (Cynthia A. Davis 323), the profound humiliation which both know can be worse than death:

> *That anybody white could take your whole self for anything that came to mind. Not just work, kill, or maim you, but dirty you.* (*Beloved* 251)

Remembering is part of reversing the "dirtying" process that robbed slaves of self-esteem.

The concentration on the horrors of the past and present—the misuse of power, the cruelty and injustice—is characteristic of apocalyptic writing. However, the traditional apocalyptic anticipation of the messianic age—the time of freedom and redemption—is missing among these slaves and ex-slaves for whom hope has come to seem a cruel trick. The members of Paul D's chain gang try to destroy that part of themselves as they crush stone: "They killed the flirt whom folks called Life for leading them on" (*Beloved* 109).

The typical format of the slave narrative is to trace the story of the individual's life in slavery, escape, and the journey to freedom (Willis 220). What Morrison reveals is that the process must be repeated twice: first to leave physical enslavement by whites and the second time to escape the psychological trauma created by their brutality. The physical escapes of both Sethe and Paul D create the patterns for their psychological escapes: archetypal journeys of courage, descents into almost certain death, and rebirths into beauty and freedom. Sethe gives birth with the help of a young White girl when she reaches the Ohio River and thus freedom. Paul D is helped by Cherokees, who "describe the beginning of the world and its end and tell him to follow the tree flowers to the North and freedom (*Beloved* 112).

But the novel opens with characters still traumatized many years after their escapes from slavery. They are numb, almost incapable of emotion because they have suffered so deeply and seen such terror. Sethe and her daughter are literally haunted by the ghost of her murdered baby. Sethe is unable to feel; every morning she sees the dawn, but never acknowledges its color. Paul D experiences his heart as a "tobacco tin lodged in his chest" (*Beloved* 113), which holds the painful memories of his own past, the memories of one friend being burned to death, of others hanging from trees, his brothers being sold and taken away, of being tortured. "By the time he got to 124 nothing in this world could pry it open" (*Beloved* 113). Paul D's arrival at 124, Sethe's home, 18 years after the two had last seen each other, begins their long and excruciating process of thawing frozen feeling.

Contemporary research on treatment for post-traumatic stress syndrome indicates that support and caring from others can help victims to heal, but that the most crucial part of healing is the unavoidable confrontation with the original trauma and feeling the pain again (Brown). *Beloved* enacts that theory. Sethe and Paul D are able to help each other to a point, but until they have intimate contact with the original pain and the feelings it created that had to be suppressed, they cannot be purged of its paralyzing effect.

What breaks open Paul D's tin heart and allows Sethe to see and love color again (color often appears in Morrison's fiction as a sign of the ability to feel) is Beloved's return from the dead, not as a ghost but a living being. She climbs fully dressed out of the water—perhaps representing the collective unconscious of African-Americans—while, appropriately, Sethe, Paul D., and Sethe's daughter Denver are at a carnival (etymologically, "festival of flesh"). Beloved has "new skin, lineless and smooth" (*Beloved* 50), no expression in her eyes, three thin scratches on her head where Sethe had held her head after severing her neck, and a small neck scar. Although Sethe does not consciously recognize her daughter for some time, her bladder fills the moment she sees her face and she voids "endless" water as if giving birth (*Beloved* 51). For each of the three residents of 124—Sethe, Paul D and Denver—relating to Beloved addresses her or his most profound individual anguish, whatever lies at the core of each identity. For Sethe, it is mothering; for Paul D, his ability to feel, and for Denver, her loneliness. Their individual reactions to her reflect their respective voids, and reveal their deepest selves.

Angela Davis has pointed out that slave women were not recognized as mothers having bonds with their children, but considered only "breeders" and workers. Thus, slaveowners had no scruples about selling children away from their mothers: "Their infant children could be sold away from them like calves from cows" (Angela Davis 7). *Beloved* is characterized by mothers losing their children: Sethe's mother-in-law barely glanced at the last of her eight children "because it wasn't worth the trouble" (*Beloved* 139). Sethe's own mother, hanged when Sethe was a small child, had not been allowed to nurse her. But Sethe defines herself as mother in definace of the near-impossibility of that role. Even 18 years after her escape, Paul D recognizes that Sethe's mother-love is risky. "For a used-to-be slave woman to love anything that much was dangerous, especially if it was her children she had settled on to love" (*Beloved* 45). It was to avoid a future in slavery for her children that led Sethe to plan escape, and to get her milk to her baby—sent ahead with the other children—that made her attempt it alone. She experiences having her milk stolen from her by the nephews of her slavemaster as the ultimate brutality, even worse than the savage beating she received just before escaping. "They handled me like I was the cow, no, the goat, back behind the stable because it was too nasty to stay in with the horses" (*Beloved* 200). Beloved's return enables Sethe to mother her abundantly with "lullabies, new stitches, the bottom of the cake bowl, the top of the milk" (*Beloved* 240).

If mothering is at the core of Sethe's identity, feeling is at the core of Paul D's. "Not even trying, he had become the kind of man who could walk into a house and make the women cry. Because with him, in his presence, they could" (*Beloved* 17). What had led to his own inability to feel was the systematic destruction of his manhood. Like many men, women and children, he had had a bit in his mouth, but the worst part of the experience for Paul D was feeling the superiority of a rooster (called Mister):

> *Mister was allowed to be and stay what he was. . . . But wasn't no way I'd ever be Paul D again, living or dead. Schoolteacher changed me. I was something else and that something was less than a chicken sitting in the sun on a tub.* (*Beloved* 72)

When Beloved seduces Paul D, making love with her breaks open the tobacco tin in his chest to release his red heart.

Sethe's anguish is about her mothering, and Paul D's, the ability to feel. Denver's is her loneliness. Its original cause is Beloved's murder, which alienated the community, made Denver afraid of her mother and of whatever was terrible enough to make her kill her own, and caused the haunting of 124 that made Denver's two brothers leave. She had gone deaf and withdrawn from others for a time after having been asked if she hadn't been in jail with her when her mother was charged with murder (*Beloved* 104). Beloved's gift to Denver is attention. Under her gaze, "Denver's skin dissolved . . . and became soft and bright" (*Beloved* 118).

But Beloved is much more than Sethe's resurrected daughter. She is the embodiment of the collective pain and rage of the millions of slaves who died on the Middle Passage and suffered the tortures of slavery. Therefore, her unconscious knows the desperately crowded conditions of a ship of the Middle Passage:

> *. . . there will never be a time when I am not crouching and watching others who are crouching too   I am always crouching   the man on my face is dead   his face is not mine   his mouth smells sweet but his eyes are locked* (*Beloved* 212)

West African religion believes that after physical death, the individual spirit lives, but because it is no longer contained by its "carnal envelope," it gains in power. Spirits "may cause havoc to people if they are spirits of people who were killed in battle or unjustly" (Mbiti 8), and the spirits feel punished if their names are obliterated or forgotten (Mbiti 9). (Beloved has no name but the epitaph on her gravestone, a word Sethe remembered from the funeral and which she could pay to have engraved only by enduring the sexual assault of the engraver). The invasion of the world of the living by Beloved's physical presence is evidence of the terrible destruction of the natural order caused by slavery. No one had thought anything about a ghost haunting the house, because ancestral spirits were known to linger in the world. But her physical presence has the effect of Judgment Day on all those whom she encounters: Sethe, Paul D, Denver, and the community. However, because the West African sense of time is non-linear, judgment can be endured and redemption still achieved.

> *. . . if the apocalypse stands as one constant pole of the black imagination, as a present possibility, the other pole is an unfashionable conviction that change is possible—that the ghosts of the past can be laid if only they are freely engaged and honestly confessed.* (Bigsby 167)

Beloved proclaims that apocalypse and change are not necessarily at opposite poles: an apocalypse—that lifting of the veil on whatever lies beyond—can stimulate change. Its catharsis can be the beginning of transformation; apocalypse can thus become a bridge to the future, passage to freedom.

This novel makes very clear that physical escape into physical freedom was only the first step for the slaves. That fact is symbolized by *Beloved*'s equivalent of Charon, the figure in Greek mythology who ferries the souls across the Acheron to the underworld. This character is an ex-slave who, after handing over his wife to his master's son, changed his name from Joshua to Stamp Paid because "whatever his obligations were, that act paid them off." By ferrying escaped slaves across the Ohio into freedom, he "gave them their own bill of sale" (*Beloved* 185), except that the freedom on the Ohio side of the river is illusory, and not only for political and economic reasons. The slaves who cross the river bring with them the memories of lynchings and torture, family members sold away, degradation, and cumulative loss, so that Stamp Paid, like Charon, actually carries them physically to an underworld, to "free" territory where, in *Beloved*, souls are dead even if bodies are alive. However, Stamp Paid also attempts to carry them out of this underworld into genuine freedom. He "extended the debtlessness [that he believed he had achieved by handing over his wife] to other people by helping them pay out and off whatever they owed in misery" (*Beloved* 185).

Stamp Paid interprets the angry mumbling of the spirits around Sethe's home as "the jungle whitefolks planted" in Black people, a jungle which grew and spread, "In, through and after life" (*Beloved* 198). Among other things, Beloved is the embodiment of the White folks' jungle, the psychological effects of slavery. The three residents of 124—Sethe, Paul D, and Denver—find out that although Beloved, once no longer a ghost, did address their deepest needs, she is also malevolent. Sethe realizes that Beloved will never accept her explanation for the murder and that Sethe can never make it up to her. Sethe becomes Beloved's slave, goes without food so that Beloved can eat, and begins to die. Paul D recognizes that making love with Beloved "was more like a brainless urge to stay alive" (*Beloved* 265). Denver is finally deserted by Beloved when her mother recognizes her dead daughter. When Denver accuses her of strangling Sethe from a distance of several feet, Beloved denies it. "The circle of iron choked it" (*Beloved* 101). Her reply reflects the complexity of her character, as both the ghost of Sethe's murdered baby who can't get enough love from her mother and as also the representative of all the angry spirits—the manifestation of the murderous rage created by Whites in enslaved African-Americans. Beloved as the spirit of slavery—the circle of iron around slave necks—did try to kill Sethe; murdered indirectly by Sethe's slavemaster, Beloved is an unquiet spirit. The enormity of the wrongs wreaked upon the "60 million and more" has produced her, obsessed with revenge, desperately needy for love, but incapable of giving it. Beloved is the tangible presence of the painful past. When Sethe finally recognizes her, Sethe is "excited to giddiness by all the things she no longer had to remember" (*Beloved* 183). Even though sex with her filled Paul D with repulsion and shame, "he was thankful too for having been escorted to some ocean-deep place he once belonged to" (*Beloved* 265).

Beloved's stream of consciousness reveals that she had waited "on the bridge" (*Beloved* 212). She herself becomes a bridge between the "other side" and the living, the apocalyptic manifestation of the world beyond the veil. Like a bridge, Beloved enables passage to knowledge of the other side that otherwise would be impossible. We know that medieval chapels were constructed in the middle of bridges so that passengers could contemplate passage from one state of being to another. Beloved's very being forces such contemplation.

In terms of Christian apocalypse, Beloved is not the anti-Christ; that role belongs to Sethe's slavemaster, representative of the Whites who oppressed African-Americans through slavery. But as the product of slavery, she could be the Anti-Christ's beast. She is a constant sign that this novel is dealing with another level of reality, but also a reminder of the paradoxes about which the novel circles: the killing of a child to protect her and the combined pathos and wrathfulness of the ancestral spirits. Yet, although Sethe's murder of Beloved is the center of the paradox, which occurred 18 years before the action that begins the novel, it is not depicted until nearly the mid-point of *Beloved*. Instead, the murder is anticipated so often that a dark foreboding is created, just as Sethe's mother-in-law sensed something "dark and coming" as the slavemaster and his accomplices were arriving (*Beloved* 139).

The slavemaster, Schoolteacher, is definitely an anti-Christ figure, the kind of character who usually functions in apocalyptic writing as a sign of the end. The Anti-Christ signals a return to chaos (Russell 36), and Schoolteacher's arrival produces chaos which permeates Sethe's life and the lives of everyone in her family and in the entire community. Schoolteacher and the three other White men: his nephew, the slavecatcher, and the sheriff, are Morrison's four horsemen of the apocalypse. Their appearance crystallizes the terror and horror of slavery, emphasized by the fact that this episode is the only one in the novel told from the point of view of a white person. When they discover Sethe's sons bleeding at her feet, her baby's head nearly severed, and her trying to kill the other infant, Schoolteacher concedes his economic loss. He believes that Sethe would be useless as a slave to him because she has "gone wild" (*Beloved* 149) due to his nephew having "overbeaten" her; she resembles a hound beaten too hard and which, therefore, can never be trusted. He reflects slavery's treatment of African-Americans as animals. Sethe's reaction to seeing the four horsemen is to protect her children in the only way she has left: to remove them from the reach of evil, to try to carry them "through the veil, out, away, over there where no one could hurt them" (*Beloved* 163).

This prefiguring of the novel's climactic, redemptive moment is the most violent episode in the novel. Although violence is characteristic of apocalyptic literature, this violence is especially notable because it consists of the victim inflicting the violence on her own children out of utter hopelessness. Stamp Paid calls this event "the Misery" and "Sethe's response to the Fugitive Act" (*Beloved* 171). It demonstrates what the characters in *Beloved* recognize—that actual battle with Whites is impossible because the odds are so stacked against Blacks: "Lay down your sword. This ain't a battle; it's a rout" (*Beloved* 244).

Biblical scholars read the four horsemen of the apocalypse as agents of divine wrath; Morrison's four horsemen are only emblems of evil. Her revision of the classic apocalyptic image suggests that she does not share with many apocalyptic writers a belief in a moral force at work in history, the invisible presence of a god who will come again to judge sinners and rescue and reward the oppressed. Instead, *Beloved* insists that if change is possible, it will happen only when individuals are integrated with the natural world and each other. The only moral agency is human, represented in *Beloved* by Denver. Born in a boat filling with the "river of freedom," she represents the generation born outside slavery—the future.

Denver is the redemptive figure in this novel. She was only a few days old when her mother murdered Beloved, and Sethe's nipple was covered with her sister's blood when she nursed. "So Denver took her mother's milk right along with the blood of her sister" (*Beloved* 152). The image can be read as an allusion to Christ in Revelation "robed in the blood of martyrs" (Rev.

19:13). Like a Christ figure, Denver often functions as an intermediary between spirits and living. Even before Beloved materialized, she saw her in a white dress kneeling beside Sethe, and she was the first to recognize Beloved. Denver not only represents the future; she brings it into being. When neither Sethe nor Beloved seem to care what the next day might bring, "Denver knew it was on her. She would have to leave the yard; step off the edge of the world," and find help (*Beloved* 243). Her efforts lead to everyone's salvation: the reunion of the community. It begins with gifts of food accompanied by the givers' names, but culminates in the women coming to the yard of 124 to exorcise Beloved.

Ella, the former slave woman who had led Sethe and the just-born Denver from the Ohio River, leads Sethe's rescue. She had guided them to the community of former slaves, then led the community's ostracizing of Sethe for 18 years when Sethe had seemed not to need anyone after Beloved's death. Now, it is the idea of Beloved's physical presence which enrages Ella, for she understands that Beloved represents the invasion of one world by the other, and specifically, "the idea of past errors taking possession of the present" (*Beloved* 256). As long as Beloved was only a ghost, even a violent ghost, Ella respected it.

> *But if it took on flesh and came in her world, well, the shoe was on the other foot. She didn't mind a little communication between the two worlds, but this was an invasion.* (*Beloved* 257).

Ella and the others recognize that Beloved's being violates the boundary between the dead and the living. They know that she is the representative of "the people of the broken necks, of fire-cooked blood" (*Beloved* 181) whose anger and suffering could not be contained in the other world as long as the living neither heard nor remembered them: the apocalyptic presence come to demand attention. When the community is forced to acknowledge what she represents in their own interior lives, Beloved can be exorcised. Like Beloved's murder, the exorcism takes place in the yard of 124. It shares several other characteristics with that appearance of the Anti-Christ: the arrival of a White man with a horse, a violent reaction by Sethe, and the demise of Beloved. But it is the contrasts that are most important. This time, the White man's mission is innocent; Sethe does not succeed; Beloved's demise is necessary and beneficial, the community supports Sethe instead of deserting her, and, most important of all, the community achieves a shared revelation that ushers in a new age.

This second momentous gathering at 124 has a fated quality. For instance, at precisely the same moment that the Black women are marching toward 124, Edward Bodwin, the White abolitionist who owns 124, is coming to take Denver to his house to work as a night maid. The women are coming to purge the house of the demon beating up on Sethe, armed with whatever they believe will work: amulets, their Christian faith, anything. It has been 30 years since Bodwin saw 124, the house where he was born, a place about which "he felt something sweeter and deeper" than its commercial value (*Beloved* 259). The thought of it takes him back to his childhood, a time when he had buried his precious treasures in the yard. It has been 18 years since the women were in the yard of 124, at the picnic Sethe's mother-in-law had given the day before Schoolteacher's arrival to celebrate Sethe's escape. If the house is symbolic for Bodwin, it has symbolic value also for the women approaching it. Seeing Beloved on the porch makes them see themselves as young girls picnicking in the yard 18 years earlier, the day before Beloved was killed. What they see is also a reminder of how the community shares responsibility for Beloved's death. The community of former slaves had been so jealous of the huge party which Sethe's mother-in-law had thrown that no one warned 124 of the approaching horsemen. Then the community had not gathered around Sethe when she climbed into the cart for the ride to jail because they felt that she held her head too high. However, Beloved's presence does enable the women to go back in time to being "young and happy" (*Beloved* 258). She also lets them recapture the paradisal time they had spent in the Clearing with Sethe's mother-in-law Baby Suggs as their spiritual leader. It is significant that by the end of the novel "rememorying" calls back positive moments instead of the painful, oppressive past. United in memories of joy and collective strength, the women can respond to the need to banish Beloved, the objectification of the angry and revengeful ancestral spirits, with the full power of their spiritual tradition. It is especially important that their leader Ella recognizes at last that she shares something very significant with Sethe. What Ella remembers is the "hairy white thing," fathered by her slavemaster, which she had let die. "The idea of that pup coming back to whip her too set her jaw working" (*Beloved* 259). And she hollers, to be joined at once by the others.

> *They stopped praying and took a step back to the beginning. In the beginning there were no words. In the beginning was the sound, and they all know what that sound sounded like.* (*Beloved* 259).

The primal sound exorcises Beloved and thus the evil of the "White folks' jungle" in their own lives as well as Sethe's family's. The moment takes them all outside of linear time into a type of apocalypse in which all is reduced to its most fundamental terms, to a purity of emotion and a brilliant clarity. In this moment the cycle has rolled around to begin again. When the women take a step back to the beginning, they touch the eschaton, the boundary, and momentarily escape from the flux of time to the place where clear vision is possible. They remind us that apocalypse is not a synonym for disaster or cataclysm; it is linked to revelation. Seeing clearly into the past, the women can take hold again of what they had lost in forgetting.

Apocalyptic literature is very like Greek tragedy in arousing emotion and creating the conditions for catharsis. Morrison's novel raises all kinds of emotion—pain, grief, remorse, anger, fear—and purges it once "intensified and given objective expression" (Robinson xiii). Beloved focuses the objective expression of emotion. When the women create the powerful, timeless sound which exorcises Beloved, they purge themselves and Sethe and Denver of the emotion which had imprisoned them. It returns them all to a new beginning where, cleansed, they can create a new life.

> *The apocalyptic imagination may finally be defined in terms of its philosophical preoccupation with that moment of juxtaposition and consequential transformation or transfiguration when an old world of mind discovers a believable new world of mind, which either nullifies and destroys the old system entirely or, less likely, makes it part of a larger design.* (Ketterer 13)

The women's song or shout creates the moment of redemptive transfiguration in *Beloved.* Still caught in the mode of forgetting which had been their method of survival after physically escaping slavery, when the women focused on the image of Beloved standing on the front porch of 124, they were themselves dragged through the veil into a world rich with memory of their personal and collective lives and of the "unnamed, unmentioned people left behind" (*Beloved* 92).

> *For Sethe it was as though the Clearing had come to her with all its heat and simmering leaves, where the voices of women searched for the right combination, the key, the code, the sound that broke the back of words.* (*Beloved* 261)

The Clearing was the open place in the woods where Sethe's mother-in-law, Baby Suggs had led the community in spiritual ceremonies. Baby Suggs had begun those ceremonies by asking the children to laugh, the men to dance, but the women to cry, "For the living and the dead" (*Beloved* 88). Then she would direct them all to love themselves deeply.

> *'Here,' she said, 'in this here place, we flesh; flesh that weeps, laughs, flesh that dances on bare feet in grass. Love it. Love it hard. Yonder they do not love your flesh.'* (*Beloved* 88)

But Baby Suggs gave up after the "Misery" and went to bed to die. When Sethe is taken back to the Clearing by the women's song in her yard, it is a sign of both personal and community redemption; the community at this apocalyptic moment has returned finally to loving themselves, but also to feeling compassion for those who have died. In the yard of 124 when the women found "the sound that broke the backs of words,"

> *it was a wave of sound wide enough to sound deep water and knock the pods off chestnut trees. It broke over Sethe and she trembled like the baptized in its wash.* (*Beloved* 261)

The women's song was powerful enough to break "the back of words"—words used to define African-Americans, such as "animal" and "breeding stock" and "slaves." It baptizes Sethe into a new life, into a radical spiritual transformation.

Ironically, Bodwin arrives at the peak of the women's song/shout. His appearance recalls Sethe to that moment when four White horsemen rode into her yard: and so she acts again to protect her child, but this time she runs to kill the oppressor—whom she sees as Bodwin—instead of her own child. Denver stops her. We should not read Sethe's seeing Bodwin as her enemy as a crazed mistake, but rather as evidence of a kind of clear-sightedness, Sethe having just been baptized in primal, sacred sound. Apocalyptic catharsis requires confrontation with hidden horror; it also provides a two-fold purgation by making the wronged one feel better and castigating the sinner. Although the Bodwins did help ex-slaves and worked for abolition of slavery, *Beloved* makes it clear that they are part of the problem, not the solution. They gave help to runaways "because they hated slavery worse than they hated slaves" (*Beloved* 137). On a shelf by their back door is the figurine of a Black child, his mouth full of money, kneeling on a pedestal with the words, "'At Yo' Service'" (*Beloved* 255). When Bodwin returns to 124, his eyes are transfixed by the sight of Beloved. After she has disappeared Beloved is described as "a naked woman with fish for hair" (*Beloved* 267) which may be an allusion to Medusa, the gorgon who turned men to stone. Perhaps Beloved has that effect on Bodwin. Perhaps he recognizes in her what Stamp Paid called "the white folks' jungle." Perhaps his encounter with Beloved—he doesn't even see Sethe approaching to stab him with the ice pick—is his experience of Judgment, occurring appropriately at the house where he was born, where his "treasure" lay hidden.

Apocalypse is a more diffuse experience in *Beloved* than traditionally conceived, and it is presented as something which can be survived, not as an event at the end of linear time. In *Beloved* it is an attempt to free African-Americans from guilt and past suffering. What *Beloved* suggests is that while the suffering of the "black and angry dead" is the inescapable psychological legacy of all African-Americans, they can rescue themselves from the trauma of that legacy by directly confronting it and uniting to loosen its fearsome hold. *Beloved*'s redemptive community of women epitomizes the object of salvation in biblical apocalyptic literature: "the creation of a new society" (Russell 27).

Thus, like much African-American writing, *Beloved* does not conclude with a climactic moment. "For the black writer, incompletion is a fact of private and public life and the basis for social and cultural hope" (Bigsby 168). The experience of suffering and guilt can begin to be transformed into knowledge, once the trauma is purged, so that the novel leaves the powerful apocalyptic scene of the community's expurgation of Beloved to observe Sethe and Paul D rejoining their stories to each other's. Paul D, who had left upon learning of the murder, must return to Sethe's house to re-establish the intimate connection which will allow them each to find his or her own self and love it. Paul D, despite his inability to feel when he had first arrived at Sethe's, has a deep understanding of the meaning of slavery and freedom, that under slavery "you protected yourself and loved small," but finding freedom means "to get to a place where you could love anything you chose" (*Beloved* 162). Linked with Sethe's mother in several ways, including the wearing of the bit, he mothers Sethe as her own mother never could, and when he does, the voice of his lynched best friend enters his mind, speaking about the woman he loved, "She is a friend of my mind. She gather me, man. The pieces I am, she gather them and give them back to me in all the right order" (*Beloved* 272–73).

Beloved is a novel about collecting fragments and welding them into beautiful new wholes, about letting go of pain and guilt, but also recovering what is lost and loving it into life. One of its most poignant images is the ribbon that Stamp Paid finds on the river bottom—"a red ribbon knotted around a curl of wet woolly hair, clinging still to its bit of scalp" (*Beloved* 180). Although he knows all the horrors of 1874—the lynchings, whippings, burnings of colored schools, rapes, and lynch fires—it is this discovery which finally weakens Stamp Paid's bone marrow and makes him "dwell on Baby Suggs' wish to consider what in the world was harmless" (*Beloved* 181).

What Morrison creates is far from harmless. She knows how painful it is to remember the horrors she presents. She has said in an interview that she expected *Beloved* to be the least read of all her books because "it is about something that the characters don't want to remember, I don't want to remember, black people don't want to remember, white people don't want to remember. I mean, it's national amnesia" (Angelo 120). However, because *Beloved* insists on remembering, the novel is able to recover and honor the symbolic spirit of the Black girl whose ribbon and piece of scalp Stamp Paid found. In so doing, it makes possible the contemplation and creation of a future in which African-Americans can respect and honor themselves and their ancestors—be beloved. As Paul D says to Sethe, "Me and you, we got more yesterday than anybody. We need some kind of tomorrow" (*Beloved* 273). What *Beloved* suggests is that tomorrow is made possible by the knowledge of yesterday, a knowledge that for contemporary African-Americans can be gained from imagining what it was like to walk in the flesh of their slave ancestors.

> *Auschwitz lies on the other side of life and on the other side of death. There, one lives differently, one walks differently, one dreams differently. . . . Only those who lived it in their flesh and their minds can possibly transform their experience into knowledge.* (Wiesel 1).

By giving its readers the inside view of slaves' lives—which bore uncanny resemblance to the holocaust—the novel enables its African-American readers to live the experience of slavery in their minds and to join in the healing primal sound of the women who come to Sethe's yard. By speaking the horror, Morrison assumes and helps to create the community that can hear it and transform it.

DAVID LAWRENCE

Fleshly Ghosts and Ghostly Flesh: The Word and the Body in Beloved

In William Faulkner's *Light in August*, Byron Bunch reflects that no matter how much a person might "talk about how he'd like to escape from living folks . . . it's the dead folks that do him the damage." The damage done by dead folks in Toni Morrison's *Beloved* points to the central position accorded to memory, the place where these dead folks are kept alive, in this novel of futile forgetting and persistent remembrance. Operating independently of the conscious will, memory is shown to be an active, constitutive force that has the power to construct and circumscribe identity, both individual and collective, in the image of its own contents. Sethe's "rememory," in giving substance to her murdered daughter and to the painful past, casts its spell over the entire community, drawing the members of that community into one person's struggle with the torments of a history that refuses to die.

In portraying the capacity of the past to haunt individual and community life in the present, *Beloved* brings into daylight the "ghosts" that are harbored by memory and that hold their "hosts" in thrall, tyrannically dictating thought, emotion, and action. The stories of the tightly woven network of characters culminate in a ritualistic sacrifice of Beloved, a ceremony that frees the community from this pervasive haunting. The supernatural existence of Beloved, who acts as a scapegoat for the evils of the past, threatens the naturalized set of inherited codes by which the community

From *Studies in American Fiction* 19:2 (Autumn 1991). © 1991 by Northeastern University.

defines itself. The climactic scene shows how a culture may find it necessary in a moment of crisis to exorcise its own demons in order to reaffirm its identity.

Morrison first exposes, however, the workings of the internal mechanisms that have generated the need for exorcism in the first place. A deeply encoded rejection of the body drives the highly pressurized haunting in *Beloved.* The black community of Cincinnati is caught in a cycle of self-denial, a suffocating repression of fundamental bodily needs and wants. The inability to articulate such embodied experience, to find a text for the desiring body within communal codes, obstructs self-knowledge and does violence to the fabric of community. Woven into the dense texture of the novel, into what Morrison has called the "subliminal, the underground life of a novel," the interaction of language and body underlies the collective confrontation with the ghosts of memory. In her representation of this psychic battle, Morrison fashions word and flesh as intimate allies in the project of constructing a domain in which body and spirit may thrive. The exorcism of Beloved, an embodiment of resurgent desire, opens the way to a rewording of the codes that have enforced the silencing of the body's story, making possible a remembering of the cultural heritage that has haunted the characters so destructively. In the end, the communal body seems ready to articulate a reinvigorated language that, in returning to its roots in the body, empowers its speakers to forge a more open, inclusive community.

In a novel that examines the dehumanizing impact of slavery, one might expect that the white man, the monstrous enforcer of slavery's brutality, would haunt the black community. The haunting occurs, however, within a social structure relatively insulated from the white community and, in its most intense form, springs from the "rememory" of an ex-slave in the form of one victimized by slavery. There is nothing mysteriously threatening about whites; on the contrary, "white folks didn't bear speaking on. Everybody knew." Of course, whites "spoke on" their slaves tirelessly, and, in the exploration of political power in the novel, ownership of body and authorship of language are shown to be insidiously linked. Under the regime of white authority, the "blackness" of the slave's body represents for "whitefolks" an animal savagery and moral depravity that, ironically, ends up remaking them in the image of their own fears:

> Whitepeople believed that whatever the manners, under every dark skin was a jungle. Swift unnavigable waters, screaming baboons, sleeping snakes, red gums ready for sweet white blood. . . . But it wasn't the jungle blacks brought with them to this place from the other (livable) place. It was the jungle whitefolks planted in them. And it grew. It spread. In, through and after life,

> it spread, until it invaded the whites who had made it. . . . The screaming baboon lived under their own white skin; the red gums were their own (pp. 198–99).

This "belief," which underlies the chilling scientific rationality of schoolteacher, abstracts the human corporeality of the slave into a sign for the other in the discourse of the dominant ideology. Further, such invasive signifying upon the black body generates a self-fulfilling prophecy, as blacks find themselves unable to assert an identity outside the expectations imposed upon them: "The more [colored people] used themselves up to persuade whites of something Negroes believed could not be questioned, the deeper and more tangled the jungle grew inside" (p. 198).

In *Beloved*, the question of authority over one's own body is consistently related to that of authority over discourse; bodily and linguistic disempowerment frequently intersect. At Sweet Home, Sethe makes the ink with which schoolteacher and his nephews define on paper her "animal characteristics"; the ink, a tool for communication produced by her own hands, is turned against her as ammunition for their "weapons" of torture, pen and paper. Shocked, she asks Mrs. Garner for the definitions of "characteristics" and "features," vainly attempting to assert control over the words that have conscripted her body in a notebook (pp. 194–95). The terror she feels at seeing herself defined and divided (animal traits on the left, human on the right) concludes her list on ways whites can "dirty you so bad you forgot who you were" (p. 251); the litany of brutality—decapitations, burnings, rapes—she provides Beloved as "reasons" for killing her ends with this bottom line: "And no one, nobody on this earth, would list her daughter's characteristics on the animal side of the paper. No. Oh no" (p. 251).

As Stamp Paid, the community's literate newsbearer, reads about the post-Civil War violence against his people, he can "smell" the bloody brutality in the very words that attempt to communicate that violence in digestible form:

> The stench stank. Stank up off the pages of the *North Star*, out of the mouths of witnesses, etched in crooked handwriting in letters delivered by hand. Detailed in documents and petitions full of *whereas* and presented to any legal body who'd read it, it stank (p. 180).

The primary means of entry into the realm of the written word for blacks is the atrocity that is inflicted upon them or that they inflict upon others. Looking at Sethe's picture in Stamp's newspaper clipping relating the story of Sethe's "crime," Paul D knows that "there was no way in hell a black face could appear in a newspaper if the story was about something anybody wanted to hear" (p. 155).

Even on Sweet Home, where Garner believes he allows his slaves to be men, the power of naming remains with the white master. Paul D wonders years later, "Is that where the manhood lay? In the naming done by a whiteman who was supposed to know?" (p. 125). Of course, schoolteacher, Garner's successor, destroys even this precarious sense of identity. Sethe recalls how schoolteacher asserted his authority as "definer" after Sixo had dexterously challenged an accusation of theft. Sixo's rhetorical artistry—stealing and eating the shoat is "improving property" since such apparently transgressive behavior actually will increase his productive capacity—is futile: "Clever, but schoolteacher beat him anyway to show that definitions belonged to the definers—not the defined" (p. 190). Sethe tells Denver that what "tore Sixo up . . . for all time" was not the beatings but the questions that schoolteacher asked them, presumably as part of his research into their animal nature. According to Sethe, it is the notebook schoolteacher carries with him containing the answers that destroys Sixo, not the gunshots that eventually end his life (p. 37).

Finally, in the first pages of the novel, Sethe remembers how she had to exchange "ten minutes" of sex with the engraver for the "one word that mattered"—Beloved (p. 5). In order to acquire the inscribing power of the white man's chisel, she must transform her body into a commodity; he will grant the cherished script provided he first be granted the right of sexual inscription. Thus Sethe must temporarily "kill off" her own body (she lies on a headstone, "her knees wide open as the grave") to purchase the text that she thinks will buy her peace. The debt owed to her murdered daughter, however, will not be so "easily" paid.

As Sethe lies in the Clearing where her mother-in-law, Baby Suggs, used to preach the Word, she thinks about how her month of "unslaved life" made her realize that "freeing yourself was one thing; claiming ownership of that freed self was another" (p. 95). This striving to claim ownership links Sethe's own horrifying story to the story of the entire community. Central to the pursuit of self-ownership is the articulation of a self-defining language that springs from the flesh and blood of physical experience and that gives shape to the desire so long suppressed under slavery. Baby Suggs discovers such self-definition immediately upon gaining her freedom. After she experiences the wonder of possessing her own body, of recognizing the pounding of "her own heartbeat" (p. 141), she renames herself "Suggs" (her husband's name), forcefully rejecting Garner's uncomprehending defense of the "legal" name on her bill of sale, Jenny Whitlow. She thus begins to fill with "the roots of her tongue" (p. 141) that "desolated center where the self that was no self made its home" (p. 140).

Of course, it is precisely this kind of "self-generating" language that has been stifled by the mortifications of flesh endured under slavery. In defending itself against the bodily depredations of enslavement, the community has learned to choke off its capacity for pleasure and love, for the experience of jouissance. "Baby Suggs, holy," the "unchurched preacher" (p. 87), tries to revise this legacy of self-denial in her self-loving exhortations, devoting "the roots of her tongue" to calling the Word. Eschewing such confining abstractions as sin and purity, Baby Suggs grounds her words in the earthly, sensual realm through which the body moves: "She told them that the only grace they could have was the grace they could imagine. That if they could not see it, they would not have it" (p. 88). Rather than a divine state of being that descends from above, grace is a humanly conceived, embodied experience. In the oral text of her "sermon," which Baby Suggs draws from the powerfully felt fact of being alive within a body, "grace" is both noun and verb, a blessed touching of one's own body: "Here in this here place, we flesh; flesh that weeps, laughs; flesh that dances on bare feet in grass. Love it. Love it hard . . . grace it, stroke it, and hold it up" (p. 88). In this open-ended, organic religion, Baby Suggs taps a bodily "organ music," imploring her listeners to love their "dark, dark liver" and "life-giving parts" (p. 88–89). And when her words cease, Sethe recalls, she "danced with her twisted hip the rest of what her heart had to say while the others opened their mouths and gave her the music" (p. 89). Using her own disfigured body as an instrument, Baby Suggs talks through dance to find the language adequate to the demands of their bodies: "Long notes held until the four-part harmony was perfect enough for their deeply loved flesh" (p. 89). Her speech, both literally and metaphorically, comes from her "big old heart," providing a kind of scaffolding for the reconstitution of the damaged communal body. The members of the community must put themselves back together—re-member themselves—so that they can remember that the heart "is the prize" (p. 89).

Sethe recalls how this "fixing ceremony" (p. 86) had begun the work of asserting self-defined ownership: "Bit by bit . . . along with the others, she had claimed herself" (p. 95). But the unwritten codes of the community cannot yet entirely accommodate such joyous self-celebration. After Baby Suggs hosts a spontaneous feast to mark the arrival of her daughter-in-law, the community finds itself resenting what they perceive as her prideful behavior. She has crossed the boundary of permissible pleasure: "Her friends and neighbors were angry at her because she had overstepped, given too much, offended them by excess" (p. 138). Her former guests transfer their self-despising outrage at the poverty of their own lives onto the person who dares to dispense such a rare commodity as love with "reckless generosity": "Loaves and fishes were His powers—they didn't belong to an ex-slave" (p. 137). Ironically, the communal voice that Baby Suggs "hears" the morning after the feast plays, in effect, the role of the white master by reprimanding the "slave" who has violated the code of acceptable behavior. The oppression enforced by slaveowners is now perpetuated by the oppressed themselves. As a unit, the community itself remains an "ex-slave," unable to define itself outside the parameters of the slave experience.

To be sure, Morrison makes it clear that under slavery the self-imposed prohibition on "reckless generosity" worked as a necessary survival strategy, an indispensable means of self-defense. Paul D learned "to love just a little bit; everything just a little bit, so when they broke its back, or shoved it in a croker sack, well, maybe you'd have a little left over for the next one" (p. 45). Loving "big," according to Paul D, "would split you wide open," so "you protected yourself and loved small" (p. 162). On the chain gang in Alfred, Georgia, Paul D and the men vent their rage in songs, fictions that permit them to act out through their labor their desire to "kill the boss" as well as "the flirt whom folks called Life for leading them on" (p. 109). But this life-killing strategy of self-defense has become, after slavery, a deadly form of self-destruction. Listening to Sethe's own story of desperate self-defense (her "explanation" of why she had to kill her children in order to protect them), Paul D reflects upon the need to find a space for uninhibited love: "To get to a place where you could love anything you chose—not to need permission for desire—well now, that was freedom" (p. 162). Freed from slavery, the community must now learn to permit itself the freedom to desire. The denial of this permission to Baby Suggs, apparently an act of collective self-assertion, only implicates the community in Sethe's self-destructive defense of own flesh and blood. Because her neighbors are furious at Baby Suggs' presumption, they do not send someone to warn her of schoolteacher's approach, a warning which might have prevented the slaughter of one of their own by one of their own.

Having moved from "the center of things" (p. 137) to the margins of the community, 124 is haunted, its residents three phantoms (after Sethe's sons run away) and a ghost. Baby Suggs, her heart "collapsed" and her voice silenced, spends the last eight years of her life contemplating the colors on her quilt. Sethe devotes herself to beating back the past that is "still waiting" (p. 44) for Denver, who goes deaf rather than remember the dark time she spent with her mother in prison (p. 104). They lead sterile, isolated lives, the ghost the only member of the family who seeks the intimacy of physical contact.

But Paul D's arrival eighteen years after "the Misery" (p. 171) disturbs the unhealthy equilibrium at 124. In evicting the ghost and touching Sethe, he initiates the process of articulating "word-shapes" (p. 99) for the past that still imprisons them. The marks of violence and humiliation must be "read," translated into a shared understanding, before that body language called by Baby Suggs in the Clearing can be rediscovered and respoken. With instinctive compassion, Paul D goes straight to the source to learn of Sethe's suffering, the network of scars inscribed by schoolteacher's nephews that has numbed her entire back: "He rubbed his cheek on her back, and learned that way her sorrow, the roots of it, its wide trunk and intricate branches" (p. 17). The sexual union that allows Sethe to "feel the hurt her back ought to" (p. 18) also brings about a psychic union; they silently recall, in tandem, the safe memory of love at Sweet Home. Morrison's narrator creates seamless transitions between their separate but simultaneous memories of Sethe and Halle's first lovemaking in the cornfield. The recollection culminates in the shared trope for sexual arousal and fulfillment expressed in the husked corn: "How loose the silk. How quick the jailed-up flavor ran free" (p. 27). This convergence of sexuality, memory, and poetic figure beautifully illustrates the intimate communion of linguistic and bodily experience enacted in the text of the novel.

As Sethe and Paul D "make talk" (p. 20), what had previously been "unspeakable" begins to be speakable: "Her story was bearable because it was his as well—to tell, to refine and tell again. The things neither knew about the other—the things neither had word-shapes for" (p. 99). In his presence, Sethe rediscovers her own capacity for bodily sensation and reestablishes contact with the outside world that induces such sensation: "Emotions sped to the surface in his company. Things became what they were. . . . Windows suddenly had view" (p. 39). After a day spent at the carnival enjoying Paul D's gregarious companionship, Sethe allows herself to imagine that the three hand-holding shadows she observes on their return will shortly be a fully fleshed unit. The desire that Paul D stirs up, however, taps a reservoir of repressed feeling that seems to trigger Beloved's emergence from Sethe's rememory. The spoken text of their love cannot accommodate Beloved, and their storytelling intimacy is soon broken by the ghost's return in full-grown, fleshly form.

Beloved acts as an embodiment of uninhibited desire, projecting a "bottomless longing" (p. 58) for love that places impossible demands upon the human body. Her appearance at 124 fresh from the waters of the Ohio causes Sethe to run desperately for the privy to relieve the incredible pressure of her own waters, an emergency evacuation reenacting Beloved's natural birth. Her touch, "no heavier than a feather but loaded with desire" (p. 58), dissolves the "tobacco tin" into which Paul D has crammed his painful, humiliating memories, moving him involuntarily from the house he thought he had claimed. She absorbs Denver's devotion only to give her more strength for consuming Sethe's love: "Sethe was licked, tasted, eaten by Beloved's eyes" (p. 57). Her appetite is an insatiable "life hunger" (p. 264), a "downright craving to know" (p. 77) the life and love that was denied her. Like a vampire, she sucks out Sethe's vitality, fattening on her mother's futile attempts to "make her understand," to explain and justify the necessity of murdering her own child to save her from the murder of slavery.

When Stamp Paid approaches the newly haunted 124, he hears "a conflagration of hasty voices" speaking a language incomprehensible save for the word *mine* (p. 172). He senses that this is the "roaring" of "the people of the broken necks, of fire-cooked blood and black girls who had lost their ribbons" (p. 181). Beloved magnetizes 124, attracting all that lost life now returning to lay claim to its own. The impossibility of articulating such possessive claims in an "earthly" language suggests the life-threatening potency of Beloved's desire. As an infant in a nineteen-year-old body, Beloved has not yet learned the codes that give shape to and control desire. Her unadulterated narcissism permits her to "seduce" her mother in the Clearing, an impulsive sensuality that probably derives from her memory of breastfeeding. Here, though, the libidinal element in normal breastfeeding becomes dominant, as Beloved's tender kisses entrance Sethe until she finds herself forced against the wall of the incest taboo: "You too old for that" (pp. 97–98). Beloved recognizes no social bounds, showing a resistance to conventional form that is registered in the disturbing "cadence" (p. 60) of her own words. While she craves adult language, particularly those stories that "construct out of the strings" of Denver and Sethe's experience "a net" to hold her (p. 76), she is incapable of such construction herself.

The sections of the novel dominated by Beloved's voice reflect her lack of a socially circumscribed identity; her "word-shapes" embody her tenuous physical and psychical shape. Before she finds "the join" with Sethe that enables her to escape the "dark place" (pp. 210–13), her "units" of self-representation are fragmented memories, word-pictures, and sensations, articulated without clearly established frames of reference—inside and outside, past and present, cause and effect. Even the gaps on the printed page suggest the danger of the disintegration of her being. After she assumes physical form (pp. 214–17), her self-projection in language integrates itself syntactically but continues to obfuscate the boundary between self and other; Beloved's image of her mother's face—"She smiles at me and it is my own face smiling" (p. 214)—suggests her inability to distinguish her own body from that of her mother.

At the end of the sections expressing the "unspeakable thoughts, unspoken" of "the women of 124" (p. 199), the voices of Sethe, Denver, and

Beloved merge into a single chorus that effaces individual identity in a possessive love sounded by the refrain

> You are mine
> You are mine
> You are mine (p. 217).

The fusion of identity expressed in this refrain can only be destructive, as Sethe and Denver lose themselves in the overpowering "mine" asserted by Beloved. In the end, their "conversation" is a monologic discourse dictated by a fleshly ghost, a univocal tyranny silencing any attempt at dialogic communication. In her insistence on absolute possession of her mother, Beloved resurrects the slavemaster's monopoly over both word and body, enforcing the internalized enslavement that has become a legacy of institutionalized slavery.

In order to free itself of the haunting past embodied in 124, the community must tap a deeper level of language, a more primitive source of cultural experience that creates communal bonds rather than destroying them. When Paul D's chain gang rescues itself from the muck flooding their below-ground cages, it discovers this kind of instinctive communication in the chain that binds them together: "They talked through that chain like Sam Morse and, Great God, they all came up" (p. 110). This "talking" is born out of the ooze, a pre-Genesis chaos—"All Georgia seemed to be sliding, melting away" (p. 111)—from which the human community is delivered. Ironically, the "best hand-forged chain in Georgia" (p. 107) acts as a linguistic tool for forging the communal identity that enables each one of them to survive the flood. Conversely, as Paul D reflects, had just one not "heard" the message, they all would have perished. Individual and community survival are thus inseparable; the trials of one body are, in some form, the trials of everybody.

This unity of the one with the whole is reaffirmed when the townswomen, alerted by Denver, come to rescue Sethe. The community resuscitates itself by again giving voice to the power of the life-affirming language that Baby Suggs had called out in the Clearing and that now demands the complete devotion of their bodily efforts. Eighteen years ago, the community, outraged at Sethe's prideful self-possession, had turned its back to her as she rode off to prison. The narrator observes that, had Sethe not been so seemingly convinced of her rectitude, "a cape of sound would have quickly been wrapped around her, like arms to hold and steady her way. . . . As it was, they waited till the cart turned about, headed west to town. And then no words. Humming. No words at all" (p. 152). The people withhold the support that their songs would have bodied forth, their words disdaining to touch the offending flesh. Now, however, the community, led by Ella, tries to sing Sethe back into its embrace. Like the singing of Paul D's chain gang and that of Sixo just before he is shot to death, the human voice in song is a potent material force. Sixo's song, triumphant because the Thirty-Mile Woman has escaped with his "blossoming seed," culminates in a laugh "so rippling and full of glee it put out the fire" (p. 229).

But when the women's singing prayer does not have the power to make contact with the "roaring" around 124, they must go all the way back to the first page of the text in their collective memory: "In the beginning was the sound, and—they all knew what the sound sounded like" (p. 259). This familiar, original sound precedes and overwhelms words, revitalizing Sethe's body and allowing her to break the lock Beloved has had upon her:

> For Sethe it was as though the Clearing had come to her with all its heat and simmering leaves, where the voices of women searched for the right combination, the key, the code, the sound that broke the back of words. Building voice upon voice until they found it, and when they did it was a wave of sound wide enough to sound deep water and knock the pods off chestnut trees. It broke over Sethe and she trembled like the baptized in its wash (p. 261).

This preverbal language seems to flex its muscles as it bursts forth from the deepest roots of human knowing, tapped by the "building" of a chorus of individual voices. Unleashed, Sethe rushes toward Bodwin (mistaking him for schoolteacher) with ice pick raised, her body partially transformed into the shape of the weapon she must use to protect her daughter: "The ice pick is not in her hand; it is her hand" (p. 262). But the reconstituted community intervenes, absorbing her in what Beloved sees as a "hill of black people falling" (p. 262). Now that Sethe and Denver have both reentered the communal fold, Beloved senses she has been left behind "Alone. Again" (p. 262), and the "devil-child" (p. 261) vanishes.

In the aftermath of her baptism, though, Sethe is devastated, her "best thing" taken from her a second time. She has taken a crucial step towards self-ownership in directing her protective violence against the oppressor (schoolteacher in the form of Bodwin) instead of against her own flesh and blood, but, alone, she cannot recuperate from the tragic repetition of her loss. To open the way to such recuperation, Paul D's own story of self-recovery is reunited with Sethe's. After he first leaves 124, ostensibly in horror at the news of Sethe's murderous past, he retreats into isolation, drinking alone in the cold church." When Stamp Paid visits him, Paul D resists his attempts to humanize Sethe's actions. But when Stamp asks whether he might have been "run off" 124 by Beloved, not Sethe, he is shocked into recognizing that his condemnation of Sethe's shameful act actually covered his own shame at his emasculation in Beloved's company (pp. 234–35). Now, returning to 124 to check on Sethe, he recalls his peculiar lovemaking with Beloved:

> Coupling with her wasn't even fun. It was more like the brainless urge to stay alive. Each time she came, pulled up her skirts, a life hunger overwhelmed him and he had no more control over it than over his lungs. And afterward, beached, gobbling for air, in the midst of repulsion and personal shame, he was thankful too for having been escorted to some ocean-deep place he once belonged to (p. 264).

His gratitude suggests a recognition that his rival for Sethe's affections had actually started the work of prying open his rusty tobacco tin and restoring to him the pulse of his "red heart" (p. 117).

Paul D must discover this "life hunger" within himself by sounding that "ocean-deep place" that the community tapped into in exorcising Beloved. To find that place "he once belonged to," he must begin drawing a "map to discover" himself (p. 140), one charting those regions of memory that block the way to the ocean-deep self. Standing over the half-conscious Sethe, not knowing what to make of this powerful woman, he suddenly recalls how Sixo described his love for the Thirty-Mile Woman: " 'She is a friend of my mind. She gather me, man. The pieces I am, she gather them and give them back to me in all the right order. It's good you know, when you got a woman who is a friend of your mind'" (p. 273). Then, "thinking about her wrought-iron back," that map of Sethe's sorrow and suffering, he remembers a moment that previously had been "packed away" in his tobacco tin:

> The mean black eyes. The wet dress steaming before the fire. Her tenderness about his neck jewelry—its three wands, like attentive baby rattlers, curving two feet in the air. How she never mentioned or looked at it so he did not have to feel the shame of being collared like a beast. Only this woman Sethe could have left him his manhood like that. He wants to put his story next to hers (p. 273).

This remembering of his haunting past is constructive rather than destructive, giving him the freedom, finally, to choose his own desire. In effect, he regains the authorship of his own text; he wants to put the story of his body, as well as the body of his story, alongside Sethe's. The next words inscribed into that text, communicated through the "holding fingers" (p. 273) of Paul D's "educated hands" (p. 99), begin the restoration of Sethe's own self-authorship: "You your best thing, Sethe. You are." Her wondering response, "Me? Me?," implies its own affirmation (p. 273). Reviving her with the knowing touch of his words, Paul D rescues Sethe from mute oblivion, reconnecting her with the talking spirit of companionship and community.

In the end, Beloved again becomes one of the "disremembered and unaccounted for" (p. 274), lurking in the liminal space of communal memory perhaps, but not a part of that community's consciousness. As Morrison's narrator puts it, "remembering seemed unwise," for Beloved's story "was not a story to pass on" (pp. 274–75). Her demonic "life hunger" simply cannot be encompassed within the "word-shapes" of the community's storytelling language. Provoked by Beloved's intrusion, the neighborhood has widened the circle of community to reincorporate Sethe and 124, but that circle must exclude the unassimilable otherness of Beloved.

Having accomplished its spontaneous "fixing ceremony" (p. 86), the kind Baby Suggs had led in the Clearing, the community is free to lay down "the heavy knives of defense against misery, regret, gall, and hurt" (p. 86), those weapons of self-defense that had turned against them as weapons of self-denial and self-destruction. Morrison has commented on the need for the novel as a way of dispensing "new information": "It should have something in it that enlightens; something in it that opens the doors and points the way. Something in it that suggests what the conflicts are, what the problems are. But it need not solve those problems because it is not a case study, it is not a recipe." In *Beloved*, Morrison suggests a way through the door of memory, even if that way entails a precarious balancing act between the danger of forgetting a past that should not be forgotten and of remembering a past that threatens to engulf the present. While the painful heritage of slavery cannot simply "pass on," cannot die away (to use another meaning suggested by that ambiguous phrase), enslavement to that heritage, Morrison implies, must "pass on," must die away, in order to undertake the task of remembering and rearticulating the individual and the communal body.

BERNARD W. BELL

Beloved: *A Womanist Neo-Slave Narrative; or Multivocal Remembrances of Things Past*

"What is curious to me," Toni Morrison occasionally says in her lectures, "is that bestial treatment of human beings never produces a race of beasts." Since her childhood in Lorain, Ohio, she has been fascinated by the uncommon efforts of common black people to deal creatively with their double consciousness and socialized ambivalence.

As first defined in 1897 by W.E.B. DuBois in "Strivings of the Negro People," double consciousness was not the sociopsychological and sociocultural experience of all ethnic immigrants and hyphenated white Americans. Rather, it was the complex double vision of Americans of African descent whose humanity and culture had been historically devalued and marginalized by people of European descent. For DuBois, it was a mythic blessing and a social burden: an ancestral gift for making sense of life, a product of institutionalized racism, and a dialectical process in American society involving the bearers of residual sub-Saharan African cultures, on the one hand, and bearers of residual Western cultures, on the other hand. For many contemporary Afro-Americans, it is the striving to reconcile one's ancestral African past—however remote, mythic, or spiritual—with one's American present, one's ascribed identity with one's achieved identity; to reconcile the politics of race with the politics of sex; to reconcile being a subject with being an object, and being an outsider with being an insider.

From *African American Review* 26:1 (Spring 1992).

In an apparent rewriting of DuBois's metaphor of double consciousness and sociologist Robert E. Park's 1928 theory of the marginal man (a racial and cultural hybrid or creole), the term *socialized ambivalence* was coined in 1937 by anthropologist Melville J. Herskovits in *Life in a Haitian Valley* to signify the anthropological adjustment of Haitians to the sociopsychological conflict that resulted from the contradictory cultural imperatives of European colonialism and African traditions. In applying this model to the United States, one notes the ambivalence expressed in the mixed emotions of most Americans of African descent about ideologies of integration and separation and in our shifting identification between white hegemonic and black nonhegemonic cultural systems as a result of institutionalized racism. *Double vision*, Ralph Ellison's 1964 rewriting of DuBois's metaphor (in *Shadow and Act*), is a fluid, ambivalent, laughing-to-keep-from-crying perspective toward life as expressed in the innovative use of irony and parody in Afro-American folklore and formal art.

How, then, do ordinary black people cope with the sexist customs, racist absurdities, and class exploitation of American life? Drawing on remembrances of her family's tradition of telling ghost stories and her longstanding fascination with literature, Morrison began attempting to answer this question creatively and expanded her commitment by joining a writers' workshop at Howard University in 1962. The short story which she began in that workshop became the nucleus of *The Bluest Eye* (1970) and the apprenticeship for her major achievements in poetic realism and Gothicism: *Sula* (1973), *Song of Solomon* (1977), *Tar Baby* (1981), and the Pulitzer-Prize-winning *Beloved* (1987).

Beloved contains Toni Morrison's most extraordinary and spellbinding womanist remembrances of things past. As Alice Walker's epigraphs to *In Search of Our Mothers' Gardens* suggest, *womanist* connotes "a black feminist or feminist of color"; a woman who, among other things, is audaciously "committed to [the] survival and wholeness of entire people, male *and* female." As Wilfred D. Samuels and Clenora Hudson-Weems remind us in their bio-critical study *Toni Morrison*, because of the silences in the slave narratives due to authorial compromises to white audiences and to self-masking from a painful past, Morrison sees her role as a writer as bearing witness to "the interior life of people who didn't write [their history] (which doesn't mean that they didn't have it)" and to "fill[ing] in the blanks that the slave narrative left."

Unlike James Baldwin, who also defined his role as bearing witness, Morrison privileges the authority and epistemology of black and Third World women in America. "I use the phrase 'bear witness' to explain what my work is for," she told Steve Cannon and Ntozake Shange in 1977.

> I have this creepy sensation . . . of loss. Like something is either lost, never to be retrieved, or something is about to be lost and will never be retrieved. Because if we don't know . . . what our past is, . . . if we Third-World women in America don't know it, then, it is not known by anybody at all. . . . And somebody has to tell somebody something.

As narrative strategy, remembrance, in Morrison's words, is "a journey to a site to see what remains have been left behind and to reconstruct the world that these remains imply." As in Marcel Proust's *The Remembrance of Things Past*, the recovery of lost experience is triggered by some external, ostensibly insignificant event. For example, in *Beloved* Sethe

> worked hard to remember as close to nothing as was safe. Unfortunately her brain was devious. She might be hurrying across a field, running practically, to get to the pump quickly and rinse the chamomile sap from her legs. Nothing else would be in her mind. . . . Then something. The plash of water, the sight of her shoes and stockings awry on the path where she had flung them; or Here Boy lapping in the puddle near her feet, and suddenly there was Sweet Home rolling, rolling, rolling out before her eyes, and although there was not a leaf on that farm that did not make her want to scream, it rolled itself out before her in shameless beauty. It never looked as terrible as it was and it made her wonder if hell was a pretty place too. Fire and brimstone all right, but hidden in lacy groves. Boys hanging from the most beautiful sycamores in the world. It shamed her—remembering the wonderful soughing trees rather than the boys. Try as she might to make it otherwise, the sycamores beat out the children every time and she could not forgive her memory for that.

On a sociopsychological level, *Beloved* is the story of Sethe Suggs's quest for social freedom and psychological wholeness. Sethe struggles with the haunting memory of her slave past and the retribution of Beloved, the ghost of the infant daughter that she killed in order to save her from the living death of slavery. On a legendary and mythic level, *Beloved* is a ghost story that frames embedded narratives of the impact of slavery, racism, and sexism on the capacity for love, faith, and community of black families, especially of black women, during the Reconstruction period. Set in post-Civil-War Cincinnati, *Beloved* is a womanist neo-slave narrative of double consciousness, a postmodern romance that speaks in many compelling voices and on several time levels of the historical rape of black American women and of the resilient spirit of blacks in surviving as a people.

As the author has explained in interviews and as a sympathetic white minister's report in the February 12, 1856, issue of the *American Baptist* reveals (see Bassett), at the center of *Beloved* is Morrison's retelling of the chilling historical account of a compassionate yet resolute self-emancipated mother's tough love. Margaret Garner, with the tacit sympathy of her sexagenarian mother-in-law, cut the throat of one of her four children and tried to kill the others to save them from the outrages of slavery that she had suffered. Guided by the spirits of the many thousands gone, as inscribed in her dedication, Morrison employs a multivocal text and a highly figurative language to probe her characters' double consciousness of their terribly paradoxical circumstances as people and non-people in a social arena of white male hegemony. She also foregrounds infanticide as a desperate act of "'thick'" love by a fugitive-slave mother "with iron eyes and backbone to match." "'Love is or it ain't,'" Sethe, the dramatized narrator/protagonist, says in reproach to a shocked friend, Paul D. "'Thin love ain't love at all.'" Indignantly reflecting on Paul D's metonymic reprimand that she "'got two feet . . . not four,'" she later expands on their oppositional metaphors in reverie: "Too thick, he said. My love was too thick. What he know about it? Who in the world is he willing to die for? Would he give his privates to a stranger in return for a carving?"

The implied author, the version of herself that Morrison creates as she creates the narrative, brilliantly dramatizes the moral, sexual, and epistemological distances between Sethe and Paul D. After their first dialogue, a trackless, quiet forest abruptly appears between them. This metaphorical silence is an ingenious, ironic use of the technique of call and response that invites the implied reader—in Wolfgang Iser's words, that "network of response-inviting structures, which impel the reader to grasp the text"—to pause and take stock of his or her own ambivalent moral and visceral responses to this slave mother's voicing of her thick love.

Thematically, the implied author interweaves racial and sexual consciousness in *Beloved*. Sethe's black awareness and rejection of white perceptions and inscriptions of herself, her children, and other slaves as nonhuman—marking them by letter, law, and lash as both animals and property—are synthesized with her black feminist sense of self-sufficiency. Sethe reconciles gender differences with first her husband Halle Suggs, and later Paul D, in heterosexual, endogamous relationships that affirm the natural and Biblical principles of the racial and ethnic survival of peoplehood through procreation and parenting in extended families. Although the implied author blends racial and sexual consciousness, the structure and style of the text foreground the ambivalence of slave women about motherhood that violates their personal integrity and that of their family.

Foregrounding the theme of motherhood, Morrison divides the text into twenty-eight unnumbered mini-sections, the usual number of days in a woman's monthly menstrual cycle, within three larger, disproportionate sections. Within these sections, Sethe experiences twenty-eight happy days of "having women friends, a mother-in-law, and all of her children together; of being part of a neighborhood; of, in fact, having neighbors at all to call her own." Also within these sections, the passion and power of memory ebb and flow in a discontinuous, multivocal discourse of the present with the past. Unlike the univocal, nineteenth-century slave narratives, in which plot rides character in the protagonist's journey of transformation from object to subject, *Beloved* is a haunting story of a mother's love that frames a series of interrelated love stories (maternal, parental, filial, sororal, conjugal, heterosexual, familial, and communal) by multiple narrators. These stories begin in 1873 and end in 1874, but flash back intermittently to 1855. In the flashbacks and reveries, the omniscient narrator invokes ancestral black women's remembrances of the terror and horror of the Middle Passage. She also probes the deep physical and psychic wounds of Southern slavery, especially the paradoxes and perversities of life on Sweet Home plantation in Kentucky, and recalls Sethe's bold flight to freedom in Ohio in 1855. Freedom, as Paul D's and Sethe's stories most dramatically illustrate, is "to get to a place where you could love anything you chose—not to need permission for desire."

The metaphors of personal and communal wholeness in the text heighten the psychological realism of its womanist themes of black kinship, motherhood, sisterhood, and love. Besides the structural analogue to a woman's natural reproductive cycle, the text frequently and dramatically highlights metaphors and metonyms for the agony and ecstasy, despair and hope, of loving, birthing, nurturing, and bonding. Heart, breasts, milk, butter, water, and trees—these recurring tropes first appear in the opening eight mini-sections as the vehicles for controlling the psychological, emotional, and moral distances among the narrators, characters, and implied reader, who participate, on various levels, in Sethe's historical and mythic quest.

After the omniscient narrator introduces us to the restless, spiteful spirit of Sethe's two-year-old daughter Beloved, we are quickly and irrevocably drawn into the vortex of conflicting values and feelings of the text. On one hand, we are drawn emotionally and psychologically closer to Sethe through her unrelenting memory of the terrible price she has paid for loving her daughter so dearly; but on the other, like Paul D and Ella, we are at first morally repelled by her gory act of infanticide. When slave catchers and schoolteacher suddenly appear in the family's Ohio yard to return Sethe and her children to slavery, she not only cuts Beloved's throat with a handsaw and attempts to kill her other three, but she subsequently trades ten minutes of sex on her daughter's grave with an engraver, as his son watches, to pay him for carving the word *Beloved* on her daughter's headstone.

Our sympathies for Sethe are strengthened, however, through her grim reverie and dialogue with Paul D. Through them we discover that, earlier in 1855, while pregnant with Denver and before she could escape with her husband Halle to join their children in Ohio with the milk to nurse her baby girl, she was outrageously violated. "I am full God damn it of two boys with mossy teeth," she remembers, "one sucking on my breast the other holding me down, their book-reading teacher watching and writing it up." Weaving into her story the additional gruesome details provided eighteen years later by Paul D, who knew her from their shared years of slavery on the ironically named Sweet Home plantation, the horror continues:

> Add my husband to it, watching, above me in the loft—hiding close by—the one place he thought no one would look for him, looking down on what I couldn't look at at all. And not stopping them—looking and letting it happen. . . . There is also my husband squatting by the churn smearing the butter as well as its clabber all over his face because the milk they took is on his mind. And as far as he is concerned, the world may as well know it.

Again we note the implied author's privileging of metaphor and metonym over black dialect to achieve just the right aesthetic balance between the poetics and polemics of the long black song of the many thousands gone that she skillfully orchestrates to engage our hearts and mind.

The collusion of many antebellum white women with the brutalization of black women is suggested by the ineffectual tears of the plantation mistress, Mrs. Garner, whom Sethe tells about the attack. In retaliation, Mrs. Garner's wryly named brother-in-law, who studies and treats slaves as animals, orders one of his nephews to whip Sethe. "'Schoolteacher made one open my back,'" Sethe tells Paul D, "'and when it closed it made a tree. It grows there still.'" The ugly scar on her back is described as having the trunk, branches, leaves, and blossoms of a chokeberry tree by Amy Denver, the runaway, ragged, and hungry indentured white girl who, in sharp contrast to Mrs. Garner, not only massages Sethe's swollen feet but also helps to deliver her baby on the Ohio River bank. Unlike most of the black female narrators, Amy, whose quest for velvet rather than love is the principal sign of her racial, sexual, and class difference, is not raped, and she stands as the implied author's brightest ray of hope for black and white sisterhood. When Paul D hears about Sethe's stolen milk and bitter-fruit tree, he bends down behind her in the kitchen, "his body an arc of kindness," and holds her breasts in his hands as he "rub[s] his cheek on her back and learn[s] that way her sorrow, the roots of it; its wide trunk and intricate branches." Symbolically, the chokeberry tree signifies the physical and psychic suffering of slavery that Paul D shares with Sethe.

As the text unfolds with the ebb and flow of characters, events, and memories, these figures of speech are developed in free association and free indirect discourse—the linguistic fusion of two narrative voices. Occasionally, the implied author's consciousness merges with the narrator's, the narrator/protagonist's with the characters', the past with the present, and the black female's with the male's. These techniques compel the reader viscerally and cerebrally to fill in the gaps in the text of the fragmented, yet complementary, embedded stories and memories of Baby Suggs, Nan, Sethe's mother, Ella, Stamp Paid, and Paul D. The implied reader is moved by these illustrative comparisons and contrasts to reconstruct and reconsider the unspeakable human cost of American slavery, racism, and sexism, then and now—to whites as well as blacks, to men as well as women—, and to sympathize with Sethe, black mothers, and black families in their struggle against white male hegemony to affirm their self-worth as a racial group.

The Gothic story of Sethe's loving and losing Beloved is thematically and emotionally emblematic of the historical struggle for survival with self-respect and love of black families that has been passed on orally and spiritually from generation to generation. "'Not a house in the country ain't packed to its rafters with some dead Negro's grief,'" Sethe's sixty-year-old mother-in-law tells her. "'You lucky. You got three left. . . . I had eight. Every one of them gone away from me. Four taken, four chased, and all, I expect, worrying somebody's house into evil.'" Sethe tells her daughters the horror story of her mother as passed on to her by Nan, the one-armed slave wet nurse and cook who became her surrogate mother. For Sethe was nursed only two or three weeks by her mother, a field slave branded with a circle and cross under her breast, before she was turned over to Nan, who, along with Sethe's mother, had been raped many times by crew members during the Middle Passage. The children fathered by these and other whites, Sethe's mother threw away. "'Without names, she threw them,'" Nan tells young Sethe in a pidgin tongue that implicitly valorizes the ancestral life-bestowing power of naming rituals, a tongue and ritual bonding that are only a dim memory for Sethe. "'You she gave the name of the black man. She put her arms around him. The others she did not put her arms around. Never. Never.'"

Ella, an agent on the Underground Railroad who twice rescues Sethe, believes in root medicine but not love. As a result of Ella's having been regularly abused sexually while in puberty by her master and his son, "'the lowest yet,'" she considers sex disgusting and love a "serious disability." She remembers having delivered, "but would not nurse, a hairy white thing, fathered by 'the lowest yet.'" While she understands Sethe's rage in the shed, she regards Sethe's reaction as prideful and misdirected. Even so, ". . . Ella didn't like the idea of past errors taking possession of the present . . . of sin moving on in the house, unleashed and sassy." Morally and emotionally, the relationship of the past to the present is relative, not absolute.

Similarly, Baby Suggs, an "unchurched preacher" who is driven to bed to think about the colors of things by the un-Christian ways of white Christians, passes on the bittersweet wisdom of her years in stories she tells to her granddaughter Denver and her daughter-in-law Sethe. Baby Suggs's heart, her faith and love, began to collapse twenty-eight days after Sethe's arrival, when white slave catchers violated her home and terrorized Sethe into killing Beloved, the daughter of the only son Baby Suggs was allowed to mother, Halle. "What she called the nastiness of life," the sympathetic implied author tells us in free indirect discourse,

> was the shock she received upon learning that nobody stopped playing checkers just because the pieces included her children. Halle she was able to keep the longest. Twenty years. A lifetime. Given to her, no doubt, to make up for *hearing* that her two girls, neither of whom had their adult teeth, were sold and gone and she had not been able to wave goodbye. To make up for coupling with a straw boss for four months in exchange for keeping her third child, a boy, with her—only to have him traded for lumber in spring of the next year and to find herself pregnant by the man who promised not to and did. That child she could not love and the rest she would not. "God take what He would," she said. And He did, and He did, and He did and then gave her Halle who gave her freedom when it didn't mean a thing.

The double consciousness and double vision here (which some readers will recognize as analogous to Mikhail M. Bakhtin's theory of double-voiced or dialogic texts) are apparent in the interplay and interweaving of the represented discourse, time frames, and perspectives of the implied author and Baby Suggs.

In addition to the three basic types of represented discourse (direct, simple indirect, and free indirect), five different yet related linguistic codes and their concomitant ideologies (i.e., their implicit, related systems of beliefs and values) are present in *Beloved*: standard American English, rural black vernacular English, black feminist discourse, black patriarchal discourse, and white male hegemonic discourse. The two dominant voices, however, are in standard American English and black feminist discourse. For example, the implied author and the dramatized narrator/protagonist, Sethe, want Beloved and the implied reader to understand that, far worse than Beloved's grisly death, is

> that anybody white could take your whole self for anything that came to mind. Not just work, kill, or maim you, but dirty you. Dirty you so bad you couldn't like yourself anymore. Dirty you so bad you forgot who you were and couldn't think it up. And though she and others lived through and got over it, she could never let it happen to her own. The best thing she was, was her children. Whites might dirty *her* all right, but not her best thing, her beautiful, magical best thing—the part of her that was clean.

In contrast, Denver tells her sister Beloved the legend of her birth and of the white girl with "no meanness around her mouth" whose name she bears.

In an apparent rewriting of Faulkner's narrative strategy in dramatizing Shreve and Quentin's reconstuction and reliving of Charles Bon and Henry Sutpen's fatal kinship in *Absalom, Absalom!*, Morrison employs Denver to voice the manner and degree to which storyteller, story, and primary audience of *Beloved* share a concord of sensibilities in a residually oral culture which sanctions the dynamic coexistence of the spoken and written word, the metaphysical and physical, the mythic and historic:

> Denver was seeing it now and feeling it—through Beloved. Feeling how it must have felt to her mother. Seeing how it must have looked. And the more fine points she made, the more detail she provided, the more Beloved liked it. So she anticipated the questions by giving blood to the scraps her mother and grandmother had told her—and a heartbeat. The monologue became, in fact, a duet as they lay down together, Denver nursing Beloved's interest like a lover whose pleasure was to overfeed the loved.

Near the end of the novel, in sections 22 and 23, the consciousness of Sethe, Denver, and Beloved merge in free indirect discourse and surrealism.

Unlike Morrison's *The Bluest Eye* and the womanist texts of Alice

Walker, in *Beloved* black men are not stereotyped as "low-down dirty dog[s]," like the nameless Assistant and the Wild Child's anonymous impregnator in *Meridian* and Mr. _____ and even God in *The Color Purple*. Although circumstances may reduce some to debasing themselves with cows, clabber, or the daughters of their lovers, Baby Suggs, Sethe, and the implied author agree: "'A man ain't nothing but a man . . .'" Even Garner, the benevolent master of Sweet Home, stands out among his white neighbors for treating his slaves (Paul D, Paul A, Paul F, Halle, and Sixo) like men. "'Bought em thataway, raised em thataway,'" he boasts with dramatic irony. Garner allows Halle to hire himself out on weekends for five years to buy his mother's freedom, allows his slaves to have guns, and even allows them to marry rather than breed them like animals. Thus, although Sethe was a desirable young girl of thirteen when she arrived at the plantation, the Sweet Home men, who were all in their twenties and "so sick with the absence of women they had taken to calves," did not rape her. They "let the iron-eyed girl be, so she could choose." Clearly, the theme, protagonist, structure, and style privilege a black woman's perspective, but sexual politics complements rather than dominates racial politics in the implied author's celebration of black people as more than the dehumanized victims of brutal social oppression.

In her multivocal celebration of the spiritual resiliency of black people, black men and women are physically and psychologically violated by slavery, racism, and sexism in the text. (These violations were exacerbated by the infamous Fugitive Slave Act of 1850, which legalized the kidnapping and enslavement of any black person anywhere in the United States.) With Garner's death, "schoolteacher broke into children what Garner had raised into men." So after Paul F is sold, the other slaves attempt unsuccessfully to escape. Sixo is burned alive and shot; Paul A is hanged and mutilated; Sethe is raped and beaten; and Halle loses his mind after witnessing his wife's violation. Paul D is forced to wear a three-spoked collar and mouth bit while waiting to be sold down river where he and other black prisoners are terrorized with fellatio and death. Paul D's reverie explains his subsequent seduction by Beloved while he is Sethe's lover as "more like a brainless urge to stay alive" than a desire to have fun. Also "dirtied" by whites, Stamp Paid, the conductor on the Underground Railroad who ferries Sethe to Ohio and snatches Denver from death in a woodshed, was born Joshua. But

> . . . he renamed himself when he handed over his wife to his master's son. Handed her over in the sense that he did not kill anybody, thereby himself, because his wife demanded he stay alive. . . . With that gift, he decided that he didn't owe anybody anything. Whatever his obligations were, that act paid them off.

For the characters, narrator, and the implied author, the scars of sexual, racial, and class oppression on the soul—the price of the ticket for the journey from slavery to freedom and from object to subject—are more horrible than those on the body.

Even so, the struggle to survive with justifiable self-respect rather than inordinate self-esteem or self-debasement prevails for those who affirm ties to their ethnic community. When the community perceives excessive pride in Sethe and Baby Suggs, as illustrated by the former's "stand offishness" and the latter's extravagant blackberry party, it feels insulted and rejected—which is why no one from the community warns them about the slave catcher's approach. After sixty years of a life with less sunshine than rain, Stamp Paid reflects, ". . . to belong to a community of other free Negroes—to love and be loved by them, to counsel and be counseled, protect and be protected, feed and be fed—and then to have that community step back and hold itself at a distance—well, it could wear out even a Baby Suggs, holy." But Ella and the community of thirty black women come praying and singing to Sethe's rescue after Denver reaches out to the community and after Beloved "t[a]k[es] flesh" in the world as a "devil-child" and nearly hounds Sethe to death.

The arrival, departure, and return of Paul D, however, provide the frame-story for Sethe's realization of personal wholeness in the community and Morrison's synthesis of sexual and racial politics. With Paul D's arrival at Sethe's haunted house, she can suddenly "trust things and remember things because the last of the Sweet Home men was there to catch her if she sank." In her mind's eye, "there was something blessed in his manner. Women saw him and wanted to weep. . . . Strong women and wise saw him and told him things they only told each other . . ." Paul D leaves Sethe after being shocked by her confession of infanticide and after responding insensitively about the number of feet Sethe has. This remark is associated in the minds of the protagonist and, with mixed emotions, the implied reader with schoolteacher's belief and value systems as dramatized in his listing of Sethe's "characteristics on the animal side."

Paul D returns to 124 Bluestone Road after Denver and the choral community of black women break Beloved's spell because he wants to take care of Sethe, who has withdrawn in despair to die in Baby Suggs's bed. As he proceeds to rekindle the will to live of the woman who, as Sixo said of his woman, is "'a friend of [his] mind'" by bathing her, he remembers how she "left him his manhood" by not mentioning his being collared like a beast. Putting "his story next to hers" as the framestory closes in a romantic vignette, he holds her hand and tells her that she is her best thing and that "'. . . we got more yesterday than anybody. We need some kind of tomorrow.'"

In her multivocal remembrances of things past, Morrison probes the awesome will to live of her characters in order to celebrate the truth and resiliency of the complex double consciousness of their humanity. What she has wrought in *Beloved* is an extraordinarily effective Gothic blend of post-modern realism and romance as well as of racial and sexual politics.

STEPHANIE A. DEMETRAKOPOULOS

Maternal Bonds as Devourers of Women's Individuation in Toni Morrison's Beloved

My focus here is the way in which Toni Morrison, in her complex and dazzling novel *Beloved*, develops the idea that maternal bonds can stunt or even obviate a woman's individuation or sense of self. The book both thematizes and problematizes the conflict between history/culture and maternal instincts. And whereas the bulk of the novel develops the twistings and turnings, the complexity, of the protagonist's maternal instincts, the conclusion of the book effects a resolution of the tension between history and nature which underlies the movement of the work as a whole.

Women are ultimately defined as different from men for one simple reason: We can be mothers. Our sexuality, aside from our ability to bear children, is different from men's, desired by men, and worriedly or viciously projected onto by men. But men are just as much prey to the sexual bonds forged within a couple as women are. The bonds of mothering are what differentiate women's lives from men's. Important books on the sociological, psychological, even clinical aspects of mothering have appeared in the last decade, many by women who are themselves mothers and know the power of the maternal bond.

Nancy Chodorow's *The Reproduction of Mothering* and Dorothy Dinnerstein's *The Mermaid and the Minotaur* are two splendid examples of feminist analyses that delve into the reasons for and meanings of this maternal

From *African American Review* 26:1 (Spring 1992). © 1992 by Stephanie A. Demetrakopoulos.

response. But no feminist analysis I have read explores with depth and honesty the dark and painful side of mothering, the fact that mothering can extinguish the developing self of the mother, sometimes even before that individuation can really begin—and sometimes forever. In Morrison's *Bluest Eye* Pecola becomes pregnant in her early teens through incest with her father; the pregnancy precipitates abuse by her community, which eventually sends her over the edge into permanent insanity *before* she can develop an adult sense of self. The teenage mother often never really enters human history: She is erased before pubescent consciousness dawns enough to solidify her sense of self. Her own biology sucks/swamps her psyche into the undifferentiated morass of Nature.

Only a few individual mothers have written of their sense of being stifled, smothered by their entrapment in the care of children. Tillie Olsen, for example, has explored a woman's turning away from this entrapment in *Tell Me a Riddle*. But the culture at large really does not want to hear about the heavy costs of mothering. The most thorough exploration of the Devouring Mother archetype has come from a male author, Erich Neumann, in *The Great Mother*. Esther Harding's *Women's Mysteries* admonishes against the dangers attendant on the woman who needs to wean herself from mothering as her children grow up so that she can develop other parts of her identity, but only Neumann explores the imagery of devouring that is connected with the mother archetype. Yet even he examines the devouring motif solely from the point of view of the fearful child or the wary male. Toni Morrison's *Beloved* is the first book-length work to examine the dangers of mothering to the individuation of the mother herself. Parallel to the theme of the devouring nature of maternal bonds, and merging with it, are Morrison's explorations of a matriarchal world turned in on itself and the pathology inherent in such female fortresses. I will separate out and analyze this important theme later in this essay. First, I want to establish Morrison's perspective on motherhood, that conundrum, that riddling force that has impelled, compelled our species forward.

We can never fully understand this massive force that has carried the species' evolution, supported it, nurtured it. Consider what the many individual mothers who have given birth to infants with newly mutated characteristics have had to face. Each individual death of a baby of our species whose mutation has rendered it unable to survive has required the personal care, and brought the attendant grief, of a mother; but we subsume this individual pain and grief under the abstract term *evolution*. Morrison said in a national broadcast shown after she received the Pulitzer Prize that motherhood is not history. It is a timeless, ahistorical force with all the glories and limitations that pure nature imposes, even when colored, camouflaged by its many cultural versions.

As I have traced elsewhere, the Demeter/Persephone or Kore (daughter) archetype can be an illuminating frame on Morrison's works. I am not the only critic who believes that Morrison identifies more with the Demeter/mother half of that dyad. The classical Demeter/Kore of the Eleusinian rites, which celebrate and delineate time's cyclical character with respect to nature and woman, symbolizes the sacredness and grace inherent in the mother-daughter chain letter that underlies our species. The Demeter/Persephone dyad is the central divine image for Western culture of the pattern that all women must follow and comprehend in all its phases in order to individuate. We all begin as Kore, the daughter, before maturing into the Demeter phase of nurturer. All women, as they leave the first bloom of youth, experience the two sides of Demeter: They age into knowing within both the kindness of Sophia, umbrella mother to the species, and the deadly killing anger of Kali.

Beloved explores the benign, benevolent, and powerful phase of this archetype in Baby Suggs, the mother-in-law of Sethe, the novel's protagonist. Baby Suggs basically shrinks herself into death when she experiences American culture's denial of and intent to destroy her daughter-in-law's mothering; and, with the annihilation of Sethe's motherhood, her own grandmothering is also obviated. But the dark, devouring phase of the aging Demeter is part of Sethe's character, not Baby Suggs's. Sethe, prematurely hurled into Kali fury by the slave owners' attempt to repossess her and her family, makes a split-second decision to kill her own children rather than allow their souls to be devoured by slavery. The institution of slavery, the atrocity of historical time, denies Sethe her mothering and destroys the natural cycles of maternal bonding.

In *Beloved*, Morrison examines motherhood in its most denied form, the mother enslaved, reduced to a brood mare. Sethe's initial bonding with her children has occurred at the ironically named Sweet Home, where slaves are allowed to marry and have families. These bonds resurge with terrifying strength as Sethe attempts to return the babies to perhaps a collective mother body, to devour them back into the security of womb/tomb death much as a mother cat will eat her babies as the ultimate act of protection. In this act, Morrison gives us the most searching portrait I know of the paradoxical polarities in motherhood. For Sethe the children are better off dead, their fantasy futures protected from the heinous reality of slavery. It is better, Sethe's act argues, to die in the cradle than to live out one's full life span soul-dead, a zombie/puppet daily treading the process requirements of someone else's life and needs. The child as the adult's fantasy of the future is obviously central to Sethe's murder of Beloved.

That the child first killed is a girl is important. Sethe has her other three children with her and is clearly planning to kill them all before taking her own life. But, like the choice Sophie makes in William Styron's 1979 novel, in which the protagonist selects her daughter to die rather than her son, the first child Sethe makes certain is dead is her toddler daughter. Sophie's daughter is a musical, artistic child, much more like Sophie than her son, even in matters beyond gender identification. For Sethe, like Sophie, to kill her daughter is to kill her own best self, to kill her best and self-gendered fantasy of the future. The act is like killing time itself, especially its redemptive gifts, which the daughter, as a potential mother, symbolizes.

Neumann's image for the devouring mother is the *vagina dentata*, a symbol obviously fraught with special dangers for men. But Morrison explores maternity, not from a male point of view or as a cultural projection, but as an interface between life and death *from within a mother*. Morrison has remarked that she likes to push things way out to the edge, to polarize a force so that it can be closely examined. Several times in *Beloved* she alludes to the iron *materia* of Sethe's soul/psyche as the vehicle that can sustain these forces in order to permit their microscopic examination. Denver tells us that her mother does not look away when a man is stomped to death by a horse, when a sow eats its litter, when Here Boy is maimed. Sethe herself wonders why she does not lose her mind, why she must carry in all its clarity her memories of the chain of atrocities her life has been. Morrison deliberately creates a character whose strength will not break under the weight of the atrocities that push her maternal bonds into such isolation—away from her community, out of history itself, so far from the rest of life that they can be scrutinized as almost the sole forces in Sethe's life. It is almost as though her mind becomes contained, bound by her motherhood. Because her own creative self, in the form of her psyche, functions as a logical extension of her biology, killing her child forces Sethe's mind outside of her body. Her mind is not lost, but by the end of the novel, when Paul D finds her in bed, apparently giving up on life, she has certainly abandoned her mind as source of how to live and cope. (Sethe's psyche and its strength also unify the novel, so her psyche is important structurally as well as thematically.)

Morrison denies Sethe even the ability to fantasize about her future in terms of suicide, which in its destruction of self means at least that a self has been acknowledged. Even when released from slavery and jail, Sethe goes on internalizing slavery; she simply holds the past at bay for her three surviving children. But she never imagines her own future. Like Son in *Tar Baby*, who ends up in the swamp of his mythic forefathers, wandering an island in isolation from any society, community, or tribe, Sethe cannot participate in the ongoingness of life; she cannot imagine herself into history. Horribly, her ultimate and only insistence on her humanity was the act of killing her best self, her daughter's extension of potential into the future.

Even her escape from slavery was not really for herself. Her swollen breasts and the baby kicking within pressed her onward to the baby waiting for her milk. Biological necessity made her create a life that would allow her children to grow up. Sethe carries Beloved on her conscience and in her heart. For the mother, the dead child is maternity ***in potentia***, the mother truncated.

Sethe curses her own future by gazing only backwards, until she conjures the past; the baby ghost haunts her sons right out of the house, isolating her into a totally female realm. Sethe further fixates on the past by never mingling with the Black community, by protecting the only child who stays with her, her daughter Denver, from the past without seeming ever to think of the girl's future or need for community. When we first enter the home, only Sethe and Denver inhabit it, and it is claustrophobic indeed.

This claustrophobic aura echoes the closed-in lack of self of Sethe herself. Paradoxically, while she appears to have a strong self because of her pride and independence, she marshalls her prodigious strength only to maintain a home for Denver and Baby Suggs. Her idea that her children are her best parts, her best self (ultimately her *only* self) becomes such a central motif in Sethe's characterization that her dilemma is resolved by Paul D's telling her, "'You your best thing, Sethe. You are.'" The reconciliation scene between them is also the denouement of the novel, for it is with the arrival of Paul D and her final acceptance of her need for him and his sense of her wonderful self that Sethe, we know, will begin to heal and plan for a future that includes a relationship that is for *her*, a relationship that embodies her release from her pathological and painfully protracted mothering.

Perhaps a woman who forever defines herself through her maternal bonds remains forever caught in the matrix of nature—indeed becomes part of the matrix of nature. When Sethe finally connects with Paul D, she moves towards individuation, becomes connected with her own animus energy and, thus, assumes a position from which she can escape the deadly toils of nature.

Beloved is, on an historical and sociological level, a Holocaust book, and like much Holocaust literature, it marvels at the indifferent and enduring beauty of nature as a frame for the worst human atrocities. This theme is central to *And the Sun Kept On Shining*, for example, in which the author loses her entire family and then is stripped of her humanity in a Nazi death camp. Similarly, in both Alain Resnais' *Night and Fog* and his recent *Shoah*, the camera lingers ironically on beautiful landscapes as a voice-over comments on the pastoral setting where Jews were slaughtered and buried in mass graves. In Morrison's novel, Sethe marvels at how the beautiful landscape of Sweet Home recurs more often in her memories as a pastoral vision than as the slaughterhouse it finally became. Nature erases atrocities, but this allows humans to repeat them.

The originality of *Beloved* lies in Morrison's delineation of the cruelty of the nature *within*. Her use of the pathetic fallacy ironically underlines the cruel absurdity of maternal passion. After Sethe gives birth to Denver, Morrison comments on the lie of fecundity in their environment. The spores of bluefern floating in the river, she writes,

> are seeds in which the whole generation sleeps confident of a future. And for a moment it is easy to believe that each one has one—will become all of what is contained in the spore: will live out its days as planned. This moment of certainty lasts no longer than that; longer, perhaps than the spore itself.

But tenuous, frail, as almost certainly doomed as newborn life is, the mother instinct takes upon itself total and crushing responsibility for the fruition of its offspring. Sethe repeatedly cites her milk as a kind of panacea, even as the bonding element of her family.

To fully understand the extent to which Sethe's maternal bonds almost destroy her, we must look closely at the life stages that her surviving daughter Denver passes through. Denver's round, brown, chubby body symbolizes the *gravitas* of social reality, of history, which she so prosaically embodies. This is the same prosaic quality suggested by Denver's name, her typically little-girl secret room in the bushes, and her adolescent response to Paul D's entering her mother's life (Denver is both waiting for her father Halle and embarrassed by her mother's sexuality). Like Nel in *Sula* and Hagar in *Song of Solomon*, Denver needs community and family, traditional ties. She is the female survivor in Western culture, the hard-headed practical one who will finally seek work and make connections with the outside world. We see this early in her discovery of Lady Jones's classes; we see her heading for a future in American culture and society at the close of the novel as a young man pursues her down the street; and we have earlier been told that perhaps she will go to Oberlin College. Denver, in short, comes to embody the history that Sethe so resists entering.

In an awesomely strong manner, Denver finally gives birth to her Self, her own Identity. Her mother has ensured Denver's life, her survival; but Sethe has not projected futures for Denver that might ensure the child's ability to step into womanhood. Denver's consciousness as a female emerges for her as she sits alone in her bower (a word that has resonated with sexual connotations since Milton and Spenser's use of bowers as symbols for prelapsarian female sexuality), and her emergent adolescent sexuality is part of what impels her identification with Beloved, who unwittingly provides one step toward maturity for Denver's Womanself, struggling to be born. Part of Denver's strength lies in her genetic heritage: When she goes to look for work, we are told that she is her father's daughter. And Paul D remarks at the conclusion of the novel on how much she looks like Halle, who offers a superb image of male nurturing, industry, and compassion. Coupled with Sethe's strength, the qualities associated with Halle will, we know, carry Denver far.

Denver actually midwives two female souls into the toils of adult individuation—her mother Sethe's as well as her own. Denver helps deliver Sethe from her deadly bond with Beloved. It is from Denver that Sethe takes the word *plans* and by the end of the book is able to apply this concept to herself. Denver uses whatever raw material she finds around her to help her out of the matriarchal cave into life. Even Beloved serves as a foothold, a rung on the ladder; as a woman one step ahead in sexual development. Also, in mothering Beloved, Denver remothers herself away from her fears of Sethe, which began when she accidentally learned of her sister's murder. When Denver tells Sethe's story to Beloved, she really *knows* it for the first time; it becomes far more than just words, the myth of her own origin. She begins to understand how her mother suffered and finally becomes protective of Sethe as she sees the actual flesh of Sethe disappearing in the devouring bond with Beloved. Denver is realistic enough to see that something must be done, and it is through her agency that the community of women mobilize to exorcise Beloved. Sethe is tied only to her past, whereas Denver is interested only in the present until she matures to become the caretaker of her caretaker and enters the future. For a time, Denver must precociously become Demeter, until Paul D returns to catalyze Sethe out of her sickbed. The live daughter as rescuer supplants the dead daughter as succubus, Sethe's girl child does finally mean her life.

Denver recovers from some terrifying clinical symptoms, such as the deafness that follows her hearing the horror of Beloved's death, to carry her mother's soul into the future, into history. But Denver has been well loved, and it is with Baby Suggs's words resounding in her ears/memory that she steps off the porch of her womb/home into the community to seek work.

Although Denver is the daughter that will save Sethe, it is not Denver that Sethe fixates on. It is through Beloved that Morrison develops the deadliness of maternal bonding for Sethe, who is complicitous in Beloved's gradual absorption of her mother's very life and flesh.

Sethe never got to live out the Kore stage of life; she was never the Persephone gathering flowers under her mother's fond eye. Mrs. Garner seems motherly with Sethe, but she still treats her as a slave. And Mrs.

Garner has no power finally, for she gives it away to the nearest white man, who never consults her about the treatment of Sethe and the other slaves. Sethe was not provided instruction in even the basic elements of mothering at Sweet Home; she has never seen a real woman engaged in mothering. That women who have not had the opportunity to see the very flawed mothering of other women often develop impossible ideals of what good mothering is finds reflection in Sethe's fevered attempt to remother both girls as soon as she decides Beloved is her returned daughter.

Thus, Sethe suffers remorse, but has no built-in mechanism for forgiving herself. Denver sees her as "a rag doll, broke down, finally, from trying to take care of and make up for." Sethe is in fact crucified symbolically, receiving Beloved's Judas kiss in the clearing where Baby Suggs preached. This Judas kiss, of course, comes from within as well as from ghostly realms; in a sense, Sethe's guilt has recreated Beloved and perhaps sustains the ghost. And she sets about remothering Beloved with a ferocity and single-mindedness that again bespeak Sethe's iron will.

Older children disallow pure mother love with their disconcerting development of too often unlovable individuality. Sethe mothers Beloved as if she were once more a toddler, for it is easier to love wholly and without reserve the preadolescent child who has not yet developed its seed flaws into full blown and aggravating ugliness. Just as Sethe does not really see Denver's sexuality (she visually sees and notes it, but has done nothing to nurture or acknowledge its needs), she returns Beloved to the purely daughter role and remains herself the fierce tigress, dispensing eager love and protecting the child from the outside world. Unfortunately, such a protected child does not grow up, as Morrison has shown in the earlier examples of Sula (in *Sula*), Milkman and Hagar in *Song of Solomon*, and Jadine in *Tar Baby*.

For a reader familiar with Morrison's motifs, Beloved's devouring propensities are uncomfortably present even in the beginning of the novel. Her hunger for sweet things recalls Guitar in *Song of Solomon*, who cannot eat sweets or love the sweet things of life because he is dedicated to revenge, and *Tar Baby*'s Valerian, a capitalist who manufactures sweets as a sort of opiate of the masses and who marries because when he first sees his wife-to-be, she reminds him of his candies. Sweets and candies always seem dangerous to Morrison's protagonists. Beloved sees Sethe as the sweet thing that will give her Self (in the Jungian sense), and it seems that Beloved must have Paul D because he is Sethe's sweet thing. Thus, the inverted and cruel maternal bonds suck Sethe into an incestuous bonding—another way for nature itself, in the guise of the family, to swallow Sethe. Beloved is excited by the turtles' copulating, an image which turns her sex with Paul D into a boxed reptilian intercourse. Part of the reason that Paul D initially flees is fear of Beloved, who makes him wonder if he is indeed lower than some sort of animal.

Paul D is an exceptionally well-drawn character, and like most of Morrison's other male characters, he is a traveling man; he is preoccupied with his feet and carries his shoes into Sethe's house. He has traveled widely geographically and through several American cultures, including those of the American Indian. His strength, like Sethe's, is prodigious and remarkable. This strength allows women to acknowledge their need for nurturing; and with that admission, their sexuality, we are told, emerges more rampant in proportion to their age. Like Samson, he almost tears the house down as he angrily exorcises Beloved's ghost. He is also a singing man around whom space rearranges itself with him as an axis. Unlike Sethe, Paul D has survived by *not* remembering, but as he accepts her past, he recalls his; it is to Sethe as Halle's woman that he seems initially attracted. Unlike Halle, he is from a group of Pauls who are not even sure they want the risks of freedom. But Paul D achieves a powerful kind of one-sided masculine individuality when he finds Sethe, though his ability to love is dead until she awakens it.

Paul D's sexual relationship with Beloved articulates the full ugliness of Sethe's lingering maternal bonds to her dead daughter, and their incestuous union results in a kind of uroboric pregnancy with the past that finally blooms itself into extinction. Until Beloved is almost full-term, she devours Sethe. Paul D's presence in Sethe's life flushes Beloved into full-bodied form, and Beloved's physical presence makes clear the deadliness of Sethe's bonds with things past.

A Jungian perspective on Sethe and Paul's relationship helps reveal its intricate depths. Paul D gives Sethe the animus quality of initiative to escape from the mother/family matrix into individuation that celebrates the self as "her best thing." Sethe helps Paul D develop his anima qualities of relatedness that make a man responsible to his family and community, that permit him to achieve intimacy and enduring relationships. Sethe is in bed, languishing in Denver's care, when Paul D finds her; his words make her get out of that bed and live. At the end of the novel, it seems that the house itself will be sold, and we foresee a home for Sethe and Paul.

The force that finally exorcises Beloved, however, is the community of mothers, led by Ella, who also killed an infant of hers, born of a white man who abused her husband, her marriage, and her. Perhaps only through other women, preferably mothers themselves, can we women traverse the stages of mothering. Mothers need community, fellow travelers.

One of Morrison's gifts to American women is her honoring of the enlightment that living out female experiences can give. The community of women who heal Sethe is Morrison's tribal metaphor that confronts and defies the way that American culture so denigrates, so desacralizes motherhood.

Only a mother knows the cost of mothering. The strength it takes to break the bonds of even the normal amount of guilt incurred in the process is prodigious; to break the bonds of guilt that Sethe carries takes many women.

Denied normal motherhood by the culture that envelops her, Sethe carries mother instinct to an absurd and grotesque length. *Enantiodromia*, the principle that any natural force suppressed will have gained demonic force by the time it finally bursts forth, is a rule of life in this novel. Beloved is a figure of maternal love that becomes psychic incest and a terrible binding force, for the child not let go is a force that binds the maternal psyche into the family to the point that the mother cannot enter history/community. In Simone de Beavoir's terms, Sethe remains trapped in immanence rather than growing into transcendence. The lost Beloved lingers on at the close of the novel as a memory, like the last notes of a plaintive melody that resounds forever in the lives of Sethe and her family. Morrison is too tough-minded even to suggest that such an event as Beloved represents could ever simply be expunged. But, by the end of the book, Beloved is peripheral. Ultimately, this rich novel examines the death of the maternal in a woman so that her Self might live.

LINDA KRUMHOLZ

The Ghosts of Slavery: Historical Recovery in Toni Morrison's Beloved

> Your country? How came it yours? Before the Pilgrims landed we were here. Here we have brought our three gifts and mingled them with yours: a gift of story and song—soft, stirring melody in an ill-harmonized and unmelodious land; the gift of sweat and brawn to beat back the wilderness, conquer the soil, and lay the foundations of this vast economic empire two hundred years earlier than your weak hands could have done it; the third, a gift of the Spirit. . . . Would America have been America without her Negro people? (Du Bois 189–90)

Toni Morrison's *Beloved* reconceptualizes American history. Most apparent in the novel is the historical perspective: Morrison constructs history through the acts and consciousness of African-American slaves rather than through the perspective of the dominant white social classes. But historical methodology takes another vital shift in *Beloved*; history-making becomes a healing process for the characters, the reader, and the author.

In *Beloved,* Morrison constructs a parallel between the individual processes of psychological recovery and a historical or national process. Sethe, the central character in the novel, describes the relationship between the individual and the historical unconscious:

From *African American Review* 26:3 (Fall 1992). © 1992 by Linda Krumholz.

> If a house burns down, it's gone, but the place—the picture of it—stays, and not just in my rememory, but out there, in the world. What I remember is a picture floating around out there outside my head. I mean, even if I don't think it, even if I die, the picture of what I did, or knew, or saw is still out there. Right in the place where it happened." (36)

If Sethe's individual memories exist in the world as fragments of a historical memory, then, by extension, the individual process of recollection or "rememory" can be reproduced on a historical level. Thus, Sethe's process of healing in *Beloved*, her process of learning to live with her past, is a model for the readers who must confront Sethe's past as part of our own past, a collective past that lives right here where we live.

Arnold Rampersad, in his discussion of W. E. B. Du Bois's *The Souls of Black Folk*, also describes the recovery of history as both a national and a personal necessity:

> [Du Bois's] point of view is clear. Admitting and exploring the reality of slavery is necessarily painful for a black American, but only by doing so can he or she begin to understand himself or herself and American and Afro-American culture in general. The normal price of the evasion of the fact of slavery is intellectual and spiritual death. Only by grappling with the meaning and legacy of slavery can the imagination, recognizing finally the temporality of the institution, begin to transcend it. (123)

In Rampersad's description, the repression of the historical past is as psychologically damaging as the repression of personal trauma. In *Beloved* Morrison, like Du Bois in *Souls*, negotiates the legacy of slavery as a national trauma, and as an intensely personal trauma as well. Both works challenge the notion that the end of institutional slavery brings about freedom by depicting the emotional and psychological scars of slavery as well as the persistence of racism. And both Morrison and Du Bois delve into the stories and souls of black folk to tap the resources of memory and imagination as tools of strength and healing.

Morrison uses ritual as a model for the healing process. Rituals function as formal events in which symbolic representations—such as dance, song, story, and other activities—are spiritually and communally endowed with the power to shape real relations in the world. In *Beloved*, ritual processes also imply particular notions of pedagogy and epistemology in which—by way of contrast with dominant Western traditions—knowledge is multiple, context-dependent, collectively asserted, and spiritually derived. Through her assertion of the transformative power of ritual and the incorporation of rituals of healing into her narrative, Morrison invests the novel with the potential to construct and transform individual consciousness as well as social relations.

To make the novel work as a ritual, Morrison adapts techniques from Modernist novels, such as the fragmentation of the plot and a shifting narrative voice, to compel the reader to actively construct an interpretive framework. In *Beloved* the reader's process of reconstructing the fragmented story parallels Sethe's psychological recovery: Repressed fragments of the (fictionalized) personal and historical past are retrieved and reconstructed. Morrison also introduces oral narrative techniques—repetition, the blending of voices, a shifting narrative voice, and an episodic framework—that help to simulate the aural, participatory dynamics of ritual within the private, introspective form of the novel. In many oral traditions, storytelling and poetry are inseparable from ritual, since words as sounds are perceived as more than concepts; they are events with consequences. Morrison uses Modernist and oral techniques in conjunction with specifically African-American cultural referents, both historical and symbolic, to create a distinctly African-American voice and vision which, as in Baby Suggs's rituals, invoke the spiritual and imaginative power to teach and to heal.

The central ritual of healing—Sethe's "rememory" of and confrontation with her past—and the reader's ritual of healing correspond to the three sections of the novel. In part one the arrival first of Paul D then of Beloved forces Sethe to confront her past in her incompatible roles as a slave and as a mother. Moving from the fall of 1873 to the winter, the second part describes Sethe's period of atonement, during which she is enveloped by the past, isolated in her house with Beloved, who forces her to suffer over and over again all the pain and shame of the past. Finally, part three is Sethe's ritual "clearing," in which the women of the community aid her in casting out the voracious Beloved, and Sethe experiences a repetition of her scene of trauma with a difference—this time she aims her murderous hand at the white man who threatens her child.

The three phases of the reader's ritual also involve a personal reckoning with the history of slavery. In part one, stories of slavery are accumulated through fragmented recollections, culminating in the revelation of Sethe's murder of her child in the last chapters of the section. In part two, the reader is immersed in the voices of despair. Morrison presents the internal voices of Sethe, Denver, and Beloved in a ritual chant of possession, while Paul D and Stamp Paid are also overwhelmed by the legacy of slavery. The last part of the novel is the reader's "clearing," achieved through the comic relief of the conversation of Paul D and Stamp Paid and the hopeful reunion of Sethe and Paul D. The novel concludes with Denver's emergence as the new teacher, providing the reader with a model for a new pedagogy and the opportunity for the reconstruction of slave history from a black woman's perspective.

Finally, while *Beloved* can be read as a ritual of healing, there is also an element of disruption and unease in the novel, embodied in the character of Beloved. As an eruption of the past and the repressed unconscious, Beloved catalyzes the healing process for the characters and for the reader; thus, she is a disruption necessary for healing. But Beloved also acts as a trickster figure who defies narrative closure or categorization, foreclosing the possibility of a complete "clearing" for the reader. Thus, as the reader leaves the book, we have taken on slavery's haunt as our own.

Baby Suggs and Rituals of Healing

Two ghosts impel the healing process in *Beloved*: Baby Suggs, holy, acts as a ritual guide, and Beloved, the ghost-woman, acts as a psychological catalyst for the three central (living) characters. The healing ritual in *Beloved* can be broken down into three stages. The first stage is the repression of memory that occurs from the traumas of slavery; the second stage entails a painful reconciliation with these memories; and the third is the "clearing" process, a symbolic rebirth of the sufferer. Baby Suggs provides a moral background for the first stage and a ritual model for the last. Beloved embodies the second stage, compelling the characters in her "family" to face all the pain and shame of their memories.

In *Beloved* the ritual methods of healing, of initiating the participant/reader, and of interpreting the world are represented by the lessons of Baby Suggs, whose spiritual power has earned her the appellation *holy* among her people. Baby Suggs conducts rituals outdoors in the Clearing, a place that signifies the necessity for a psychological cleansing from the past, a space to encounter painful memories safely and rest from them. The day Baby Suggs becomes free, after more than sixty years of slavery, she notices her own heartbeat and is thrilled at owning her own body for the first time. Baby Suggs then "open[s] her great heart to those who could use it" by becoming an "unchurched preacher" (87). Baby Suggs creates a ritual, out of her own heart and imagination, to heal former slaves and enable them to seek a reconciliation with their memories, whose scars survive long (even generations) after the experience of slavery has ended.

Baby Suggs's rituals in the Clearing manifest the Freudian psychoanalytic process of healing as well as a spiritual process of healing that combines

African and Christian religious elements. Morrison uses Freudian psychological constructs to depict the response of slaves to their psychological torment, thus putting the construction of the African-American psyche into the most ubiquitous model of the psyche in Western literature and philosophy. According to Freud, the repression of traumatic memories directs energy away from social and sexual satisfaction to the construction of symptoms. The psychoanalytic treatment involves unedited associational speech that is meant to elude the unconscious censors, transference of emotions onto the analyst, and finally an acting out or narrativizing of the trauma in order to free the diverted energy and to reintegrate (to some extent) the ego and the libido. The metaphor of "clearing" suggests the process of bringing the unconscious memories into the conscious mind, and thus negotiating and transcending their debilitating control.

Morrison also uses African and African-American rituals to facilitate the psychological cure, suggesting that African religious ritual provides an antecedent for the psychoanalytic method and that Freudian theories are modern European derivations from longstanding ritual practices of psychic healing. The healing ritual combines Christian symbolism and African ritual expressions, as is common in the African-American church. In the spiritual context the metaphor of "clearing" suggests a process of cleansing and rebirth.

Baby Suggs's preaching and her spiritual vision invest the world with meaning without making that meaning static or rule-bound. In *Beloved*, as in all of Morrison's novels, meaning is multiple; contradictions stand intact. For example, black people and white people are essentially and irrevocably different; they are also essentially and eternally the same. Both statements are true at once, confounding the logical, objective ideology that forms the basis of Western culture.

The spiritual and subjective basis of ritual also has pedagogical implications. In ritual, the cultural specificity of knowledge and the multiple possibilities of interpretation, as well as the implied spiritual sanction, make ritual education different, at least conceptually, from the objective, scientific model of knowledge that is prevalent in American educational institutions. Baby Suggs's ritual methods of healing, teaching, and interpreting challenge basic pedagogical and epistemological premises of the United States' social system. Thus Morrison demonstrates how the reconstruction of the past makes possible a reconceptualization of the future, which is the power of history-making.

Baby Suggs is the moral and spiritual backbone of *Beloved*. Her morality is based on a method of engagement and interpretation rather than on static moral dictates. The most significant difference between Baby

Suggs's version of spirituality and that of the white religions depicted in the novel is her disdain for rules and prohibitions to define morality, as well as her rejection of definitions in general. Her actions contrast with those of white men like Mr. Bodwin's father, "a deeply religious man who knew what God knew and told everybody what it was" (260).

Baby Suggs rejects the definitions of formal religions, definitions which, as the history of slavery has shown, can be easily manipulated to justify anything. Baby Suggs preaches instead the guidance of a free heart and imagination:

> She did not tell them to clean up their lives or to go and sin no more. She did not tell them they were the blessed of the earth, its inheriting meek or its glorybound pure.
>
> She told them that the only grace they could have was the grace they could imagine. That if they could not see it, they would not have it. (88)

Baby Suggs represents an epistemological and discursive philosophy that shapes Morrison's work, in which morality is not preset in black and white categories of good and evil; "good" or "evil" spring from the *methods* of categorizing and judging, of understanding and distributing knowledge.

The only character in *Beloved* who represents a moral absolute of evil—the unnamed "schoolteacher"—is an embodiment of the wrong *methods*. Schoolteacher, the cruel slaveholder who takes over Sweet Home after the death of the "benevolent" slaveholder, Mr. Garner, has interpretive methods that are the opposite of Baby Suggs's. Rather than an engagement of the heart and imagination, schoolteacher's pedagogical tools are linguistic objectivity and scientific method.

His methods are shown to have devastating effects. For example, it is only when Sethe overhears schoolteacher teaching the nephews—and she is the subject of the lesson—that she fully comprehends her status as a slave. He says to the nephews, "'I told you to put her human characteristics on the left; her animal ones on the right. And don't forget to line them up'" (193). Schoolteacher's educational method adopts the clarity of Manichean oppositions and scientific discourse. The notebooks and neat lines verify his definitions as facts for his students. From our cultural position we can see that these "facts" are the product of a preset organization of categories and suppositions made invisible by the use of "objective" methods. Nonetheless, the social authority of the schoolteacher and the logical clarity of his methods give his words the power of "truth."

Morrison depicts schoolteacher's pedagogical and interpretive methods as morally bereft, and through him she condemns not only slavery but also the United States' educational system. Schoolteacher's practices are basic to the institutional educational system of the United States, which may have gotten past the worst of schoolteacher's racial model, but still presents politically motivated versions of knowledge and history while masking these representations in a rhetoric of "facts" and scientific method. Through schoolteacher Morrison demonstrates that discourse, definitions, and historical methods are neither arbitrary nor objective; they are tools in a system of power relations. When Sixo, the African slave at Sweet Home, deftly talks his way out of charges of theft, Morrison writes, ". . . schoolteacher beat him anyway to show him that definitions belonged to the definers—not the defined" (190).

According to Baby Suggs's morality, good and evil are undefinable, not based on absolute knowledge; they are part of a situational ethics. "'Everything depends on knowing how much,' she said, and 'Good is knowing when to stop'" (87). Slavery exemplifies the connection between a lack of morality and a lack of limitations. Baby Suggs made this her last pronouncement before she died—"the lesson she had learned from her sixty years a slave and ten years free: that there was no bad luck in the world but white people. 'They don't know when to stop,' she said" (104). The lack of limitations of the white people is shown over and over as the destruction of the slaves. The story of Halle's going mad, Sethe's murder of her baby, Paul D's memories of Mister and the bit—all demonstrate the connection to the white slaveholding society's immorality, its lack of human limitations on its actions, that reciprocates in the minds of its victims as too much suffering to be endured. In Morrison's powerful description of double consciousness, Stamp Paid thinks, " . . . it wasn't the jungle blacks brought with them to this place from the other (livable) place. It was the jungle whitefolks planted in them" (198).

Although Baby Suggs's dying words of despair condemn white people, Morrison makes it clear that race is not an absolute division either. Clearly within the context of American slavery, racial oppression is inseparable from social domination and abuses of power. But in *Beloved* the white "slave," Amy Denver, helps Sethe to cross the river to freedom and acts as a midwife for the birth of Denver (i.e., Sethe's daughter, who is named after Amy Denver). The similarity between the two women's situations supercedes their mutual, racially based mistrust, indicating that class relations (as well as differences in inherited cultural values) are central in shaping racial differences.

Because the white people don't know "'when to stop,'" as Baby Suggs says, slavery pushes the limits of the human capacity for suffering. The overwhelming pain of the past necessitates a closing down of memory, as it does for Sethe, who "worked hard to remember as close to nothing as was safe"

(6). But traumatic repression causes neurosis, and although Sethe's suppression of memory enables her to survive and remain sane, it also leads to a stultifying and isolated life. Paul D has a concrete image of his repression:

> He would keep the rest [of his past] where it belonged: in that tobacco tin buried in his chest where a red heart used to be. Its lid rusted shut. He would not pry it loose now in front of this sweet sturdy woman, for if she got a whiff of the contents it would shame him. And it would hurt her to know that there was no red heart bright as Mister's comb beating in him. (72–73)

Paul D and Sethe have found it necessary to lock away their memories and their emotions as a means of surviving the extreme pains of their past. Baby Suggs understands the lack of moral limits of the white slaveholders and the limits of psychological endurance of the black slaves that make up the devastating dynamic of slavery. Baby Suggs is already dead when the novel begins, but her ritual in the Clearing is a model of the process of healing that Paul D and Sethe must undergo to free their hearts from the pain and shame of the past.

Beloved as the Trickster of History

Amy Denver tells Sethe that "'anything dead coming back to life hurts'"(35). Beloved makes this maxim literal, as the physical manifestation of suppressed memories. Beloved is both the pain and the cure. As an embodiment of the repressed past, she acts as an unconscious imp, stealing away the volition of the characters, and as a psychoanalytic urge, she pries open suppressed memories and emotions. In a sense she is like an analyst, the object of transference and cathexis that draws out the past, while at the same time she is that past. Countering traumatic repression, she makes the characters accept their past, their squelched memories, and their own hearts, as beloved.

Beloved is the incarnation of Sethe's baby girl and of her most painful memory—the murder of her daughter to protect her children from slavery. Beloved is Sethe's "ghost," the return of her repressed past, and she forces Sethe to confront the gap between her motherlove and the realities of motherhood in slavery. But Beloved is also everyone's ghost. She functions as the spur to Paul D's and Denver's repressed pasts, forcing Paul D to confront the shame and pain of the powerlessness of a man in slavery, and enabling Denver to deal with her mother's history as a slave. Beloved initiates the individual healing processes of the three characters, which subsequently stimulate the formation of a family unit of love and support, in which the family members can provide for each other in ways that slavery denied them. And Beloved is the reader's ghost, forcing us to face the historical past as a living and vindictive presence. Thus Beloved comes to represent the repressed memories of slavery, both for the characters and for the readers. Beloved catalyzes Sethe's memories as the novel *Beloved* catalyzes the reader's historical memories (and according to Sethe's idea of "rememory" personal memories come to exist independently in the world and thereby become historical memories).

Beloved symbolizes the past and catalyzes the future. But Beloved cannot be reduced to a symbol as she manipulates the characters with her sweet, spiteful, and engulfing presence. The contradictions of her symbolic position, along with her enigmatic personality, her thoughts and speech fired with the fragmented and vague images of a baby as woman and the once-dead as living, make Beloved a character too complex to be catalogued and contained. Morrison succeeds in creating more in her novel than a sense of history; she makes the past haunt the present through the bewildered and bewildering character of Beloved.

Beloved also develops as a character, from a soft, voracious baby-woman to her final form as a beautiful pregnant woman. During the ritual in which she is exorcised the women see her at last:

> The devil-child was clever, they thought. And beautiful. It had taken the shape of a pregnant woman, naked and smiling in the heat of the afternoon sun. Thunderblack and glistening, she stood on long straight legs, her belly big and tight. Vines of hair twisted all over her head. Jesus. Her smile was dazzling. (261)

Beloved embodies the suffering and guilt of the past, but she also embodies the power and beauty of the past and the need to realize the past fully in order to bring forth the future, pregnant with possibilities. In her last moments, Beloved stands as a contradictory image, both as the African ancestor, the beautiful African mother, connecting the mothers and daughters of African descent to their pre-slavery heritage and power, and as the all-consuming devil child. The spirit of the past has taken on a personality in this novel, and thus Morrison makes the writing of history a resurrection of ancestral spirits, the spirit of the long buried past. Morrison resurrects the devil child, the spiteful, beautiful, painful past, so that Beloved—and the novel—will live on to haunt us.

To look further at the way the unfathomable and disruptive Beloved works in the novel, it is useful to turn now to a literary ancestor of Morrison's novel—the trickster tale. The trickster has long been a part of African and

African-American storytelling. Most recently in African-American literary criticism, the trickster has been evoked as a deconstructive force in culture and in texts, as in Henry Louis Gates, Jr.'s version of the signifyin(g) monkey. Gates argues, in "The Blackness of Blackness," that the African-American rhetorical tradition has always denied the monolithic voice of the white father that white poststructuralists have only recently identified and (to varying degrees) challenged. In any case, the trickster has always been part of African-American culture, signifying on itself and on the "white masters" who "know what God knows."

One basic function of the trickster as deconstructor is to bring about role reversals in which a weaker animal or character outwits and outtalks a more powerful one—although the trickster's success is never guaranteed. In *Beloved*, Sixo, the African slave, combines this role of the trickster with the image of a heroic slave who resists slavery to his dying breath. Even his name—"Sixo"—keeps him outside the signifying system, with "a number for a name."

The trickster tales are also employed in healing processes. In his work *Black Culture and Black Consciousness*, Lawrence Levine argues that "the propensity of Africans to utilize their folklore quite consciously to gain psychological release . . . needs to be reiterated if the popularity and function of animal trickster tales is to be understood" (102). Levine goes on to quote anthropologist R. S. Rattray, who concludes, "beyond a doubt, that West Africans had discovered for themselves the truth of the psychoanalysts' theory of 'repressions,' and that in these ways they sought an outlet for what might otherwise become a dangerous complex" (102).

The trickster is also the manifestation of the irrationality of life. Levine argues that, although the antebellum trickster figure often represents the slave, as the weak outwits the strong, other tricksters are best understood to represent the masters, to expose the deceit of the powerful. The trickster defies categorization as good or evil, expressing the amorality of the world. Levine writes that trickster tales "emphasize in brutal detail the irrationality and anarchy that rules Man's universe" (117).

By placing Morrison's novel in the trickster tradition we can see how her narrative strategies derive from the multiculturalism of the American novel, as well as from the African-American storytelling tradition. Beloved represents the irrationality of the world by defying definition and categorization, while at the same time participating in the novel as sister, daughter, lover, and finally, perhaps, mother. Her relations to the characters are both "real" and symbolic; her confused words and thoughts are perplexing, even her physical form is shifting and multiple. Beloved, as a trickster figure, participates in the healing function of the novel, but by refusing to be fixed by a unitary meaning she also remains unhealed—a rift in the attempt to close meaning and thereby close off the past from the present. The character Beloved, like the novel *Beloved*, works to fight a complacency toward history by both healing and disturbing the readers.

Sethe's Healing Ritual

Sethe's healing process is the focal point of the novel, as she gradually and painfully recollects the repressed past. Like Paul D's tobacco tin, Sethe's repressed past is like a rusted box closed inside of her. When she finally realizes that Beloved is the reincarnation of her dead baby, she feels as if she's found buried treasure:

> A hobnail casket of jewels found in a tree hollow should be fondled before it is opened. Its lock may have rusted or broken away from the clasp. Still you should touch the nail heads, and test its weight. No smashing with an ax head before it is decently exhumed from the grave that has hidden it all this time. No gasp as a miracle that is truly miraculous because the magic lies in the fact that you knew it was there for you all along. (176)

Beloved's resurrection exhumes the past Sethe has buried deep inside her. The treasure chest combines images of great discovery and wealth with images of death, the casket and the grave. As Amy Denver says, "'Anything dead coming back to life hurts,'" and Sethe's attempts to prove her love to Beloved and gain Beloved's forgiveness nearly destroy Sethe.

Beloved is the murdered child, the repressed past, Sethe's own guilt and loss, and so Beloved can never forgive Sethe. But the former slave women understand the context within which Sethe acted; they shared in many of her miseries. And so her fellow sufferers come to her aid to exorcise the ghost of her past preying on her life, because Beloved is in some sense their ghost, too. Another local woman, Ella, had also killed her child, although it was not out of love, and when she found out about Beloved's presence "there was also something very personal in her fury. Whatever Sethe had done, Ella didn't like the idea of past errors taking possession of the present" (256). Ella brings the local women to Sethe's house to banish the ghost, and their chanting summons Sethe and Beloved from the house.

The power of the women's voices joined together has a creative capacity that symbolizes and ritualizes Sethe's cycle from spiritual death to rebirth. In the chapter in which Sethe kills her baby, the imagery is from the

Book of Revelations, beginning with the apocalyptic image of the four horsemen and concluding with a sense of doom and judgment (148 ff.). In the exorcism ritual, near the end of the novel, the women's voices carry Sethe back to an original creative power:

> They stopped praying and took a step back to the beginning. In the beginning there were no words. In the beginning was the sound, and they all knew what that sound sounded like. (259)

The women's voices carry Sethe from the apocalyptic end to a new beginning. But in contrast to the Gospel of John, which begins, "In the beginning was the Word, and the Word was with God, and the Word was God," the women bring Sethe to a beginning of voices without words. Just as Baby Suggs rejected religious dicta, the spiritual power of the purgation ritual lies beyond the meaning of words, in sound and sensation rather than in logical meaning and the Logos.

The exorcism of Beloved is a purgation ritual, a baptismal cleansing and rebirth, and a psychological clearing:

> For Sethe it was as though the Clearing had come to her with all its heat and simmering leaves, where the voices of women searched for the right combination, the key, the code, the sound that broke the back of words. Building voice upon voice until they found it, and when they did it was a wave of sound wide enough to sound deep water and knock the pods off chestnut trees. It broke over Sethe and she trembled like the baptized in its wash. (261)

The other women's voices, sound without words, have the power of cleansing waters, bringing Sethe back to the "clearing" and to Baby Suggs's rituals during Sethe's brief period—between slavery and the return of schoolteacher—of freedom (95).

The cleansing ritual also brings Sethe back to the original scene of repression and enables her to relive it with a difference. When Denver's white employer arrives in the midst of the ritual, the confused Sethe believes him to be one of the white men who has come to take her and her children back into slavery, and Denver must hold her mother back as Sethe launches a murderous attack on the white man. As a freed woman with a group of her peers surrounding her, Sethe can act on her motherlove as she would have chosen to originally. Instead of turning on her children to save them from slavery, she turns on the white man who threatens them. The reconstruction of the scene of the trauma completes the psychological cleansing of the ritual, and exorcises Beloved from Sethe's life. Sethe can finally "lay down the sword and shield" that she has needed to fend off her memories (86).

The author and reader, too, have gone through a ritual recovery *of* history and *from* history. Sethe's ritual and her memories are Morrison's story, a story that—like the voices of the women—reaches beyond meaning to the unconscious pains of the past. Morrison's story combines the creative and cleansing power of the women's voices surrounding Sethe, as well as the spiritual power of Baby Suggs and the disturbing power of Beloved, to construct the story as a ritual both healing and painful for the reader. Finally, Sethe's daughter Denver represents both the future and the past: Denver will be the new African-American woman teacher, and she is Morrison's precursor, the woman who has taken on the task of carrying the story through the generations to our storyteller.

Denver and the History of Slavery

Denver's favorite story is the story of her birth, in which Sethe bears her into a nether world between freedom and slavery. Born on the river that divides "free" and slave land in the midst of Sethe's flight from slavery, the dual inheritance of freedom and slavery tears Denver apart. When schoolteacher comes to take Sethe and her children back to Sweet Home as slaves, Denver drinks the blood of her murdered sister with her mother's milk, and she goes to jail with Sethe. A mirror image of her mother's repressed past, Denver goes deaf when she is asked about her time in prison. From then on Denver lives in seclusion, with only Sethe, Baby Suggs, and the baby ghost as companions. In her lonely withdrawal from the world, due in part to Sethe's isolation, Denver is as trapped by Sethe's past and Sethe's inability to find psychological freedom as Sethe herself is.

Sethe intentionally keeps Denver in the dark: "As for Denver, the job Sethe had of keeping her from the past that was still waiting for her was all that mattered" (42). But the unacknowledged past keeps Denver from moving into the future. She is jealous of her mother's past, and her exclusion from that past increases her loneliness and bitterness. Beloved, on the other hand, thrives on stories of the past, on pulling from Sethe details of her past, and Denver's love for Beloved forces her to confront the past she hates.

Denver's relation to the past is primarily historic rather than personal. Denver's personal stake in retrieving the past, like the reader's, involves a familial and ancestral inheritance, and her encounter with the past is "necessarily painful," just as Arnold Rampersad suggests a black

American's historical encounter must be. Without knowledge of her mother's past, Denver must remain in isolation from history and from her position in the world that can only be understood through history.

As I've argued throughout this essay, history for Morrison is not an abstract factual recital; it is a ritual engagement with the past. Denver begins to experience the past through the stories she tells Beloved. When she repeats her birth story for Beloved, "Denver was seeing it now and feeling it—through Beloved. Feeling how it must have felt to her mother. Seeing how it must have looked" (78). But Denver does not fully remember her past and her mother's past until she undergoes a "ritual of mergence" in part two of the novel.

Four chapters in the middle of part two form a ritual of mergence and possession for Sethe, Denver, and Beloved. These four chapters emerge from the minds of the three characters, who are left alone after Paul D is gone. Sethe has recognized Beloved as her baby girl and is submerged in her attempt to prove her love and atone for her murder, while Denver tries to stay inside the intense circle of possession Sethe and Beloved have created. In the first three chapters, Sethe first proclaims her possession of her daughter Beloved, then Denver of her sister Beloved, then Beloved of her mother. The fourth chapter is in the form of a poetic chant, in which the memories and minds of the three combine in a mutual song of possession—"You are mine" (217). While Denver is possessed by the past she remembers everything—her own past and her mother's past, her fear of her mother as a child murderer, and her imaginary reunions with her father. The ritual of possession breaks through her isolation and grants Denver an experience of the past that can lead her into the future.

After the winter of possession, Denver decides she must leave the house to save her mother from madness and from the ravenous Beloved. In her last moment of fear as she reaches the door, Baby Suggs speaks to her. Baby's words conjure up the history of her "family" struggle for survival and freedom as well as Baby Suggs's own defeat against the horrors of slavery. Denver silently asks Baby:

> But you said there was no defense.
> "There ain't."
> Then what do I do?
> "Know it, and go on out the yard. Go on." (244)

Although Baby Suggs gave up struggling at the end of her life, her knowledge and spirit, and the knowledge of the past, make possible Denver's emergence into the world. With understanding comes the power to endure and to change.

Denver's position parallels the reader's in her historic relation to her mother's past. But Denver also takes on another role by the end of the novel—that of the teacher, the historian, and the author. Denver will become a schoolteacher, taking up the educational task from her teacher, Lady Jones, and Baby Suggs, and taking over the tools of literacy and education from the white schoolteacher. Paul D worries when he hears of her intentions to go to college, silently cautioning her: "Watch out. Nothing in this world more dangerous than a white schoolteacher" (266). But this is the very reason that Denver must usurp schoolteacher's position; she must take away from him the power to define African-Americans and make their history in a way that steals their past, their souls, and their humanity.

Denver is Morrison's precursor, the historian with her roots in African-American history and culture, who has a relationship with her ancestors. Sixo chooses another course, rejecting Halle's offer to be taught English, as Denver recalls:

> One of than with a number for a name said it would change his mind—make him forget things he shouldn't and memorize things he shouldn't and he didn't want his mind messed up. But my daddy said, If you can't count they can cheat you If you can't read they can beat you. (208)

While Halle discovers that the white man can cheat and beat you whether or not you are literate, Sixo keeps his cultural integrity and his oral tradition intact. But Denver, as a member of a different generation, must "know it and go on." With the knowledge of this cautionary tale, Denver points the way to a recovery of literacy, one that is suspicious of white definitions and discourse, and one that uses the African oral and cultural heritage and African-American values to take over the task of African-American history-making.

Conclusion: A Haunting History

In *Beloved* Morrison brings together the African-American oral and literary tradition and the Euro-American novel tradition to create a powerful and intensely personal representation of slavery in America. In this way, Morrison indirectly critiques historical and pedagogical methods prevalent in the United States. She counters a fact-based objective system with a ritual method, based in initiatory and healing rituals, in which the acquisition of knowledge is a subjective and spiritual experience. Through the conceptualization of knowledge as culturally constructed, Morrison points the way to a reconstruction of history, both national and personal, to combat the persistent intellectual and spiritual oppression of African-Americans and other Americans and bring about a freedom of the heart and imagination, as Baby Suggs dreamed.

In the last chapter of part one of *Beloved*, Sethe tries to tell Paul D about the secret she has never spóken of before—her killing of her baby girl. Throughout this chapter, as Sethe attempts to explain her past, she is described as "spinning. Round and round the room" and "turning like a slow but steady wheel" around Paul D (159); "Circling him the way she was circling the subject" (161). Like Sethe, Morrison proceeds circuitously toward the revelation of this central secret. Morrison's circularity and indirection correspond to the process of healing undergone by Sethe, as well as to the depiction of the character of Beloved. Sethe's spinning motion around the room, around her subject, describes the necessity for approaching the unutterably painful history of slavery through oblique, fragmented, and personal glimpses of the past—that is, through means most often associated with fiction.

Beloved depicts a healing ritual, or "clearing," for Sethe, whose inability to confront her painful memories of slavery, and especially her guilt for killing her child, keeps her mentally and emotionally enslaved despite eighteen years of freedom. Morrison's fragmented revelation of Sethe's terrible act works to postpone the reader's judgment. By weaving together the complex and emotion-laden incidents and images of the past, Morrison situates Sethe's act within the historical and personal context of slavery. But Morrison's indirection also has to do with the nature of memory itself. The process of the novel corresponds to Sethe's healing ritual, in which the unspoken incident is her most repressed memory, whose recollection and recreation are essential to her recovery. The nature of repression makes this event indescribable—it is part of the inarticulate and irrational unconscious, like an inner ghost plaguing and controlling Sethe's life.

In the last chapter of part one, as Sethe moves in circles around Paul D, she comes closest to explaining the murder of her baby, but her revelation is still internal and silent. Morrison writes:

> Sethe knew that the circle she was making around the room, him, the subject, would remain one. That she could never close in, pin it down for anybody who had to ask. If they didn't get it right off—she could never explain. Because the truth was simple, not a long-drawn-out record of flowered shifts, tree cages, selfishness, ankle ropes and wells. Simple: she was squatting in the garden and when she saw them coming and recognized schoolteacher's

> hat, she heard wings. Little hummingbirds stuck their needle beaks right through her headcloth into her hair and beat their wings. And if she thought anything, it was No. No. Nono. Nonono. Simple. She just flew. Collected every bit of life she had made, all the parts of her that were precious and fine and beautiful, and carried, pushed, dragged them through the veil, out, away, over there where no one could hurt them. Over there. Outside this place, where they would be safe. (163)

In this passage, the simple truth is not suited to a logical, causal description. The narrator describes Sethe's reaction as an emotional and physical response. The hummingbirds suggest frenzy and confusion, as well as an unnatural event, signified by their beaks thrust into Sethe's hair. The hummingbirds also represent Sethe's physical urge for flight, and at the same time the small jewel-like birds signify Sethe's children—"all the parts of her that were precious and fine and beautiful." The repetition of the single sound—"No. No. Nono. Nonono"—contains the visceral and inarticulate reaction, the protective reaction that compels Sethe to take her children "through the veil." The veil, used by Du Bois to represent the "colorline," the division between black and white flesh and vision (16), here represents the division between life and death, as if at this moment the only escape from the threat of the white world is death.

Sethe can never explain what she did because the event is outside of the logic of words and justifications, of cause and effect. Her act was a physical and emotional reaction, the culmination of her life up to that moment. Even her circling, repeatedly, around the subject with stories and contexts can never really reconstruct the moment, the event, that is beyond explanation. Similarly, Morrison's novel reconstructs slave history in a way that history books cannot, and in a way that cannot be appropriated by objective or scientific concepts of knowledge and history. By inscribing history as a trickster spirit, Morrison has recreated our relationship to history in a process baffling and difficult, but necessary. Through the character Beloved, Morrison denies the reader analytical explanations of slavery. Instead, the reader is led through a painful, emotional healing process, leaving him or her with a haunting sense of the depth of pain and shame suffered in slavery.

Beloved is the forgotten spirit of the past that must "be loved" even if it is unlovable and elusive. As Morrison tells us in the end, "This is not a story to pass on" (275). This line recapitulates the tension between repression and rememory figured throughout the novel. In one reading, the story is not one to pass by or to pass over. At the same time, the more evident meaning is intensely ironic—"This is not a story to pass on," and yet, as the novel shows us, it must be.

ELIZABETH FOX-GENOVESE

Unspeakable Things Unspoken: Ghosts and Memories in the Beloved

> Everybody knew what she was called, but nobody anywhere knew her name. Disremembered and unaccounted for, she cannot be lost because no one is looking for her, and even if they were, how can they call her if they don't know her name? Although she has claim, she is not claimed. . . .
> It was not a story to pass on. . . .
> So they forgot her. Like an unpleasant dream during a troubling sleep. . . .
> This was not a story to pass on.

The concluding pages of Toni Morrison's novel, *Beloved*, from which these words are taken, evoke the difficulty of telling the story of women's experience of slavery—of the cost of slavery for enslaved mothers and their children. Beloved, the ghost of the murdered, "crawling already?" baby, remains not lost, but disremembered and unaccounted for, because no one is even looking for her. The story of her murder by her own mother, which implicated slavery in its entirety, including the other members of the community of slaves, was not one that anyone—black or white, slave or free—chose to tell. So they forgot. And their forgetting, even more than the original event, becomes a story that cannot be passed on.

From *The 1992 Elsa Goveia Memorial Lecture presented at The University of the West Indies, Mona, Jamaica, 26 March 1992.*

The woman's story of slavery has challenged historians no less than it has challenged novelists and autobiographers. Since the nineteenth century it has been common to assert that slavery was necessarily worse for women than for men, since they were subjected to special brutality and indignity on account of their sex. In general, however, historians have primarily focused upon the injustice and indignities of slavery for men. Those who defended the freedom of labor, soil, and men readily identified the enslavement of men as a violation of the fundamental principles of individualism to which they were committed. It was not that historians have lacked sympathy for the violation of women's sexuality, but that many have found it difficult to write of it from a subjective perspective—from the "inside."

The recent historians who have devoted most attention to understanding the history of African-American slaves in the United States have written, in large measure, from a commitment to documenting and representing the strength and vitality of slave culture. They have, accordingly, emphasized the slaves' commitment to marriage and family. At the extreme, Robert Fogel and Stanley Engerman have even argued that the slaves developed and enforced a sense of family loyalty and sexual morality that remarkably resembled the values of their masters. The recent debates among these and other historians have primarily concerned the respective elements of African and American culture that the slaves forged under adversity.

Yet more recently, scholars such as Deborah White, who have focused explicitly on the experience of slave women, have more directly emphasized the sexual exploitation of slave women by white men, notably their masters. Yet even as White exposed and deplored the abuse of slave women's sexuality, she especially argued that the experience of slavery, combined with African traditions, led African-American women to develop a greater sense of autonomy and independence than their white contemporaries. Thus even she did not explore the possible consequences of sexual exploitation for slave women's minds and hearts, much less their relations with the other members of the slave community.

While working on *Within the Plantation Household*, I came increasingly to believe that slavery had taken a higher toll upon the sexual relations of African-American men and women than most of us were prepared to face. With this matter, even more than with others, the evidence tended to be oblique, veiled, indirect. Through the disguises and reticences, it nonetheless seemed to me that there lurked a troubling story. Countless slave infants may indeed have died from Sudden Infant Death Syndrome, from disease, and from inadequate supplies of maternal milk, but some undetermined number also fell victim to infanticide. No less disturbing, it seemed clear that the sexual exploitation of black women by white men might poison those women's relations with the men of their own people who might, in all too human a fashion, turn their rage against the victim. As a result, in any given instance, the most violent abusers of slave women's sexuality might be black rather than white men.

Given the paucity of direct evidence and my wish to respect the reticence of others, and perhaps even succumbing to a measure of cowardice, I decided to avoid extensive discussions of sexuality. African-American slave women had not left extensive accounts of their objective lives, and I was loath to probe their silence. My decision was bolstered by the knowledge that even when those, like Harriet Jacobs, who had written of their personal experience, had written of extra-marital sexual relations and of sexual exploitation, they had refrained from exposing what must have been the most painful aspect of their experience—their own dehumanization. For, from a woman's perspective, the worst of sexual exploitation is never simply that "he" desired me and (perhaps violently) overpowered my resistance: The worst of sexual exploitation is that "he" treated me as a thing—not as a unique object of his desire, but as an indifferent object of his lust.

The appearance of Toni Morrison's novel, *Beloved*, just as I was completing my own book provided welcome assurance that I was not alone in what I thought I was discerning in the fragmentary sources. It further confirmed my deepest sense that if slavery had indeed been the oppressive system most of us believed it to have been, those who endured it could not have emerged unscathed. Notwithstanding my having had formal psychoanalytic training and the high value I place upon the insights that psychoanalysis can contribute to the understanding of history and culture, I have always recoiled from—more properly resented—the mechanical use of psychoanalytic theory that treats other people as intellectual fodder for the analytic mind—that makes complex and sometimes troubled lives and motivations conform to someone else's rigid model. But my sense of the complexity of slave women's experience and of the extraordinary mixture of courage and frailty, anger and love their survival entailed continued to haunt me.

Recent years have brought thoughtful new attempts to map and circumscribe the activities of slave women and their central role with the community of slaves. But even now, with more than a century of distance, it remains difficult, perhaps impossible, to recapture the subjective story of slave women's experience. In rare instances, as in the case of *Beloved*, fiction can powerfully supplement elusive psychological "facts." And so I turned to *Beloved* for a plausible, if imaginative, representation of the feelings of some women who endured slavery and, like Sethe, continued to bear its scars. Even more I turned to *Beloved* as itself a source for another history, namely the history of the elusiveness of women's experience of slavery until our own time. For *Beloved* is less the story that could not be passed on—the story that was impossible to tell—than it is the story of how the story that could not be passed on was forgotten and, to borrow from psychoanalytic language, the reasons for which it was repressed.

Although slave women, like slave men, suffered oppression as laborers, some of their coerced labor permitted them to develop skills and expertise in which they could take the pride of craft, and even hard monotonous labor, which did not, did not necessarily inflict lasting scars on their sense of themselves. But as women—as sexual partners and mothers—they confronted a constant threat. The culture of domesticity and separate spheres that prevailed in the non-slave, and even in modified form in the slave, states during the mid-nineteenth century emphasized women's purity as sexual beings and their selfless devotion as mothers. No less important, it steadfastly repudiated women's sexual passion and, perhaps even more, their anger.

African cultures were generally less obsessive about women's sexual purity, although they did favor marital fidelity, but they placed high value upon children and upon women's roles as mothers. So even if African-American slave women were not normally predisposed to take the cult of sexual purity very seriously and even if their circumstances too frequently permitted their observing it, they were strongly predisposed to take their roles as mothers and their responsibilities to their children as seriously as their circumstances permitted. And the sources movingly attest that they took the separation of a mother from one or more of her children as a slaveholder's ultimate violation both of the system's professed values and of his minimal responsibilities.

Before emancipation, the majority of slave women, being illiterate, had virtually no opportunity to write of their outrage at the violation of their sexuality and, especially, their motherhood. In the measure that committed free white women wrote of it for them, they invariably wrote in their own idiom of domesticity. We know, from occasional accounts in the narratives of former slaves, that they spoke of their outrage to each other. But the narratives collected during the 1930s from those who had been children during slavery times could only tell of the outrage at a generational remove. And, as the African-American community reconstructed itself following the Civil War, it too tended to adopt the idiom of domesticity, perhaps less out of conviction than as a defense of respectability and a wish to hide their scars from the curiosity of outsiders.

All of the stories we tell depend heavily upon the ways in which stories have previously been told. Not surprisingly, the story of baby-killing has had limited possibilities. Most commonly, it has taken the form of a cautionary tale, closely associated with the horrors of war. That evil men kill babies serves to underscore their malignant overreaching of the boundaries of civilized existence. Think of King Herod. And if men who kill babies in the public arena evoke horror, how much more so do women who kill them under the veil of domestic privacy? And if women in general, what of mothers in particular? Medea has not been easy to inscribe in conventional images of motherhood.

All cultures have valued motherhood, but nineteenth-century bourgeois culture raised it to unprecedented heights of sentimentality and thus made it especially difficult for women to tell stories about its dangers and conflicts. Bourgeois idealization of mothers' natural inclinations for nurture and self-sacrifice virtually prohibited women from writing realistically of motherhood from a subjective stance. Or, to put it differently the sanctity that shrouded the conventions of motherhood virtually dictated that women would have to embrace prescribed motherly feelings when writing of their own emotions and experience. Occasionally, a female author would touch upon a woman's possible resentment of, or failure at, motherhood by including an explicitly bad mother, but this projection would not include an empathetic exploration of the unfortunate woman's feelings. More frequently, one might write an orphaned girl whose situation would permit an indirect exploration of women's feelings about motherhood.

As for motherhood, so for sexuality. It is difficult to find a proper nineteenth-century woman who wrote forthrightly of desiring sexual relations. To be sure, bourgeois women's limited experience narrowed the topics of which they could write with authority. But even more than women's limited experience since women did, felt, and especially knew many more things than they were acknowledged as doing, feeling, and knowing, the conventions of women's narratives hedged women in. Thus even the most daring women writers found it difficult, if not impossible, to explore those aspects of women's subjective experience that frontally challenged narrative conventions of womanhood.

That the experience of female slaves openly mocked the conventions was not lost on all white women. During the late antebellum period, many American women, notably Harriet Beecher Stowe and Harriet Jacobs, began to insist that slavery indeed extracted an especially heavy price from women—that the evils of slavery ran so deep as to threaten the most sacred domestic bonds and virtues. In *Incidents in the Life of a Slave Girl*, Harriet Jacobs unambiguously insisted that if slavery is terrible for men, "it is far more terrible for women. Superadded to the burden common to all, *they* have wrongs, and sufferings, and mortifications peculiarly their own" (p. 77).

Jacobs has primarily, and deservedly, been appreciated for her brave and perhaps unique account of slavery from a woman's perspective. Jacobs, possibly following Stowe's example, left her readers no doubt that she was indicting slavery as a social system. Not least, she insisted, the evil of slavery made it impossible to judge a slave woman by the standards to which free women were held—"the slave woman ought not to be judged by the same standard as others" (p.56). Yet even Jacobs never unambiguously stated that slavery made it impossible for women to be good mothers. In her narrative, she tried to expose the aspects of slavery that made it impossible for slave women to conform to prevailing standards, but she remained reticent about slave women's personal motivations. Attentive readers can easily recognize that the anger instilled by her personal experience frequently threatens to explode her narrative, but only indirectly and without ever fully disrupting the conventions within which she deemed it prudent to write.

Accepting the dominant discourse of womanhood and motherhood as normative, Jacobs, who candidly admitted to having had children by a man to whom she was not married, attempted to justify her actions as the product of her inescapable circumstances. Thus *Incidents*, which superficially accepts northeastern, middle-class female norms and simply asks forgiveness for her inability to conform to them, on another level suggests that the norms entirely miss the realities of slave women's experience. Jacobs' anger obviously derived from her outrage at a social system the logic of which was to reduce a woman to a thing—from her own refusal to be treated as a thing. But it may also have derived from her recognition that there was no way that she could candidly tell her story, for there was no way that she could publicly admit to having been treated like a thing.

In acknowledging the impossibility of telling her real story, Jacobs presumably made a calculated judgment about the expectations of her prospective readers, shrewdly determining that it was better to meet those expectations than not to be read at all. And she assuredly could not have expected a sympathetic reading—perhaps not any reading at all—had she not respected the most cherished myths of those she hoped to reach. By the time Jacobs published *Incidents*, anti-slavery women, like Stowe herself, were insisting that slavery's greatest evil lay in its violation of domestic relations. But, by the same stroke, anti-slavery women had also ensconced their own standards of motherhood and womanly virtue as the ultimate justification for opposition to slavery.

Stowe had mapped the imaginative universe into which Jacobs apparently felt obliged to write her own story. The strength of Stowe's vision lay in her uncompromising insistence that, as the systematization of absolute power, slavery corrupted everyone it touched—made it impossible for anyone to be a good person. Jacobs unquestionably concurred in Stowe's indictment, but nonetheless found it impossible to press her understanding to its bitterest and most naked conclusions. It is not difficult, as I have argued elsewhere, to demonstrate that Jacobs' text may more profitably be read as the account of her direct contest with the power of her master than as the remorseful confession of her fall from virtue. But even as she permits us to doubt that the protection of womanly virtue ranks as her primary concern, she attempts to strengthen free white women's identification with her feelings of motherhood.

The hard truth is that there are feelings that Jacobs could not share with her readers and maintain their identification and respect. Notwithstanding her evocation of the support and assistance that her protagonist, Linda Brent, received from other women, she tellingly distances her from the mass of slave women whose plight she purportedly embodied. Jacobs thus represents Linda Brent and the members of her immediate family as speaking in the purest English, while representing other slaves as speaking in dialect. For similar reasons, she relegates her harshest examples of slaveholders' brutality, notably the sexual exploitation of slave women, to castes of which Linda Brent has heard, but has not personally experienced. Jacobs never shows Linda as beaten or raped, as dirty or disfigured. She never describes her as scantily clad or even as calloused. The scratches she receives derive from the difficulties of her escape, not from the degradation of her everyday life. Above all, the persecution she endures never seriously compromises her membership in a recognizable narrative, never pushes her literally beyond the pale of civilized discourse.

For understandable reasons, Jacobs sought the identification of her readers, sought to convince them to accept her as a woman like themselves. No wonder then that she introduces the worst specific abuses of slavery as reports rather than as subjective experiences. How could she have been expected to do otherwise? If rather than representing Linda Brent—and by implication herself—as the object of corrupt male desire, she had represented her as the victim of indiscriminate lust, she would have reduced her to that status as thing to which the logic of chattel slavery pointed. And she would, thereby, have decisively undercut her own claims of empathy and respect. Worse, to do so would have forced her to acknowledge that, through the eyes of Dr. Flint, Linda Brent was little more than an animal—one occasion, among many, for the casual satisfaction of his lust.

Accordingly, Jacobs' protagonist, Linda Brent, experiences little that an unfortunate free white protagonist might not have experienced, and, in the measure that she does, the experience remains abstract. Even when slavery exposes Linda Brent to the threat of separation from her children, loss of the power to determine their fates, and even the possibility of their being sold away from her, her role as mother remains intact. She conveys the assaults that might easily have been taken to compromise her identity as mother in the most conventional bourgeois idiom. Thus Jacobs, even as she harshly indicts slavery for its violation of the minimal norms of womanhood, especially motherhood, sustains the prevailing fictions about women's innate feelings of virtue and mother love. She cannot bring herself to represent the full corruption of slavery lest that attempted representation erase her entirely from an acceptable plot. Her goal remains to indict slavery for its violation of womanly virtue motherhood, while leaving the identity of the virtuous woman and mother intact. In Jacobs' account, slavery prohibits slave women from behaving as they would want to behave, but does not penetrate, much less permanently scar, the inner reaches of their hearts and minds.

Tellingly, Jacobs represents Linda Brent as revering the memory of her own mother, whom she barely knew. "When I was six years old, my mother died; and then, by the talk around me, I learned that I was a slave" (p.6). Everyone spoke warmly of her mother, "who had been a slave merely in name, but in nature was noble and womanly" (p.7). When, years later, Linda Brent enters the church for the baptism of her children, "recollections of my mother came over me, and I felt subdued in spirit" (p.78). Subsequently, at the moment of her flight, Linda Brent visits her mother's grave. "I had," she remembers, "received my mother's blessing when she died; and in many an hour of tribulation I had seemed to hear her voice, sometimes chiding me, sometimes whispering loving words into my wounded heart" (p.90). And it grieves her to think that "when I am gone from my children they cannot remember me with such entire satisfaction as I remembered my mother" (p.90).

It seems likely that Jacobs has reshaped Linda Brent's memories of her mother for narrative purposes, although a child who loses her mother at six may well not remember much. More important, such comforting memories serve the important mission of sustaining the ideal of motherhood among a people whose circumstances frequently threatened the reality. The interviews with former slaves collected during the 1930s abound with recollections of mothers, which, for painfully obvious reasons, significantly outnumber those of fathers. Many of those who had been children during the final years of slavery fondly remembered their mothers' skills as cooks or weavers, specific acts of kindness, or their general devotion to their children. Many others allowed that they could not remember their mothers, who had died or run off when the children were young. As best we can tell, most slaves had a strong bias in favor of emphasizing the strength of mothers' love for their children under what were too often dishearteningly difficult circumstances.

Thus from the midst of shattered families and in the absence of legal protection for the most basic family ties, slaves and former slaves fashioned a collective memory of the resilience and devotion of mothers. But whatever the accuracy of the memory in individual cases, its collective version coexisted with the unsettling knowledge that slavery could lead individual women to behave in ways that might indeed be considered unmotherly. The former slave Lou Smith recalled that her mother had told her of a woman whose master had sold her first three children before they were three years old. It broke her heart that she was not allowed to keep them and, after the birth of her fourth child, she determined to forestall its sale herself. "She just studied all the time about how she would have to give it up," and decided that she would not. So one day she "got up and give it something out of a bottle and pretty soon it was dead." At what may be presumed to have been devastating cost to herself, that slave mother had enforced her right to define herself as mother, not as breeder.

Orlando Patterson has argued that the essence of enslavement lies in condemning those who suffer it to social death. Slavery severs the ties that bind people into society, effectively leaving isolate individuals to fend for themselves. Slavery denies the enslaved the right to establish and enforce social identities, including family identities, and also minimizes their possibilities, which is not exactly the same thing of doing so. We know that in the Americas the latitude that slaves enjoyed or seized to sustain their own families and communities varied considerably from one slave society to another. As a rule, the greater the ratio of slaves to free people, and the greater the ratio of blacks to whites (again, not exactly the same thing), the stronger the elements of African culture remained and the greater the opportunities that slaves enjoyed to sustain de facto community relations, including marriages. But even under the most favorable conditions, the absence of legally sanctioned marriage left the sexuality and motherhood of slave women vulnerable.

The inherent violence of slavery in this regard appears to have been most intense and most fraught with contradiction in the slave society of the southern United States. For there, the ratio of blacks to whites was lowest, the rate of reproduction was highest, the survival of African culture was most precarious, and the influence of bourgeois culture was greatest. Consider the implications of this situation. By the first quarter of the nineteenth century, slave importations had virtually ceased, many slaves had embraced aspects of Protestant Christianity, and African-American reproduction was steadily increasing. Increasingly for the slaves of the southern United States, such marriage as was possible embodied bourgeois rather than African norms, which slaveholders as well as slaves sought to promote. The self-respect and

Christian concerns of southern slaveholders as a class depended heavily on promoting the idea of slave marriage, even when economic fluctuations or simple convenience might lead any given slaveholder to break up marriages by sale. Similarly, the self-respect of southern slaveholders precluded a crass view of slave women as mere breeders, although we know that many valued the natural increase of their slaves for economic reasons.

Both slaveholders and slaves had their own reasons to promote a version of the bourgeois ideal of domesticity and motherhood for African-American slaves. Both also knew that the reality remained so fragile as frequently to look like a hypocritical fiction. The precise blend of black African and white bourgeois values in the slaves' minds and identities will always remain elusive. But the evidence is strong that throughout the first six decades of the nineteenth century the force of the bourgeois ideals of marriage and motherhood steadily grew. It is at least clear that following the Civil War innumerable former slaves struggled mightily to ensure those ideals for themselves, which suggests that they had, in important ways, claimed them as their own. Clearly, this commitment to the ideals informed the way in which Harriet Jacobs wrote of a woman's experience of slavery. No less clearly, the commitment deterred her from a forthright subjective description of the most horrendous costs of slavery for a woman whom the realities of slavery continuously exposed to being stripped of all the conventional attributes of domesticity and motherhood.

More than a century after the appearance of *Incidents in the Life of a Slave Girl*, Toni Morrison, in *Beloved*, explicitly reopened the discussion of how to tell the story of women's experience of slavery. Gone is the gentility that dominates the tone of *Incidents*. None of the former slaves whose stories make up the novel speak in the conventions of domestic fiction, or even in standard English. Drawing upon reference, images, and figures of speech that derive from southern black culture as Morrison envisions it, their words evoke a distinct social, cultural, and material universe. In sharp contrast to *Incidents*, *Beloved* anchors the experience of the slave mother in the horrifyingly tangible indignities of slavery. It is as if the examples of abuse from which Jacobs had so carefully distanced Linda Brent had come to life. No longer things that happen to others, the atrocities that slavery can perpetrate have become things that happen to you or me.

As a novel rather than a confessional narrative, *Beloved* does not present the harrowing events that occurred at 124 Bluestone Road or the history of the house's inhabitants through a single consciousness, but rather successively shows various characters' perceptions of them. In the end, *Beloved* figures less as the story of a former slave woman who killed her own child than as the story of a community's rememory (to borrow Morrison's word) of that killing and of the events that led up to it, and, especially, of the ways of telling unspeakable things. *Beloved* is a novel about personal and collective history. Like *Incidents*, *Beloved* embodies an attempt to come to terms with the legacy of slavery, or, to put it differently, the attempt of former slaves finally to break slavery's shackles. But where *Incidents* had preserved the mantle of bourgeois discretion, thus effectively neutralizing the very horrors it sought to mobilize opposition against, *Beloved* lays the horrors bare, inviting readers to confront the ways in which slavery ate into the consciousness of all of those it touched.

Although the narrative of *Beloved* is infinitely complex, the story is chillingly simple. It is the story of a group of slaves who had, in the 1850s, lived on the Sweet Home plantation in Kentucky. When the slaveholder, Mr Garner, had died, Sweet Home had been bought by Schoolteacher, who rapidly made life for the slaves intolerable. Eventually, the main character, Sethe, young mother of three and expecting a fourth, escapes to join her mother-in-law, Baby Suggs, in Cincinnati. En route, she gives birth to the child, a girl whom she names Denver. Some time after her arrival at Baby Suggs' house at 124 Bluestone Road, Schoolteacher appears with a small band of men (the four horsemen) to reclaim his property. Sethe, recognizing his hat, flees to the woodshed, kills her oldest daughter, and is about to kill the other children when Stamp Paid, another former slave, stops her.

Such is the prehistory of the events of the novel, which begin in the early 1870s, when Paul D, another former Sweet Home slave, arrives at 124. Just as he and Sethe begin to build a free love, Beloved, who is apparently the ghost of Sethe's oldest daughter arrives and turns all of their lives inside out. The novel concludes with Beloved's departure, and Sethe's acceptance, by her world—Denver, the women of the black community, and Paul D, who gently tells her, "'me and you, we got more yesterday than anybody. We need some kind of tomorrow.'" And then insists, "'You your best thing, Sethe. You are'" (p.273)

The core of *Beloved* lies in Sethe's murder of her cherished, "crawling already?" baby—the still nursing, not-yet-two-year-old girl, for whom she had braved nearly inconceivable horrors in order to provide the milk of her own breasts, which the baby needed to survive. "Why I did it. How if I hadn't killed her she would have died and that is something I could not bear to happen to her" (p.200). Throughout *Beloved*, Morrison returns time and again to slavery's implacable war against motherhood. Baby Suggs bore eight children and was stripped of them all—"four taken, four chased, and all, I expect, worrying somebody's house into evil" (p.5). Approaching death, she can remember only that her first-born loved the burned bottom of bread. "Can you beat that? Eight children and that's all I remember" (p.5).

Sethe reproaches her own mother for never having let her be a daughter. A daughter is what she wanted to be "and would have been if my ma'am had been able to get out of the rice long enough before they hanged her and let me be one" (p.203). Sethe's ma'am had had the bit so many times that she always smiled, but Sethe "never saw her own smile" (p.203). Eventually she was caught and hanged, but Sethe did not know why or what she was doing. She could not have been running. "Because she was my ma'am and nobody's ma'am would run off and leave her daughter would she?" (p.203). But then how would Sethe know about a ma'am who had only suckled her daughter for a week or two and then left her in the yard with a one-armed woman who had to nurse the white babies first and frequently did not have enough left over for Sethe. "There was no nursing milk to call my own" (p.200). She would never allow that to happen to any daughter of hers. Beloved had to understand that Sethe had cut her own daughter's throat precisely to ensure that she could be a daughter—that Sethe could be a mother.

The figure of Sethe, standing in the woodshed, dripping with the blood of the murdered baby girl, whose body she will not relinquish, offering her blood-dripping nipple to the surviving infant, challenges any recognizable image of motherhood. Schoolteacher, the leader of the four white horsemen, who have come to return her to slavery, sees only "a nigger woman holding a blood-soaked child to her chest with one hand and an infant by the heels in the other." Never fuming to look at the invaders, "she simply swung the baby toward the wall planks, missed and tried to connect a second time," while two bleeding boys lay in the sawdust at her feet (p.149). Schoolteacher, who was not looking for a mother, saw none. He saw nothing there to claim at all. He saw only a woman gone wild, "due to the mishandling of the nephew who'd overbeat her and made her cut and run"—the same nephew, although Schoolteacher does not see the connection, who had, back at Sweet Home, held her down and stolen the milk she was saving for her baby girl (p. 149). Schoolteacher had tried. He "had chastised the nephew, telling him to think—just think—what would his own horse do if you beat it past the point of education. Or Chipper, or Samson. Suppose you beat the hounds past that point thataway" (p. 149).

Small wonder that Schoolteacher, seeing Sethe as a breeder, a skilful ironer of shirts, a maker of excellent ink, cannot understand her motivations. For him she is a domesticated animal to be handled and if mishandled should be expected to go wild. It would not cross his mind that her excesses could result from the violation of her humanity and the denial of her mother's love. Paul D, who had his own knowledge of the worst that slavery had to offer, who had known Sethe at Sweet Home, and who had loved her there and at

124, is another matter. Confronted by Stamp Paid with the newspaper account of Sethe's action, Paul D refuses to believe that the woman who killed her baby could be Sethe. "That ain't her mouth" (p. 154). "You forgetting," Paul D told Stamp Paid, "I knew her before . . . Back in Kentucky. When she was a girl. . . . I been knowing her a long time. And I can tell you for sure: this ain't her mouth. May look like it, but it ain't" (p. 158). And Stamp Paid himself, looking at the "sweet conviction" in Paul D's eyes, almost wonders if it really happened, if eighteen years ago, "while he and Baby Suggs were looking the wrong way, a pretty little slave girl had recognized a hat, and split to the woodshed to kill her children" (p. 158).

Paul D never asks Sethe directly if she killed her baby, he merely confronts her with the newspaper clipping, implicitly asking her to tell him that the woman it describes is not she. Showing it to her he smiles, ready for her to "burst out laughing at the joke—the mix-up of her face put where some other colored woman's ought to be" (p.161). It may have been his smile or "the ever-ready love she saw in his eyes" that made her try to explain. Her trying led her back to Sweet Home, about which she did not have to tell him, and to what he may not have known, "what it was like for me to get away from there" (p.161). For the getting away was her own doing. "Me having to look out. Me using my own head" (p. 162). And it was also more, "It was a kind of selfishness I never knew nothing about before. It felt good. Good and right" (p.162). It was a selfishness that allowed her to love her children more than she ever had before. "Or maybe I couldn't love em proper in Kentucky because they wasn't mine to love." When she got to Ohio, a free woman, "there wasn't nobody in the world I couldn't love if I wanted to" (p.162).

That Paul D could understand all too well. For him, slavery had meant the necessity to protect yourself and love small. Under slavery, you picked "the tiniest stars out of the sky to own" so that your love would not be competing with that of the men who owned the guns. "Brass blades, salamanders, spiders, woodpeckers, beetles, a kingdom of ants. Anything bigger wouldn't do. A woman, a child, a brother—a big love like that would split you wide open in Alfred, Georgia." Oh yes, Paul D "knew exactly what she meant: to get to a place where you could love anything you chose—not to need permission for desire—well, now, that was freedom" (p. 162). Threatened with the loss of that freedom, Sethe explained to Paul D, "I took and put my babies where they'd be safe" (p.163). The "safe" shakes Paul D, who knows it is precisely what 124 was lacking when he had arrived, who thought he had made it safe, and who thought that if Sethe her own self had not it was because she could not.

Sethe's definition of her murder as assuring her baby's safety shows Paul D how wrong he has been. "This here Sethe was new. . . . This here

Sethe talked about love like any other woman; talked about baby clothes like any other woman, but what she meant could cleave the bone. This here Sethe talked about safety with a handsaw. This here new Sethe didn't know where the world stopped and she began" (p.164). All of a sudden, Paul D could see what Stamp Paid had wanted him to see: "More important than what Sethe had done was what she claimed. It scared him" (p. 164). Paul D tells Sethe that her love is too thick, that what she did didn't work. It did work, Sethe counters. How, Paul D queries, can she calculate that? Both her boys have run off, one of her girls is dead, and the other will not leave the yard. "They ain't at Sweet Home. Schoolteacher got em" (p. 165). Maybe, Paul D responds, there is worse. "It ain't my job to know what's worse. It's my job to know what is and to keep them away from what I know is terrible. I did that" (p.165). But what she did, Paul D insists, is wrong, there could have been some other way. And when she asks what way, without stopping to think, he rejoins, "You got two feet, Sethe, not four" (p. 165).

No more than Schoolteacher, can Paul D understand Sethe's motivations and, to the extent that he can understand something, he ultimately shares Schoolteacher's view of Sethe's deed as the deed of an animal. In his eyes, Sethe's desperate act of claiming her motherhood, her children and her love for them shatters the bounds between self and other, self and the world. What Sethe sees as her ultimate act of self-definition, Paul D can only see as an act of madness. Frightened like her sons, Howard and Buglar, who survived her murderous attack but ran away from home as soon as they were old enough, he leaves, leaving 124 to Sethe, Denver, and Beloved and the three women to each other. Stamp Paid, having suffered the pain of knocking and not gaining entrance, left 124 to its own devices and the women inside it "free at last to be what they liked, see whatever they saw and say whatever was on their minds." But behind the freedom of their words, which Stamp Paid could recognize if not decipher, lurked their thoughts, "unspeakable thoughts, unspoken" (p. 199).

From the start of the novel, we know that 124 is inhabited by the ghost of a murdered baby. No sooner than Paul D reappears after eighteen years, bathes Sethe's scarred back and moves into her bed, takes Sethe and Denver to the carnival, and begins to rebuild a family at 124, does Beloved herself reappear as a material presence. Entrancing, demanding, seductive, Beloved gradually wreaks her revenge by consuming Sethe's life—by confronting Sethe with a love as totally demanding as that which led Sethe to kill her baby. Beloved, the ghost-become-presence, defies any neat interpretation. But complexities notwithstanding, she must in part be understood as a narrative device that Morrison saw as necessary to telling the story she wanted to tell. Beloved embodies some essential residue of the experience of all the other characters, embodies the parts of the story that still cannot be told—the unspeakable thoughts unspoken.

For Sethe, Beloved is the daughter who has come back to her. "She mine. See. She come back to me of her own free will and I don't have to explain a thing" (p.200) Beloved is the child to whom she can tell of Sweet Home, to whom she can talk of the things that Denver does not want to hear. For Denver Beloved, "is my sister. I swallowed her blood right along with my mother's milk. . . . Ever since I was little she was my company and she helped me wait for my daddy." Denver loves her mother, but knows "she killed one of her own daughters, and tender as she is with me, I'm scared of her because of it" (p.205). Denver knows that there is something in her mother "that makes it all right to kill her own." And she constantly fears that "the thing that happened that made it all right for my mother to kill my sister could happen again" (p.205). Denver does not know and does not want to know what that thing might be. She only knows that it comes from outside 124, and so she never leaves the house, carefully watching over the years "so it can't happen again and my mother won't have to kill me too" (p. 165). More frightening yet, maybe "the thing that makes it all right to kill her children" is still in her mother (p.206).

The ghost of the victim—the name on the tombstone of the victim—of an infanticide prompted by too-thick love, Beloved is the custodian of the story that was not to be passed on. Her arrival at 124 signals her refusal to lay it down and get on with things. Nothing can be laid down or got on with until the story is told. The story belongs to no one person but to them all—the folks from Sweet Home who made it to 124. Baby Suggs feared that the murder had occurred because of the Sweet Home escapees' too great arrogance about their freedom. Twenty days after Sethe's safe arrival, Baby Suggs had given a party for ninety people who "ate so well, and laughed so much, it made them angry" (p.136). So when they awoke the next morning the odor of their disapproval at what they took to be Baby Suggs' overstepping hung in the air, masking the odor of the "dark and coming thing" that was the four horsemen in pursuit of Sethe (p.138). Had it not been for the party, Baby Suggs worried, might they not have recognized the threat soon enough to take steps to avert it?

Baby Suggs' worries link Sethe's infanticide to the free black community. Sethe's and Paul D's memories link it to Sweet Home and, beyond Sweet Home, to slavery as a social system. For Paul D fully corroborates Sethe's fragmented account of life at Sweet Home, demonstrating that we should not mistrust her memories. It was that bad. In fact, under Schoolteacher, it was so bad as to cast doubt upon their belief that it had really been any better under the Garners. The issue is not a good or a bad master. The issue is slavery. And a slavery that leaves the definition of men to the good will of a master, rather than to the identity of the men themselves, is also a slavery that destroys the definition of women—especially mothers. Sethe, having barely known her own mother and lacking the companionship of other women, knew of the practices of mothering. But by the time she arrived at 124, she knew that her very identity depended upon her children's being absolutely hers.

There are strong reasons to accept Sethe's infanticide as a desperate act of self-definition: By claiming her child absolutely, she claimed her identity as a mother, not a breeder But in grounding her defense of her identity as a mother in the murder of her own child, she opened new possibilities of being viewed as an animal. The responses of Denver and Paul D, like the absence of Howard and Buglar, remind us that Sethe's self-definition was also the "crawling already?" baby's murder. Was it a thing outside or a thing inside that made Sethe do what she did? Was slavery an external force or an internal presence? By giving Beloved a consciousness, however briefly and elliptically, Morrison seems to suggest that we cannot entirely cast the murder of a baby as an act of heroic, if tormented, resistance. By peopling Beloved's consciousness with memories that evoke the slave ships of the middle passage, she seems to suggest that we cannot entirely divorce the murder of this baby from the slavery that shaped its murdering mother's life.

In her own way, Harriet Jacobs insisted that slavery corrupted everyone it touched. But, in sternly repressing her most painful personal angers, she left the impression that it affected behavior more than identity. Linda Brent's personal war with slavery, as embodied in her master, left her identity as mother largely intact, blemished only by a few understandable lapses. Significantly, her daughter seems almost bemused that her mother feels obliged to ask her forgiveness. Morrison, in contrast, shows slavery as cutting to the quick of Sethe's innermost being—jeopardizing any possibility of even beginning to sort out rights and wrongs. And the anger that Jacobs cloaks with a veneer of respectable discourse, emerges in Beloved as the unquietable rage of the murdered "crawling already?" baby girl, whose ghost also embodies the boundary-obliterating love that joins mother and child.

The parallels between the two narratives bridge the chilling and the reassuring, leaving us only with the certainty that each embodies a different way of telling an impossible story. Slavery's contempt for the humanity of motherhood corrupted everyone it touched—black and white, slave and free, female and male. Jacobs could only begin to hint at the elements of the story, steadfastly distancing her protagonist from personal experience of the most searing pain and humiliation. Morrison has bravely attempted to capture the subjective perspective—to tell the story that was not fit for passing on and to explain the story of the forgetting. But to do so, even she had to create a ghost since memory alone demonstrably would not serve.

Throughout American slave societies, mothers have enjoyed a special place in humanizing a too-frequently dehumanizing social system, in standing as the last bastion against the full horror of social death. Many have chosen to see the predominance of mothers in different African-American communities as a sign of pathology or social breakdown. From another perspective, mothers constituted the last bastion against the evil that slavery could wreak. And the power to define and defend motherhood emerged as the battleground over the irreducible minimum of the slaves' social identities. In that struggle, it understandably appeared threatening to expose the worst horrors for fear that they confirm the worst consequences of enslavement. In this perspective, slavery's power to define motherhood becomes the power to define the slaves' humanity and the slaves' power to defy the definition becomes the cornerstone of collective resistance. What, then, to do with the ghosts—the "unspeakable thing unspoken"? For Harriet Jacobs, the risks of speaking were too high. But in the hands of Toni Morrison the speaking of unspeakable thoughts has emerged as the necessary recovery of a buried history—the cornerstone of a new resistance.

Thus Morrison, in the frontispiece to *Beloved*, quotes Romans 9:25: "I will call them my people, which were not my people; and her beloved, which was not beloved." Beloved, the ghost, acquired her name at the moment of her burial when Sethe had to provide a name for the tombstone of the "crawling already?" baby girl who had had no name in life. Her choice resulted from her having loved the words of the minister at the funeral service, "Dearly beloved, we are gathered together. . . ." Had that baby been killed in the name of the too-thick love that sought to put her beyond the claims of slavery, or had she been sacrificed to her mother's fierce determination to define her own identity as a mother? In the end, the choice is no choice at all, for the baby died, her ghost born as a result of the intertwining of both.

Sethe had grown up with the knowledge that a mother's love and behavior did not always observe the conventions that enshrined it. Had she not insisted that her own mother could not have been killed when she was running away, for no little girl's mother would run away and leave her? And does not the reader, like some part of Sethe herself, know that running away was precisely what her mother was doing? If slavery did make it almost impossible for women to be mothers, then, in the measure that they could not, the children and frequently the children's children suffered the consequences. The horror of slavery, Morrison seems to be saying, lies in the intractability of two opposing truths: Mothers might murder their own babies out of love and in an act of resistance, but that expression of love and of resistance nonetheless resulted in the extinction of a baby they had suckled and loved. There is no easy way to construct a vision of humanity out of the murder of children—especially one's own children. Only by telling the real story—by refusing the superficially ennobling conventions and relinquishing the pretension that the inequities of slavery as a social system left the hearts and minds of the enslaved untouched—would it be possible to reclaim an impossible past as the foundation for a possible future. Only by exposing their scars, could African-Americans as a people expose the full costs of the oppression they had suffered.

ASHRAF H.A. RUSHDY

Daughters Signifyin(g) History: The Example of Toni Morrison's Beloved

Despite the dangers of remembering the past, African American artists have insistently based a large part of their aesthetic ideal on precisely that activity. John Edgar Wideman prefaces his novel *Sent For You Yesterday* with this testament: "Past lives in us, through us. Each of us harbors the spirits of people who walked the earth before we did, and those spirits depend on us for continuing existence, just as we depend on their presence to live our lives to the fullest." This insistence on the interdependence of past and present is, moreover, a political act, for it advocates a revisioning of the past as it is filtered through the present. Wideman elsewhere has asked, "What is history except people's imaginary recreation?" Racial memories, he suggests, "exist in the imagination." They are in fact a record of "certain collective experiences" that "have been repeated generation after generation."

As Toni Morrison has said, "if we don't keep in touch with the ancestor . . . we are, in fact, lost." Keeping in touch with the ancestor, she adds, is the work of a reconstructive memory: "Memory (the deliberate act of remembering) is a form of willed creation. It is not an effort to find out the way it really was—that is research. The point is to dwell on the way it appeared and why it appeared in that particular way." This concern with the appearance, with the ideology of transmission, is, though, only part of the overall trajectory of her revisionary project. Eventually her work, she states, must "bear

From *American Literature* 64:3 (September 1992).

witness and identify that which is useful from the past and that which ought to be discarded."? It must, that is, signify on the past and make it palatable for a present politic—eschewing that part of the past which has been constructed out of a denigrative ideology and reconstructing that part which will serve the present.

Morrison is both participant and theorist of this black aesthetic of remembering, and she has recently set out some of the mandates for establishing a form of literary theory that will truly accommodate African American literature—a theory based on an inherited culture, an inherited "history," and the understanding of the ways that any given artistic work negotiates between those cultural/historical worlds it inhabits. Moreover, not only does Morrison, following the line of Pauline Hopkins, delineate the "dormant inmost feelings in that history"; she takes up, delicately yet resolutely, the task of reviving the very figures of that history.

By taking a historical personage—a daughter of a faintly famous African American victim of racist ideology—and constructing her as a hopeful presence in a contemporary setting, Morrison offers an introjection into the fields of revisionist historiography and fiction. She makes articulate a victim of a patriarchal order in order to criticize that order. Yet she portrays an unrelenting hopefulness in that critique. She does not inherit, as Deborah McDowell maintains some writers do, "the orthodoxy of victimage," nor does she reduce her narrative to anything resembling what Henry Louis Gates Jr. has called a "master plot of victim and victimizer." She, like Ralph Ellison, returns to history not to find claims for reparation or reasons for despair, but to find "something subjective, willful, and complexly and compellingly human"—to find, that is, something for her art. She does so, moreover, by doing what Hortense Spillers claims Ishmael Reed does with the discursive field of slavery in his *Flight to Canada*: "construct[ing] and reconstruct[ing] repertoires of usage out of the most painful human/historical experience." In articulating a reconstructive—critical and hopeful—feminist voice within the fields of revisionist historiography and contemporary fiction, what Morrison does is create daughters Signifyin(g) history.

Raising *Beloved*: A Requiem that is a Resurrection

Morrison thought that her most recent book would be the least read of her novels because it would be perceived to be a work dealing with slavery, an institution that is willingly placed under erasure by what she calls a "national amnesia": "I thought this has got to be the least read of all the books I'd written because it is about something the characters don't want to remember, I don't want to remember, black people don't want to remember, white people don't want to remember." But *Beloved* is not about slavery as an institution: it is "about those anonymous people called slaves."

Morrison's sense of ambivalence, of wishing to forget and remember at the same time, is enacted in her attitude to the story and its characters. Speaking about the writing of *Beloved*, she declares her wish to invoke all those people who are "unburied, or at least unceremoniously buried," and go about "properly, artistically, burying them." However, this burial's purpose, it would appear, is to bring them back into "living life." This tension between needing to bury the past as well as needing to revive it, between a necessary remembering and an equally necessary forgetting, exists in both the author and her narrative. We might better understand that tension by attending to the author's construction of the scenes of inspiration leading her to write this novel.

Morrison has said that the idea of *Beloved* was inspired by "two or three little fragments of stories" that she had "heard from different places." The first was the story of Margaret Garner, a slave who in January 1856 escaped from her owner Archibald K. Gaines of Kentucky, crossed the Ohio River, and attempted to find refuge in Cincinnati. She was pursued by Gaines and a posse of officers. They surrounded the house where she, her husband Robert, and their four children were harbored. When the posse battered down the door and rushed in, Robert shot at them and wounded one of the officers before being overpowered. According to Levi Coffin, "at this moment, Margaret Garner, seeing that their hopes of freedom were vain, seized a butcher knife that lay on the table, and with one stroke cut the throat of her little daughter, whom she probably loved the best. She then attempted to take the life of the other children and to kill herself, but she was overpowered and hampered before she could complete her desperate work." Margaret Garner chose death for both herself and her most beloved rather than accept being forced to return to slavery and have her children suffer an institutionalized dehumanization. The story of Margaret Garner was eventually to become the historical analogue of the plot of *Beloved*.

Morrison said that what this story made her realize was that "the best thing that is in us is also the thing that makes us sabotage ourselves" ("Conversation," 585). The story of Margaret Garner stayed with Morrison, representing, albeit unclearly, something about feminine selflessness. It took another story to clarify more precisely what Margaret Garner and her story meant.

Morrison found that story in Camille Billops's *The Harlem Book of the Dead*—an album featuring James Van Der Zee's photographs of Harlem funerals. These were photographs, Morrison has said, that had a "narrative quality." One photograph and its attendant story in particular caught her attention:

> In one picture, there was a young girl lying in a coffin and he [Van Der Zee] says that she was eighteen years old and she had gone to a party and that she was dancing and suddenly she slumped and they noticed there was blood on her and they said, "What happened to you?" And she said, "I'll tell you tomorrow. I'll tell you tomorrow." That's all she would say. And apparently her ex-boyfriend or somebody who was jealous had come into the party with a gun and a silencer and shot her. And she kept saying, "I'll tell you tomorrow" because she wanted him to get away. And he did, I guess; anyway, she died. ("Conversation," 584)

After reading the narrative of Margaret Garner, Toni Morrison had thought she glimpsed an opaque truth that she had always known, somehow: "But that moment, that decision was a piece, a tail of something that was always around, and it didn't get clear for me until I was thinking of another story."

When Van Der Zee provided that next story, Morrison saw clearly what she'd glimpsed through a darker glass: "Now what made those stories connect, I can't explain, but I do know that, in both instances, something seemed clear to me. A woman loved something other than herself so much. She had placed all of the value of her life in something outside herself. That the woman who killed her children loved her children so much; they were the best part of her and she would not see them sullied" ("Conversation," 584). In 1978, nine years before the publication of *Beloved*, Morrison started attempting to formulate the terms of that tension between remembering and forgetting, burying and reviving. In the Foreword to *The Harlem Book of the Dead* she writes: "The narrative quality, the intimacy, the humanity of his photographs are stunning, and the proof, if any is needed, is in this collection of photographs devoted exclusively to the dead about which one can only say, 'How living are his portraits of the dead.' So living, so 'undead,' that the prestigious writer, Owen Dodson, is stirred to poetry in which life trembles in every metaphor." "'One of Owen Dodson's "living" poems is on the page facing the picture of the young girl as she lies in her coffin:

> They lean over me and say:
> "Who deathed you who,
> who, who, who, who. . . .

> I whisper: "Tell you presently . . .
> Shortly . . . this evening . . . '
> Tomorrow . . ."
> Tomorrow is here
> And you out there safe.
> I'm safe in here, Tootsie. (52–53)

If Van Der Zee's photographs give renewed life to the dead, so does Dodson's poetry give renewed voice. Across from a picture of a girl in a coffin resides her living voice, her expression of the safety of death. As early as 1973, Morrison had been concerned with making the dead articulate. When Sula dies, she feels her face smiling: "'Well, I'll be damned,' she thought, 'it didn't even hurt. Wait'll I tell Nell.'"

In 1987, with *Beloved*, Morrison goes further in giving the dead voice, in remembering the forgotten. *Beloved* is, in effect, a requiem that is a resurrection. The most obvious example of this commemoration is Beloved herself, the ghost of Margaret Garner's unnamed child: "So I just imagined the life of a dead girl which was the girl that Margaret Garner killed, the baby girl that she killed. . . . And I call her Beloved so that I can filter all these confrontations and questions that she has in that situation" ("Conversation," 585). Beloved is more than just a character in the novel, though. She is the embodiment of the past that must be remembered in order to be forgotten; she symbolizes what must be reincarnated in order to be buried, properly: "Everybody knew what she was called, but nobody anywhere knew her name. Disremembered and unaccounted for, she cannot be lost because no one is looking for her."

In the end, though, Beloved is not the most important character in Morrison's revisionist strategy. That character is Denver, the other daughter. Morrison's original intent in the novel, she said in 1985, was to develop the narrative of Beloved into the narrative of Denver. First she would imagine the life of the murdered child, "to extend her life, you know, her search, her quest, all the way through as long as I care to go, into the twenties where it switches to this other girl." This "other girl," Denver, is the site of hope in Morrison's novel. She is the daughter of history. Nonetheless, as Morrison emphasizes, even when Denver becomes the focus of the narrative's attention, "Beloved will be there also" ("Conversation," 585). Before turning to the novel, and determining how Morrison inscribes hope into a critical revision of history, let us return briefly to the narrative of Margaret Garner in order to see the history that she revises.

Towards *Beloved*: Margaret Garner

It was sometime in January 1856 that Margaret Garner attempted her escape and killed her daughter. The story and the ensuing court case were reported in the Cincinnati newspapers and reported again in *The Liberator* in March 1856. Another detailed narrative appeared in the *Annual Report of the American Anti-Slavery Society* in 1856. The newspaper coverage may have been motivated by a variety of reasons, some of them, one intuits, having to do with the exoticism of the story. In much the same way, Jim Trueblood of Ralph Ellison's *Invisible Man* becomes the focus of white attention after he commits incest with his daughter:

> The white folks took up for me. And the white folks took to coming out here to see us and talk with us. Some of 'em was big white folks, too, from the big school way across the State. Asked me lots 'bout what I thought 'bout things, and 'bout my folks and the kids, and wrote it all down in a book. . . . That's what I don't understand. I done the worse thing a man could ever do in his family and instead of chasin' me out of the country, they gimme more help than they ever give any other colored man, no matter how good a nigguh he was.

In *Beloved* Morrison has Paul D respond to the media attention Sethe gets for infanticide in much the same way as the "invisible man" responds to Trueblood's story:

> Because there was no way in hell a black face could appear in a newspaper if the story was about something anybody wanted to hear. A whip of fear broke through the heart chambers as soon as you saw a Negro's face in a paper, since the face was not there because the person had a healthy baby, or outran a street mob. Nor was it there because the person had been killed, or maimed or caught or burned or jailed or whipped or evicted or stomped or raped or cheated, since that could hardly qualify as news in a newspaper. It would have to be something out of the ordinary—something whitepeople would find interesting, truly different, worth a few minutes of teeth sucking if not gasps. And it must have been hard to find news about Negroes worth the breath catch of a white citizen of Cincinnati. (155–56)

As Levi Coffin noted, the Margaret Garner case "attracted more attention and aroused deeper interest and sympathy" than any other he'd known (I'll return to the importance of this critique of print media later).

The case became a forum for "that noble anti-slavery lawyer" John Jolliffe, counsel for the defence, to argue that the 1850 Fugitive Slave Law was unconstitutional. Lucy Stone, who visited Garner in jail, spoke to the crowd outside her trial, describing Garner as a quintessentially American hero: "I thought the spirit she manifested was the same with that of our ancestors to whom we had erected a monument at Bunker Hill—the spirit that would rather let us all go back to God than back to slavery." A year and a half after her trial, Garner had become a symbol for what Frederick Douglass called his "philosophy of reform." Addressing an assembly celebrating the twenty-third anniversary of West Indian Emancipation, Douglass proclaimed:

> The whole history of the progress of human liberty shows that all concessions yet made to her august claims, have been born of earnest struggle. The conflict has been exciting, agitating, all-absorbing, and for the time being, putting all other tumults to silence. It must do this or it does nothing. If there is no struggle there is no progress. . . . This struggle may be a moral one, or it may be a physical one, but it must be a struggle. Power concedes nothing without a demand. It never did and it never will. Find out what any people will quietly submit to and you have found out the exact measure of injustice and wrong which will be imposed upon them. . . . The limits of tyrants are prescribed by the endurance of those whom they oppress. . . . If we ever get free from the oppressions and wrongs heaped upon us, we must pay for their removal. We must do this by labor, by suffering, by sacrifice, and if needs be, by our lives and the lives of others.
>
> Hence, my friends, every mother who, like Margaret Garner, plunges a knife into the bosom of her infant to save it from the hell of our Christian Slavery, should be held and honored as a benefactress.

As late as 1892, the story of Margaret Garner could be used to signify the extreme measures a person would take to escape what the lawyer Jolliffe called the "seething hell of American slavery" and Douglass the "hell of our Christian Slavery."

In Frances E. W. Harper's *Iola Leroy*, Margaret Garner's case symbolized in the heroine's life what the author calls "school-girl notions." Iola is the daughter of the slaveowner Eugene Leroy and his wife Marie, who has "negro blood in her veins"; Iola, when she attends school in the North, does not yet know her maternal racial background. In discussion with her fellow school-girls in the Northern school, Iola defends the institution of slavery, claiming that their slaves are "content." One of her schoolfriends disagrees: "'I don't know,' was the response of her friend, 'but I do not think that that slave mother who took her four children, crossed the Ohio River on the ice, killed one of the children and attempted the lives of the other two, was a contented slave.'" Significantly, when Iola does discover her racial heritage she begins a mission of education, the biggest part of which is the paper she reads to the Council Meeting at Mr. Stillman's house, a paper entitled "Education of Mothers." Nameless now, Margaret Garner had become a political symbol for discontent. By 1948, Herbert Aptheker would cite the Margaret Garner case to argue why "the Negro woman so often urged haste in slave plottings." By 1981, Angela Y. Davis would echo him in arguing that the Margaret Garner case demonstrated not only the willingness of slave women to organize insurrections but also the unique desperation of the slave mother.

By 1987, Margaret Garner's story would inspire a Pulitzer prizewinning novel. Morrison has said that she does not know what eventually happened to Margaret Garner. There are conflicting reports. According to Coffin and *The Liberator*, while Garner was being shipped back to Kentucky she jumped overboard with her baby; she was saved but her baby drowned. According to a report in the Cincinnati *Chronicle* and the Philadelphia *Press*, Margaret and her husband Robert worked in New Orleans and then on Judge Bonham's plantation in Mississippi until Margaret died of typhoid fever in 1858. Whatever her fate, at Morrison's hands she has been buried in order to be resurrected into a new life, and she has been remembered in order that the institution she suffered may be forgotten.

Signifyin(g) on History

Beloved, according to Stanley Crouch, one of its harshest reviewers, "means to prove that Afro-Americans are the result of a cruel determinism." This criticism is a good place to start our discussion of the novel, not because Crouch has hit upon some truth regarding *Beloved* or Morrison (he has not) but because he demonstrates the sort of conclusion a reader may reach if unburdened by knowledge of the historical place of *Beloved*'s writing, its historical analogue, and its critical position in the African American aesthetic and politics of remembering history.

Beloved is the product of and a contribution to a historical moment in which African American historiography is in a state of fervid revision. The debate currently rages between those who argue that slavery led to the "infantilization" of adult Africans because the most significant relationship in any slave's life was that between the slave and the master, and those who argue that slaves formed viable internal communities, family structures, and protective personae that allowed them to live rich, coherent lives within their own system of values. One premise underlying this debate is the question of whether slaves were acquiescent or resistant to the institution, whether they conformed to the "Sambo" or "Mammy" stereotypes who accepted their stations or whether they were in perpetual opposition to them—both in daily resistance and in sensational insurrections. It is within this revisionary fray that *Beloved* may profitably be examined. As I hope to demonstrate below, the novel both remembers the victimization of the ex-slaves who are its protagonists and asserts the healing and wholeness that those protagonists carry with them in their communal lives. Crouch, unfortunately, reads the novel as if it were a rendition only of victimization, only of determinism; in other words, he misreads it.

Morrison has on more than one occasion asserted that she writes from a double perspective of accusation and hope, of criticizing the past and caring for the future. She claims that this double perspective is the perspective of a "Black woman writer," that is, "one who look[s] at things in an unforgiving/loving way . . . , writing to repossess, re-name, re-own." In *Beloved*, this perspective is described as "the glare of an outside thing that embraces while it accuses" (271). It is on precisely this issue of a dual vision that she marks the distinction between black men's writing and black women's: "what I found so lacking in most black writing by men that seems to be present in a lot of black women's writing is a sense of joy, in addition to oppression and being women or black or whatever."

Morrison writes out of a dual perspective in order to re-possess, as I've suggested earlier, by remembering the ancestor, not only an aesthetic act but an act of historical recovery: "roots are less a matter of geography than sense of shared history; less to do with place, than with inner space." Each act of writing a novel is for her an act of discovering deep within herself some relationship to a "collective memory." Memory itself, write Mary Frances Berry and John Blassingame, is for African Americans "an instrument of survival." It is an instrument, writes Morrison, that can be traced back to an African heritage: "it's true what Africans say: 'The Ancestor lives as long as there are those who remember.'"

In the novel this truth is expressed by Sethe's mother-in-law. Baby Suggs knows that "death was anything but forgetfulness" (4). That remembering is both a resurrection and a pain is testified to by Amy Denver, who assisted in the birthing of Sethe's daughter: "Anything dead coming back to life hurts." The daughter Amy delivered testifies to that: "A truth for all times, thought Denver" (35). Let us now turn our attention to the novel in which all the double perspectives of this black woman writer are expressed—remembering and forgetting, accusing and embracing, burying and reviving, joy and oppression.

Reading *Beloved*

The obvious place to begin a reading tracing Morrison's signifyin(g) on the story of Margaret Garner is the site of infanticide. One of the recurrent tropes of the African American novel of slavery is the possible response to an institution attempting to render meaningless the mother-child relationship. In William Wells Brown's *Clotelle*, the slave mother Isabella would rather commit suicide than face slavery for herself and her children. Hunted by a crowd of dogs and slavecatchers, Isabella leaps into the Potomac as an act symbolizing the "unconquerable love of liberty which the human heart may inherit." The chapter is entitled "Death Is Freedom." In Zora Neale Hurston's *Moses, Man of the Mountain*, slavery is described as an institution in which only death can give freedom. As Amram tells Caleb, "you are up against a hard game when you got to die to beat it." It is an even harder game, Morrison would add, when you have to kill what you love most.

Coffin explicitly states Margaret's motivation: "the slave mother . . . killed her child rather than see it taken back to slavery" (557). Like Harriet Jacobs, Margaret, in Coffin's reading of her history, sees death as a better alternative than slavery. "It seemed to me," writes Jacobs, "that I would rather see them [her children] killed than have them given up to his [the slaveowner's] power. . . . When I lay down beside my child, I felt how much easier it would be to see her die than to see her master beat her about."

Sethe killed Beloved, according to Stamp Paid, because she "was trying to outhurt the hurters." "She love those children" (243). Loving as a slave, according to Paul D (whom Stamp Paid is trying to persuade with his assessment of Sethe's motivation), meant loving small, loving in an unobvious way so that whatever was loved did not become part of a technique of punishment. Paul D's advice, and his credo, was to "love just a little bit" so that when the slave owners took whatever or whoever the slave loved and "broke its back, or shoved it in a croaker sack, well, maybe you'd have a little love left over for the next one" (45). Ella another ex-slave who was loved by no one and who considered "love a serious disability" (256), lived by the simple dictum "Don't love nothing" (92). When Paul D learns of Sethe's infanticide he tells her that her love is "too thick." She responds by telling him that "Love is or it ain't. Thin love ain't love at all" (164). Although Paul D lives by his philosophy of loving small as a protective measure, he knows what Sethe means. "He knew exactly what she meant: to get to a place where you could love anything you chose—not to need permission for desire—well now, *that* was freedom" (162). Although Paul D knows the conditions of freedom and Sethe knows the conditions of love, each has to learn to claim that freedom, to claim that love, and thereby to claim genuine community and begin the process of healing.

Sethe's process of healing occurs when she acknowledges her act and accepts her responsibility for it while also recognizing the reason for her act within a framework larger than that of individual resolve. Here perhaps, is Morrison's most powerful introjection into the Margaret Garner story—the establishing of a context for Sethe's act. Sethe's own mother kills all the children fathered by the whites who raped her. As Nan, Sethe's grandmother tells her, "She threw them all away but you. The one from the crew she threw away on the island. The others from more whites she also threw away. Without names, she threw them" (62). Another important person helping Sethe through the exorcising of her painful memories is Ella, who, it is hinted, has also committed infanticide. By placing such a frame around Sethe's story, Morrison insists on the impossibility of judging an action without reference to the terms of its enactment—the wrongness of assuming a transhistorical ethic outside a particular historical moment. Morrison is not justifying Sethe's actions; she is writing about them in the only way she knows how—through eyes that accuse and embrace, through a perspective that criticizes while it rejoices. Towards that end, she has constructed two daughterly presences in her novel who help Sethe remember and forget her personal history, who embody the dual perspective of critique and rejoicing.

Beloved, the incarnation of the ghost of the murdered daughter, is the most obvious revisionist construction in Morrison's novel. Through Beloved, she signifies on history by resurrecting one of its anonymous victims. When Beloved comes back to haunt Sethe for murdering her, Beloved becomes the incarnated memory of Sethe's guilt. Moreover, she is nothing but guilt, a symbol of an unrelenting criticism of the dehumanizing function of the institution of slavery. In this, she is the daughter representing a severe critique, demonstrating the determinism in slave history. She represents, however, only half of Morrison's work: the accusing glare, the unforgiving perspective, the need to forget—"It was not a story to pass on." There is another daughter in the novel, another daughter of history—representing the embracing glance, the loving view, the need to remember.

When Sethe first sees the reincarnated Beloved, her "bladder filled to capacity." She runs immediately to the outhouse, but does not make it: "Right in front of its door she had to lift her skirts, and the water she voided was endless. Like a horse, she thought, but as it went on and on she thought, No, more like flooding the boat when Denver was born. So much water Amy said, 'Hold on, Lu. You going to sink us you keep that up.' But there was no stopping water breaking from a breaking womb and there was no stopping now" (51). She would later, in a retrospective moment, remember this scene in trying to discover who Beloved could be (132). What is worth noticing, though, is that at that precise moment she does not remember the birth of Beloved but the birth of Denver. Denver is the fictional recreation of Margaret Garner's other daughter, the daughter who survives. Coffin describes Garner and this daughter in the courtroom: "The babe she held in her arms was a little girl, about nine months old, and was much lighter in color than herself, light enough to show a red tinge in its cheek" (562–63). In *Beloved*, Denver becomes the daughter of hope.

Denver is the first to recognize that Beloved is the incarnation of the ghost that had haunted 124; and she is also the first who lives through that recognition and develops the understanding necessary for an affirmative return to life. Like everyone else in the novel, she must learn to confront the past in order to face the future. She, too, must deal with what she has been repressing for most of her life: "the hurt of the hurt world" (28). Denver begins, like her mother, by attempting to prevent the past from intruding upon her life: "she had her own set of questions which had nothing to do with the past. The present alone interested Denver" (119). Denver is not able to avoid the past for long, though, because the past becomes an immediate pain to her present life and an incipient danger to her future. What Denver must do is remember, and she must do so by revising her memory—her history and her mother's history—in a collective anamnesis. Denver is pre-eminently in this novel the signifyin(g) daughter.

The first recognition Denver has of the danger Beloved represents to Sethe—the danger of the past's taking over the present—occurs in the Clearing. When Sethe goes to the Clearing to commune with her dead mother-in-law Baby Suggs, a spiritual force begins to choke her. Sethe reflects on the moment: "But one thing for sure, Baby Suggs had not choked her as first she thought. Denver was right, and walking in the dappled tree-light, clearer-headed now—away from the enchantment of the Clearing—Sethe remembered the touch of those fingers that she knew better than her own" (98). Denver will later accuse Beloved, who is the incarnated memory of her own murder, of choking her mother:

> "You did it, I saw you," said Denver.
> "What?"
> "I saw your face. You made her choke."
> "I didn't do it."
> "You told me you loved her."
> "I fixed it, didn't I? Didn't I fix her neck?"
> "After. After you choked her neck."
> "I kissed her neck. I didn't choke it. The circle of iron choked it."
> "I saw you." Denver grabbed Beloved's arm.
> "Look out, girl," said Beloved and, snatching her arm away, ran ahead as fast as she could along the stream that sang on the other side of the woods. (101)

For Denver, this is the first of her two crucial moments. She has not gone to the other side of the woods in years because she has willfully isolated herself in the house and the yard: "124 and the field behind it were all the world she knew or wanted." There had been a time when "she had known more and wanted to."

Reflecting on what she thinks she has just witnessed—Beloved's attempt to choke her mother—and looking out at Beloved's flight, Denver remembers the moment that caused her willful isolation. When she was seven she had wandered beyond the confines of the house and yard and entered the children's class Lady Jones conducted. For a full year, she learned to write and read: "She was so happy she didn't even know she was being avoided by her classmates—that they made excuses and altered their pace not to walk with her. It was Nelson Lord—the boy as smart as she was—who put a stop to it; who asked her the question about her mother that put chalk, the little *i* and all the rest those afternoons held, out of reach forever." Denver never went back to Lady Jones's, but she also did not ask anybody whether Nelson Lord's question was true. Reflecting now both on the latest incident in the Clearing and on the moment Nelson Lord had ended her adventurousness forever, Denver begins to confront questions regarding the ways the past shapes the present—she begins to ask herself whether she has a complicitous role in her mother's history: "Walking toward the stream, beyond her green bush house, she lets herself wonder what if Beloved really decided to choke her mother. Would she let it happen? Murder, Nelson Lord had said. 'Didn't your mother get locked away for murder? Wasn't you in there with her when she went?'" (104). It was "the second question that made it impossible for so long to ask Sethe about the first." Because Denver knows her mother's loving care, she finds it impossible to ask about the moment Sethe might have expressed her love murderously.

At age seven, Denver chose not to ask Sethe to explain; she preferred the comfort she received from the ghost haunting 124: "Now it held for her all the anger, love and fear she didn't know what to do with" (103). It is Denver who hears and identifies her dead sister's presence in the ghost. And by recognizing the ghost's identity, Denver begins the process of confronting the ramifications of the past: "The return of Denver's hearing, cut off by an answer she could not bear to hear, cut on by the sound of her dead sister trying to climb the stairs, signaled another shift in the fortunes of the people of 124. From then on the presence was full of spite" (103–04). For ten years, Denver prefers to live in the ambivalence wrought of suspicion without desiring any explanation.

At age fifteen, confronted with the incarnated memory of her mother's crime, Denver again chooses the ghost: "The display she witnessed at the Clearing shamed her because the choice between Sethe and Beloved was without conflict." Ironically, although Denver thinks that the present alone is what interests her, she luxuriates in the past, in dwelling in a shadowy history which she is unwilling to confront or confirm. Now though, she has realized that she must make a choice—a choice she defers for now but must eventually make.

She makes an initial choice based on her fear for her own life: "I love my mother but I know she killed one of her own daughters, and tender as she is with me, I'm scared of her because of it" (205). Because of this Denver feels the onus of protecting Beloved: "It's all on me, now, but she can count on me. I thought she was trying to kill her that day in the Clearing. Kill her back. But then she kissed her neck and I have to warn her about that. Don't love her too much. Don't. Maybe it's still in her the thing that makes it all right to kill her children. I have to tell her. I have to protect her" (206). There is only so long Denver can nurture this resentment; there is only so much the past can inform her living present. Beloved becomes demanding: "Anything she wanted she got, and when Sethe ran out of things to give her, Beloved invented desire" (240). It takes an act of seeing how this memory is literally consuming her mother for Denver to realize that her initial choice must be altered: "Then Sethe spit up something she had not eaten and it rocked Denver like gunshot. The job she started out with, protecting Beloved from Sethe, changed to protecting her mother from Beloved" (243).

This is the second crucial moment in Denver's life, when she must assume responsibility for having nurtured resentment, for having kept the past alive for selfish reasons. She will now have to leave 124 and face the larger community. She will have to stop dwelling on her mother's history and recognize the larger communal history of slavery's suffering. In doing so, she must understand her mother's act in light of a larger narrative. Beloved had responded to Denver's accusation of choking Sethe's neck by referring to an institution: "I didn't choke it. The circle of iron choked it." Slavery, Beloved is saying in a lower frequency, is the thing to blame. Denver will have to learn to listen to that lower frequency.

As she stands on the steps, Denver remembers her grandmother's final words: "Lay down your sword. This ain't a battle; it's a rout." Standing uneasily on the steps she has not left since Nelson Lord asked her that painful question. Denver is visited by Baby Suggs's ghost:

> Denver stood on the porch in the sun and couldn't leave it. Her throat itched; her heart kicked—and then Baby Suggs laughed, clear as anything. "You mean I never told you nothing about Carolina? About your daddy? You don't remember nothing about how come I walk the way I do and about your mother's feet, not to speak of her back? I never told you all that? Is that why you can't walk down the steps? My Jesus my."
>
> But you said there was no defense.
>
> "There ain't."
>
> Then what do I do?
>
> "Know it, and go on out the yard. Go on." (244)

"Know it": historical knowledge, if it isn't the defense, is at least the only way to integrity. It is a knowledge of the larger collective—of her father, her mother, her grandmother, Carolina, Sweet Home, slavery. It is understanding the forces of slavery that compelled her mother to do what she did. There is another story besides Beloved's, a larger narrative besides her family's, a deeper pain than suspicion and fear and spite. She follows her grandmother's advice and leaves the yard. By leaving the house, she enables herself to know.

She is first of all initiated into maturity and then understanding. The first place she goes is to Lady Jones's. When Lady Jones recognizes her and says, "Oh, baby . . . Oh, baby," Denver passes an indefinable threshold: "Denver looked up at her. She did not know it then, but it was the word 'baby,' said softly and with such kindness, that inaugurated her life in the world as a woman. The trail she followed to get to that sweet thorny place was made up of paper scraps containing the handwritten names of others" (248). Those paper scraps represent her place in history—both within the family as a literate daughter of an unlettered mother and within the culture as a remembering being.

A woman now, Denver begins to glean the inner meaning of a larger reality, to comprehend the dangers that dwelling on the past holds. Denver's discovery, though, occurs when she becomes imbricated into a story Sethe is telling Beloved. The passage in which Sethe's relationship to Beloved is delineated must be quoted in full:

> *Denver thought* she understood the connection between her mother and Beloved: Sethe was trying to make up for the handsaw; Beloved was making her pay for it. But there would never be an end to that, and seeing her mother diminished shamed and infuriated her. Yet she knew Sethe's greatest fear was *the same one Denver had in the beginning*—that Beloved might leave. That before Sethe could make her understand what it meant—what it took to drag the teeth of that saw under the little chin; to feel the baby blood pump like oil in her hands; to hold her face so her head would stay on; to squeeze her so she could absorb, still, the death spasms that shot through that adored body, plump and sweet with life—Beloved might leave. Leave before Sethe could make her realize that worse than that—far worse—was what Baby Suggs died of, what Ella knew, what Stamp saw and what made Paul D tremble. That anybody white could take your whole self for anything that came to mind. Not just work, kill, or maim you, but dirty you. Dirty you so bad you couldn't like yourself anymore. Dirty you so bad you forgot who you were and couldn't think it up. And though she and others lived through and got over it, she could never let it happen to her own. The best thing she was, was her children. Whites might dirty *her* all right, but not her best thing, her beautiful, magical best thing—the part of her that was clean. . . . This and much more, *Denver heard* her say from her corner chair, trying to persuade Beloved, *the one and only person she felt she had to convince*, that what she had done was right because it came from true love. (251, emphasis added)

This moment of understanding, the moment when Sethe articulates her recognition of the reasons she killed Beloved, is filtered through Denver's hearing and understanding; it begins with Denver's thinking and ends with her hearing. Although Sethe thinks she is attempting to convince only one daughter of her love, in reality she is convincing the other daughter too. Denver had, "in the beginning," wished Beloved to stay because Beloved represented the ambiguity she felt about her mother—because Beloved was an accusation always readily available. Denver has since understood that because of a larger communal history, her mother's deed might not be so heinous as she had at first thought. That is not to say that Morrison is trying to negate the guilt Sethe feels, or even attempting to palliate it by reference to an institutional context. Rather, by having both of the daughters listen to Sethe's realization, Morrison represents for us the ambivalent duality of what she considers primarily the black woman writer's way of looking at the world—as she puts it, "in an unforgiving/loving way." Each daughter in this novel represents one way. Beloved accuses while Denver embraces; Beloved is unforgiving while Denver is loving; Beloved will be "Disremembered and unaccounted for" while Denver is the source of remembering. Two things occur when Denver finally follows Baby Suggs's advice and steps out of 124—one that leads to a personal healing and another that leads to a communal.

First, she tells the community that Beloved, the murdered baby, has returned to punish Sethe. It is a story that must be narrated for its subjects to be cured: "Nobody was going to help her unless she told it—told all of it" (253). The community responds in three ways: "those that believed the worst; those that believed none of it; and those, like Ella, who thought it through" (255). It is Ella, finally, who initiates the exorcism of Beloved; and it is significant that Ella is the one to do this. First of all, Ella, like the matured Denver, has outgrown the need to dwell on the past: "Whatever Sethe had done, Ella didn't like the idea of past errors taking possession of the present. Sethe's crime was staggering and her pride outstripped even that; but she could not countenance the possibility of sin moving on in the house, unleashed and sassy. Daily life took as much as she had. The future was sunset; the past something to leave behind. And if it didn't stay behind, well, you might have to stomp it out" (256). Moreover, Ella too has a place in the larger narrative of slavery. Her puberty was spent "in a house where she was shared by father and son, whom she called 'the lowest yet.' It was 'the lowest yet' who gave her a disgust for sex and against whom she measured all atrocities" (256). And Ella's personal history has hints of infanticide in it too: "Ella had been beaten every way but down. She remembered the bottom teeth she had lost to the brake and the scars from the bell were thick as rope around her waist. She had delivered, but would not nurse, a hairy white thing, fathered by 'the lowest yet.' It lived five days never making a sound. The idea of that pup coming back to whip her too set her jaw working" (258–59). By registering her narrative within a framework of determinism and forgiveness, Ella has learned how to free herself. She offers that possibility to Sethe. For twenty-eight days, Sethe had been free—the time between crossing the Ohio River and the time she killed her baby daughter. Sethe had known then that "freeing yourself was one thing; claiming ownership of that freed self was another" (95). In that twenty-eight days, she had claimed herself. After murdering Beloved, she lost that claim. Ella, by exorcising Beloved, by not allowing the past to consume the present, offers Sethe the opportunity to reclaim herself. In the end Sethe does, and does so by an act of community. In this her life is following the pattern established by her daughter Denver.

Denver's personal healing is attested to when she meets Nelson Lord for the first time since he had asked her the question that had deafened her. This is the second thing that happens when she leaves 124. She sees Nelson: "All he did was smile and say, 'Take care of yourself, Denver,' but she heard it as though it were what language was made for. The last time he spoke to her his words blocked up her ears. Now they opened her mind" (252). This encounter demonstrates Denver's growth. She knows now her shared history—her family's, her community's, her culture's. As much as Nelson's original question had been the closure of language for her, so now is his amiable comment a renewal of communication.

Sethe, after Denver, will make a successful return to life in the same way. When she told Paul D how she killed Beloved, he made a comment that caused a forest to spring up between them (165). It will take Paul D's own education, and Sethe's attempts to understand herself and make Beloved understand her actions, before they are able to reunite. Paul D finally realizes that he "wants to put his story next to hers." Not only is this an act of a shared narrative, but it is also an affirmation that Sethe has a claim to herself:

> "Sethe," he says, "me and you, we got more yesterday than anybody. We need some kind of tomorrow."
>
> He leans over and takes her hand. With the other he touches her face. "You your best thing, Sethe. You are." His holding fingers are holding hers.
>
> "Me? Me?" (273)

Like Denver, who finds the ability to discover herself in Nelson Lord's words, Sethe finds the ability to reclaim, to recover, herself in Paul D's. Before she told Paul about Beloved, she had thought that theirs was a shared narrative: "Her story was bearable because it was his as well—to tell, to refine, and tell again. The things neither knew about the other—the things neither had word shapes for—well, it would come in time" (99). The full story does come in time, but it is a product of extreme stress and pain, of the effort to remember what each desires to forget. It is a story told in a language that deafens while it enlightens: "This was not a story to pass on."

Hearing *Beloved*

It is a story, however, that does get passed on—and it is passed on through the ear. While Sethe thinks she is trying to convince only Beloved of the reasons she committed murder, Denver is *listening*. As I suggested earlier, Denver is the filtering ear for Sethe's process of self-discovery: "This and much more Denver heard her say. . . ." It is important that Denver, the signifyin(g) daughter, *hears* what Sethe has to say. It alerts us to how this novel situates itself in the African American literary tradition. *Beloved* belongs to that class of novels Gates characterizes as "speakerly texts"—those texts "whose rhetorical strategy is designed to represent an oral literary tradition" and to produce the "illusion of oral narration." Within the structure of the broadest frame of *Beloved*'s "speakerly text" there exists what we might call the "aural being." It is this being who represents our belonging to this novel, and this being is represented within the novel by the signifyin(g) daughter.

Peter Brooks has suggested that meaning in novels resides in the dialogical relationship between "tellers and listeners," in the transmission of the "'horror,' the taint of knowledge gained." The reader of narratives, that is, is "solicited not only to understand the story, but to complete it." That reader—when constructed within the novel, that aural being—is, like Marlowe's auditor, a creation of the speakerly text. Moreover, and this is distinctly an aspect of the African American literary tradition, the voice of the speakerly text is a product of a generational memory. We may find the protocols for this sort of generational memory represented in at least two other novels written by African American women: Hurston's *Their Eyes Were Watching God* (1937)—the prototype, Gates tells us, of the speakerly text—and Sherley Anne Williams's *Dessa Rose* (1986).

Beloved is also a novel that constructs its ideal "listener." Denver will tell and re-tell the story that she now understands. Like Pheoby in *Their Eyes Were Watching God*, Denver uses the knowledge of "horror," transmitted to her aurally, to perform a healing narrative—orally. And, like Pheoby, Denver represents the implied community of ideal readers, the "aural being." What, finally, Denver is to *Beloved* is the space for hearing the tale of infanticide with a degree of understanding—both as sister of the murdered baby and as the living daughter of the loving mother. Denver, that is, is a site of participation.

Morrison has said on various occasions that she writes into her narratives the "places and spaces so that the reader can participate." It is a dialogic form that she has suggested is akin to music and to black preaching. These are art forms which, she suggests, are part of the repertoire of "Black art," which is difficult to define but does have "major characteristics,"

> One of which is the ability to be both print and oral literature: to combine those two aspects so that the stories can be read in silence, of course, but one should be able to hear them as well. It should try deliberately to make you stand up and make you feel something profoundly in the same way that a Black preacher requires his congregation to speak, to join him in the sermon, to behave in a certain way, to stand up and to weep and *to cry and to accede or to change and to modify*—to expand on the sermon that is being delivered. In the same way that a musician's music is enhanced when there is a response from the audience. Now in a book. . . . I have to provide the places and spaces so that the reader can participate. (Emphasis added)

She intends her novels to be healing, belonging to a form she calls "village literature"—literature that should "clarify the roles that have become obscured," literature that is able to "identify those things in the past that are useful and those things that are not," a literature, finally, that is able to "give nourishment." The novel as a form of "Black art" works with history as its subject in order to criticize and to revise—to cry and to modify.

Morrison claims that it is precisely because the black oral historical tradition is now a thing of the past that the African American novel is so necessary: "the novel is needed by African Americans now in a way that it was not needed before. . . . We don't live in places where we can hear those stories anymore; parents don't sit around and tell their children those classical, mythological, archetypal stories that we heard years ago." Those stories must have a place in African American culture, and they've found their place in the novel. The novel becomes for Morrison what Aunt Sue was for Langston Hughes—the site of an oral history passed from generation to generation:

> And the dark-faced child, listening,
> Knows that Aunt Sue's stories are real stories.
> He knows that Aunt Sue never got her stories
> Out of any book at all,
> But that they came
> Right out of her own life.

Because all those ancestors, like Aunt Sue, are no longer available, there must evolve within the African American tradition an art form that gives them voice. *Beloved* is but one more novel in a tradition doing just that. But it also does one more thing: it situates itself not only theoretically, but also performatively, as an oral literature.

I noted earlier that Morrison provides a criticism of print media through Paul D's assessment of what newspapers will or will not write about black people. Like other novels in the tradition of African American letters, Morrison criticizes the ideological imperative of print media in order to establish the value of oral historical relation. This criticism of print media is very much part of the overall, revisionist motive in criticizing the historiography of slavery. It is, after all, only when slave narratives and slave accounts began to be taken seriously as historical documents that the other side of slavery could be articulated. The contemporary novel of signifyin(g) history, or the speakerly text, represents this struggle for the validation of orality. In Williams's *Dessa Rose*, for instance, the slave Dessa is given two voices—one as the white pro-slavery polemicist Adam Nehemiah "reconstructs" her voice in his journal, and the other as she orally tells her story to her grandchildren in her own voice. Dessa, that is, can save herself only by telling a story different from the one she is written to fit, by refusing to be written and asserting herself in voice. In *Beloved* it is schoolteacher who uses writing in a detrimental way. Schoolteacher attempts to read and write Sethe as a subhuman thing by listing what he calls her "animal" characteristics alongside her human ones. Sethe resolved that "no one, nobody on this earth, would list her daughter's characteristics on the animal side of the paper" (251). Like Dessa, Sethe refuses to allow the written to usurp her humanity, and she finds that her humanity is best represented by the spoken word. To discover how *Beloved* is constructed to represent its own orality, we must first of all delineate the variety of oral communities in the novel.

Paul D belongs to a chain gang that had its own language, signifying nothing to those who didn't belong to its community: "They sang it out and beat it up, garbling the words so they could not be understood; tricking the words so their syllables yielded up other meanings" (103). Like the chain gang described by Frederick Douglass, the slaves would sing songs that "to many would seem unmeaning jargon, but which, nevertheless, were full of meaning to themselves." But when he enters the community of Sethe and her two daughters, Paul D finds himself unable to comprehend their language: "Hearing the three of them laughing at something he wasn't in on. The code they used among themselves that he could not break" (132). When Sethe first converses with Ella, after escaping from the Sweet Home plantation, what Sethe says yields up a surplus of meaning to Ella because of her ear for the silences: "she listened for the holes—the things the fugitives did not say; the questions they did not ask. Listened too for the unnamed, unmentioned people left behind" (927). When Ella initiates the exorcism with a holler, language becomes wholly oral: "In the beginning was the sound, and they all knew what that sound sounded like" (259).

Finally, though, the most important oral community in this novel is comprised of those able to understand the mode of discourse necessary to relating the crux of this story—the murder of Beloved:

> Sethe knew that the circle she was making around the room, him, the subject, would remain one. That she could never close in, pin it down for anybody who had to ask. If they didn't get it right off—she could never explain. Because the truth was simple, not a long drawn-out record of flowered shifts, tree cages, selfishness, ankle ropes and wells. Simple: she was squatting in the garden and when she saw them coming and recognized the schoolteacher's hat, she heard wings. Little hummingbirds stuck their needle beaks right through her headcloth into her hair and beat their wings. And if she thought anything, it was No. No. Nono. Nonono. Simple. She just flew. Collected every bit of life she had made, all the parts of her that were precious and fine and beautiful, and carried, pushed, dragged them through the veil, out, away, over there where no one could hurt them. Over there. Outside this place, where they would be safe. And the hummingbird wings beat on. (163)

Paul D has trouble understanding this discourse, just as he had trouble understanding the code existing between Sethe and her daughters. "At first he thought it was her spinning. Circling him the way she was circling the subject. . . . Then he thought, No, it's the sound of her voice; it's too near" (161). Eventually, Paul D understands only that Sethe murdered Beloved; he suggests that it was because her love was "too thick." It will take him the rest of the novel to understand that for Sethe "Love is or it ain't. Thin love ain't love at all" (164).

It takes memory and articulation for Sethe to understand her own action. What she had to remember is another oral community between her grandmother and herself; "she was remembering something she forgot she knew" (61):

> Nan was the one she knew best, who was around all day, who nursed babies, cooked, had one good arm and half of another. And who used different words. Words Sethe understood then but could neither recall nor repeat now. She believed that must be why she remembered so little before Sweet Home except singing and dancing and how crowded it was. What Nan told her she had forgotten, along with the language she told it in. The same

> language her ma'am spoke, and which would never come back. But the message—that was and had been there all along. Holding the damp white sheets against her chest, she was picking meaning out of a code she no longer understood. (62)

The story Nan tells her is that of Sethe's mother's killing those children fathered by whites. The story is remembered when Beloved returns and asks about Sethe's mother. It is a story that has a progressive effect on Sethe, exactly as the story of Sethe's murder of Beloved has on Denver: "As small girl Sethe, she was unimpressed. As grown-up woman Sethe she was angry, but not certain at what." Now, in remembering her own relationship to her two daughters, she is able to understand her mother's acts and her grandmother's code. By situating herself within a communal narrative of grandmother-mother-daughter relationships, Sethe is able to understand herself. The code becomes unlocked and available for her hearing.

I have suggested that part of the significance of Denver's "hearing" her mother explain to Beloved the reasons for her action is that she becomes the "aural being" of this speakerly text. Moreover, the act of hearing symbolizes Denver's overcoming her deafness—wrought, as it was, of her first hearing of her mother's act. For Sethe, telling her story allowed her to understand *her* mother's history. For Denver, telling her mother's story allows her to understand the communal history and her place in it. As we saw, Sethe's final healing occurs in imitation of Denver—as Denver places her story next to Nelson Lord's, Sethe places hers next to Paul D's. Denver is, then, in a very real sense, completing her mother's story. That, finally, is what an aural being is to the speakerly text's unfolding—both the space for the reader's participation and, as Brooks suggests, a symbol of the illusion of completeness, of closure.

It is worth noting the differences between aural beings and their roles in the novels we can designate as speakerly texts. *Their Eyes Were Watching God* gives us a framed story, with the hearer—Pheoby—being presented at the beginning and end of the relation. She is the gauge of our understanding of Janie's tale and the source of Janie's justification in the eyes of the community: "Nobody better not criticize yuh in mah hearin." In Hurston's novel, then, the scene of the grandmother's relating her story to her granddaughter is part of the overall enactment of the telling of the tale. Much as Nanny attempted to justify her life in an oral story to her granddaughter, so does Janie—that very granddaughter—attempt to justify her life by telling it to her friend. In *Dessa Rose*, we find out only in the epilogue that the aural beings are Dessa's grandchildren By exposing the fact that this is an enactment of the grandmother's oral narration at the very end, Williams forces us to reconsider our relation to textual history. "Afro-Americans," she writes in her prefatory note, "having survived by word of mouth—and made of that process a high art—remain at the mercy of literature and writing" (ix). In a bold gesture, Williams makes Dessa's orality the foundation of any textual record of her. The white Nehemiah's records become illegible and blank sheets; Dessa's story is recorded by her son and *said* back to her. The oral transmission, then, is the enactment of part of this novel's polemical trajectory: the establishing of the primacy of a told tale.

Beloved differs from these two means of organizing orality within the speakerly text in that it is based on a variety of discrete oral linguistic communities; and its story is about the establishment of a communal narrative. The critique of the newspaper's report and the condemnation of schoolteacher's racist anthropology attest to the ex-slaves' refusal to be written. They are, nonetheless, discrete individuals prevented by various deafnesses from *hearing* the communal story to which they belong. Paul D must learn to understand the community of mother and daughters, just as he must learn to hear Sethe's story of her infanticide (he had felt her *voice* was too close, we recall). Denver must understand Sethe's story, as well, because she is the one who must go out and tell it—tell it in order to save her mother. Likewise, Sethe learns to understand how to claim herself as her own best thing only after she is able to understand what her grandmother told her, only after she is able to understand her mother's actions as part of a larger framework of experience.

The scenes of hearing the mother's tongue, understanding the mother's code, knowing the mother's history—these are themselves the very enactment of an ongoing generational oral transmission. In themselves, they represent the organization of this novel's speakerliness. Unlike *Dessa Rose* and *Their Eyes Were Watching God*, each of which enacts a single scene of oral transmission of one person's story to her grandchildren or to her friend, *Beloved* is concerned with demonstrating the variety and continuousness of oral transmissions necessary for any person to understand her own story. In this, each of the major characters in the novel signifies on the story of each of her or his fellow characters in order to establish a communal narrative—*Beloved* itself. The best figure for this (internal) formal revision is Paul D's desire to place his story next to Sethe's. The novel is, finally, about putting stories together and putting them to rest.

Putting to rest, of course, for Morrison means giving renewed and energetic life. From this rest, she gives her characters resurrection. In the end, perhaps the greatest achievement of Morrison's novel is that she gives the murdered victim of history *voice*; she resurrects the unjustly killed and allows that daughter to have renewed historical life by criticizing the sort of history that has hitherto excluded her and her rebellious spirit. In the end, this impetus is best expressed in one of W. E. B. Du Bois's most lyrical moments, in a passage that can almost act as a commentary on the novel which would be published nearly eighty-five years later: "It is a hard thing to live haunted by the ghost of an untrue dream; to see the wide vision of empire fade into real ashes and dirt; to feel the pang of the conquered, and yet to know that with all the Bad that fell on one black day, something was vanquished that deserved to live, some thing killed that in justice had not dared to die." In giving that "ghost" a renewed voice and life, Morrison not only criticizes the institution responsible for Beloved's death but also shows the healing knowledge that accrues to those attentive to the ghost's presence. What Morrison does in *Beloved* is to remember in order to revive, to survive, to rename, to re-possess. At the end of *The Color Purple*, Alice Walker, signing herself as author and medium, writes, "I thank everybody in this book for coming." In the preface to *Dessa Rose*, Williams claims to have the feeling of "owning" a summer in the nineteenth century. Resuscitating historical figures may indeed give one the feeling of belonging to a larger community, of being at one with the ancestors—in Walker's metaphor, of being in the temple of the familiar; in Morrison's metaphor, of burying the dead to revive them. Nothing serves more persuasively to delineate how an author feels when she has revised and revived history than Morrison's own commentary on her novel. At the end of her conversation with Gloria Naylor, Toni Morrison reflects on what her creative act continues to mean to her:

> It was a conversation. I can tell, because I said something I didn't know I knew. About the "dead girl." That bit by bit I had been rescuing her from the grave of time and inattention. Her fingernails maybe in the first book; face and legs, perhaps, the second time. Little by little bringing her back into living life. So that now she comes running when called—walks freely around the house, sits down in a chair; looks at me. . . . She is here now, alive. I have seen, named and claimed her—and oh what company she keeps.

JOSEF PESCH

Beloved: *Toni Morrison's Post-Apocalyptic Novel*

The uneasy relation of Toni Morrison's Pulitzer-Prize novel to the American apocalyptic tradition has been noted (Bowers 1992), but does it fit into a category of work described as post-apocalyptic? No doubt there are more obvious examples: Peter Freese, who seems to be the first to use the term, writes about Bernard Malamud's *God's Grace*. Walter M. Miller's *A Canticle for Leibowitz*, Ray Bradbury's *Fahrenheit 451*, and García Márquez's *Love in the Time of Cholera* are discussed elsewhere (Buehrer; Spencer; Dorris). Paul Auster's *In the Country of Last Things*, Margaret Atwood's *A Handmaid's Tale*, Timothey Findley's *The Wars*, Kurt Vonnegut's *Cat's Cradle* and *Slaughterhouse-Five*, perhaps Michael Ondaatje's *The English Patient*, and certainly Russell Hoban's *Riddley Walker* are novels one may think of. But *Beloved*? And: what does "post-apocalyptic" mean?

Apocalypse is generally understood to be the final catastrophe, and apocalyptic literature usually closes in a cataclysmic climax. However, post-apocalyptic literature tells us that this catastrophe might not have been really final—and tells us of the story after. In post-apocalyptic writing the apocalypse has happened before the narration sets in. For example, in *Riddley Walker* or in *A Canticle for Leibowitz* an apocalypse has destroyed a civilisation but humanity somehow survived. Had it been an apocalypse, there would not be a story to tell. Thus, the story of the post-apocalypse can

From *Canadian Review of Comparative Literature* 20:3–4 (September–December 1993).

be told in fiction. In this way writers mourn the loss of something—our culture, our civilisation which we may not have lost yet; but which we will no longer be able to mourn when humanity has become extinct—and there will be peace on earth at last.

"Post-Apocalypse" in this sense is a fictional construct presenting a reality that we may not perceive as ours, though it could be ours. Many of the novels of this type are called elsewhere "nuclear fiction," "dystopias," "fiction of the remade world," "post-holocaust novels," even "science fiction," although the latter is only one aspect of post-apocalyptical writing (e.g., Schwenger; Brians; Dowling; Yoke).

In the Webster's *Third International Dictionary*, the *Oxford English Dictionary*, and in the *Duden*, we find the following definitions of "apocalypse":

a) [ME apocalipse Revelation of St. John (book of the New Testament), revelation, vision, fr. LL apocalypsis, fr. Gk apokalypsis, lit., uncovering, revelation, fr. apokalyptein to uncover, reveal (fr. apo- + kalyptein to cover, to conceal) + -sis—more at HELL] l: a writing professing to reveal the future; esp.: such a pseudonymous writing in Jewish or early Christian circles between about 200 B.C. and A.D. 150 predicting the future shape of eschatological events by means of a symbolism understandable to the faithful but hidden from others 2: something viewed as a revelation: Disclosure (*Webster's* 100);

[ad.L. apocalypsis ... apo- off; -kalyptein to cover]
1. The "revelation" of the future granted to St. John in the isle of Patmos. The book of the New Testament in which this is recorded.
2. by extension: Any revelation or disclosure. (*Oxford English Dictionary* 97);

[kirchenlat. apocalypsis <griech. apokálypsis, eigtl. = Enthüllung]: 1. (Rel.) Schrift, die sich in Visionen, Träumen, Abschiedsreden, Weissagungen mit dem kommenden Weltende befaßt. 2. <o. Pl.> (bildungssprr.) Untergang; Unheil; Grauen; (*Duden* 131).

These definitions appeared surprising and confusing to me at first. No doubt, the books mentioned above do reveal eschatological events (and often in rather symbolic and obscure ways)—and they do contain visions of the future. Hence, this kind of writing "after the end" should properly be termed "apocalyptic." Unfortunately, this term is commonly used for novels ending in climactic cataclysm. "Post-apocalyptic" is therefore proposed and used here to differentiate cataclysmic writing from novels in which this cataclysm is but a distant memory.

However, there is more to "post-apocalyptic" than suggested and this is where the notion becomes interesting. For what if the "future," revealed in apocalyptic writings, has already begun; what if the revelation is so cryptic that only a few realize or want to realize what has taken place? When Paul

Auster's novel *In the Country of Last Things* was described as "grounded in the dystopian or post-holocaust tradition of science-fiction," Auster complained, "As far as I'm concerned, the book has nothing to do with science-fiction. It's quite fantastic at times, of course, but that doesn't mean it's not firmly anchored in historical realities. It's a novel about the present and the immediate past, not about the future" (Auster 1992, 306). What if Auster were right, and we are no longer in perpetual crisis, waiting for the end—as Kermode suggested in "The New Apocalyptists" and in *The Sense of an Ending*; what if we are past that end—without noticing or acknowledging the uncomfortable truth? Holding on to the great tradition of literature and the order of Western values, Kermode, for instance, evades facing the disruption he has before him. With his concept of "crisis," even perpetual crisis, he fights off ideas of a break in that tradition with all means at his disposal, to the point of conceding that "our own epoch is the epoch of nothing positive, only of transition" (1966, 345). Transition to what? Kermode does not see what Benjamin had observed earlier: "The concept of progress is to be grounded in the idea of the catastrophe. That things 'just go on' is the catastrophe. It is not that which is approaching but that which is" (Benjamin 50). The notions of historic "progress"—religious, economic, political—towards an abstract and ideal state of affairs, which a concept of "transition" would seem to suggest, are significantly absent from post-apocalyptic texts. Here catastrophe is indeed a (timeless) presence before which characters often literally "just go on," becoming wanderers (as well as wonderers) like Riddley Walker (a walking riddle to himself and others), Paul D., Billy Pilgrim (Vonnegut 1983)—or Slothrop (Pynchon).

Despite early modernist claims to the contrary, Kermode simply incorporates early Modernists such as Yeats, Eliot, Pound, and Joyce into his continuous great tradition (cf. Materer; Pesch). Wherever writers deviate into anything disruptive, this is linked to their fascist, Catholic, etc., creeds. As this does not work with Joyce, who always kept his distance from wars, politics, and religion, Kermode has to put forward a reading of *Ulysses* which is reductive (at best); what is more, his reading of Joyce is telling: Joyce's last book, *Finnegans Wake* is not even mentioned. Yet this book, a post-apocalyptic WAKE, a book beginning with a great fall on its first page, is a book of disruptions, death, and mourning; it alone is enough to falsify much of what Kermode has to say. Here not one history, but stories of all ages and of none are told; here it is not one voice, but voices; no master narrative, but a plurality of narration; and no linear, but cyclical structures; no end (and thus no "Sense of an Ending")—or beginning, but a circular closure, completing the first sentence.

Kermode ignores all that, turning instead to Beckett—Joyce's friend and companion through much of *Work in Progress* (Ellmann 563 and *passim*)—and calls Beckett "the perverse theologian of a world which has suffered a Fall, experienced an Incarnation which changes all relations of past, present and future, but which will not be redeemed" (1966, 355). Here Kermode touches upon something central to "post-apocalyptic" writing: for what is "an Incarnation which changes all relations of past, present and future" if not an apocalypse? Kermode, however, drops the subject almost immediately to write about order, which he perceives as "the Christian paradigm" (1966, 355). To Kermode, "it is this order, however ironized, this continuously transmitted idea of order, that makes Beckett's point" (1966, 355).

There may be order here, but it is the kind of order to be found in the *Wake*—hardly that of Christian theology or the great tradition. Kermode touches upon what is now addressed as Postmodernism, but which I would rather call the "post-apocalyptic phase of modernism." In less extreme cases than the *Wake*, the features referred to appear in a variety of techniques and variations in other novels. Cut off from their past and with no bright future in sight, protagonists or narrators, or arrangers, often use a multiple narrative in which one line follows the on-going narrative development of the novel's present, into which other narratives of past events intrude disruptively; there often are several narrators or voices, and intertextual incorporations of documents or tales and myths of the pre-apocalyptic and apocalyptic past. These tell their own story and supply their own view of things.

The recent Nobel Prize Winner of literature, Toni Morrison, is one of these writers of the "new apocalypse," who have taken apocalyptic writing a step further, into post-apocalypse. Her writing is not oriented towards the future, but towards the past, a past not connected in a linear fashion to the present, as it has been painfully disrupted by an apocalyptic event which questions "the justification of ideas of order," in ways Kermode only hints at (1966, 361). To Kermode, "our order, our form, is necessary" to keep the Great Tradition going (1966, 361). Post-apocalyptic writers, however, have had to develop their own ideas of orders to find forms that will suffice in accommodating the narration of "unspeakable horrors." These are integral parts of another Great Tradition of Western order and culture that is disregarded by Kermode, but traced through the history of philosophy by other scholars, for instance in Ulrich Horstmann's *Das Untier* (1985). This aspect of the Great Tradition is hardly ever acknowledged by proponents of that tradition: wars (the legalized ritual mass-slaughter of mostly innocent human beings by skilled, but otherwise civilised human beings, perfected in our century), racism, persecution, pogroms, concentration camps, the elimination of animals and plants, the poisoning of water and soil, the wasting of natural resources—and all this often in the name of "Enlightenment," of rationality—and rationally and lawfully calculated private profits.

The fact that Morrison's *Beloved* is apocalyptic has already been commented on by Susan Bowers. In her essay "Beloved and the New Apocalypse," she places Morrison's novel within the American apocalyptic tradition, but makes important observations questioning *Beloved*'s relation to that tradition. Bowers's assertion that in *Beloved*, Morrison creates "a revised apocalyptic which principally looks backward, not forward in time" is a first indication that, although part of an apocalyptic tradition, *Beloved* is indeed different:

> The narrative does not drive toward the apocalyptic moment, but recounts the struggle of living through and beyond the reign of the Anti-Christ and of surviving the "numbing of the black and angry dead." *Beloved*'s focus on the past may seem contrary to the forward-looking spirit of apocalypse, especially in American literature, where the apocalypse is considered fundamental.

What Bowers is describing here is a significant deviation from the traditional apocalyptic mode of writing, a writing in which the apocalypse has already taken place and which should thus properly be called "post-apocalyptic." After all, the specific apocalypse of *Beloved* has happened eighteen years before the novel begins, "When the four horsemen—schoolteacher, one nephew, one slave catcher and a sheriff" arrive (*Beloved* 148). The story is told from a point of view in which the apocalypse is a (distant) memory. Thus, it can hardly be surprising that there is very little drive towards apocalypse. How could there be, when it has already happened?

The apocalypse itself is strange, too. A mother killing her baby to save her, another "dead black." Here, the reference to apocalypse seems arbitrary. One dead person hardly counts. Yet, this is the fictional convention in post-apocalyptic writing, the end of the world is never total because there would be no story-telling if it were. Furthermore, this is a matter of perspective, but from Beloved's point of view, the schoolteacher's coming indeed signals the end of the world.

The apocaylpse is also an apocalypse of Enlightenment's rationality. This is presented in its primitive form in the schoolteacher who empirically and rationally constructs reasons for his idea of racial superiority, using a "scientific" method. The integrity of this rationality is questioned, however, when Sethe finds herself in the position of having to make a decision which forces her beyond its limits.

It should have become clear by now that life in the post-apocalypse is not what Christian (or Jewish) ideology wants us to believe. There is judgement—although not divine—but, and this is another convention of post-apocalyptic writing, no return to organic wholeness, no War-to-End-All-Wars and no paradise waiting on the other side, either. Bowers has aptly noted this feature of Morrison's novel:

> Biblical scholars read the four horsemen of the apocalypse as agents of divine wrath; Morrison's four horsemen are only emblems of evil. Her revision of the classic apocalyptic image suggests that she does not share with many apocalyptic writers a belief in a moral force at work in history, the invisible presence of a god who will come again to judge sinners and rescue and reward the oppressed. (69)

It is not that history is rejected—and there is little point in rejecting it. It is rather that the belief in the moral force at work in history has been shattered. From a post-apocalyptic perspective traditional morality is no longer credible. The post-apocalyptic novel picks up the debris, assembles the fragments, and shocks in juxtapositions of difference. It aspires to unity, knowing full well—as Modernists do—that while unity may be constructed by the artists in their works, it is a unity of fragments, of debris, of shreds and patches. It opposes concepts of a unified History by proposing histories—which present voices unheard, and, in oral tradition, often unrecorded. For proponents of the concept of a unified History, this must indeed suggest something like *post-histoire*, in so far as it presents a dissolution of history into stories.

Morrison's novel also revises another myth, that "the Bomb-fueled vision of a possible material end of history" is at the root of this deconstruction (Gitlin 353). Morrison reminds us that the effectiveness of destruction—physical, mental, and spiritual—does not necessarily depend on nuclear missiles. Even before the bomb, man was the worst enemy of man. In this and other post-apocalyptic novels the moral force supposedly at work in history (or apocalypse) is revealed to be little more than a cover for common self-righteousness, creating totalitarian ends for the killed, and hell on earth for the survivors. In Morrison's novel the "traditional messianic age—the time of freedom and redemption—is missing among these slaves and ex-slaves for whom hope has come to seem a cruel trick" (Bowers 63); it is missing because—as post-apocalyptic experience teaches us—there is no such age.

Baby Suggs's advice, "Lay them down . . . sword and shield. Don't study war no more. Lay all that mess down. Sword and shield" is foolish and wise

(*Beloved* 86). War and killing are no solution, but simply putting sword and shield aside without reflecting on what one is doing, is no solution either. Baby Suggs's statement, "There is no bad luck in the world but whitefolk" and her subsequent capitulation marks the collapse of a world of absolutes (*Beloved* 89). After all, "we are left with the frightening realization that Sethe, by trying to destroy the monster that had deprived her and her family of their humanity, had herself become one" (Samuels and Hudson-Weems 111). Thus Sethe's absolute mother-love is placed against Paul D.'s relativistic insight: "The best thing was to love just a little bit; everything, just a little bit, so when they broke its back . . . well, maybe you'd have a little love left over for the next one" (*Beloved* 45). This is not a view arrived at on the basis of a theory or philosophy—or rational argument—as it often is in modernist or postmodernist thinking; it rather is sheer necessity, sheer pragmatism, if one is to survive in a post-apocalyptic world.

Nonetheless, there is moral significance to an apocalypse in which "the only moral agency is human" (Bowers 69). Metaphysical agencies, powers beyond human control can no longer be blamed for what has taken place. Responsibility rests—for better or for worse—on human shoulders. This is the unbearably heavy burden of living in post-apocalyptic times.

The dilemma is focused on Sethe, who "had murdered Beloved to save her from the future, [. . . and who] raises Denver by 'keeping her from the past'" (Mobley 194). Both past and future, it seems, are fraught with danger: time is clearly out of joint in *Beloved* and Morrison comments on time as one of the features notably absent from this novel: "especially no time because memory, pre-historic memory, has no time" (Morrison 1990, 229). It is this shell-shocked timelessness that generates the postmodern "blankness" in which everything takes place in the present, "here" (Gitlin 350). If time is eliminated, past, present, and future become one and death no longer is the barrier to communication. A deliberate free play can begin, in which ghosts are simply accepted as facts of life.

One vexing problem, however, remains. How can there be memory, how can there be history, if there is no time? On the one hand, the timelessness is not universal: there is progress in the story line of the novel from Paul D.'s arrival at the beginning of the book to his return to Sethe at the end. There is progress also in Paul D.'s and Sethe's stories from Sweet Home to 124 Bluestone Road. On the other hand, timelessness implies a different concept of time. An apocalypse that "is repeatable and survivable" does indeed suggest a notion of cyclical time, as Bowers states (61). This view stands against the teleological concept of a singular apocalypse at the end of time in the Judeo-Christian tradition. Cyclical concepts, however, are not as unknown in Western philosophical or literary tradition as Bowers, for instance, seems to think. They are basic to the mythical cycles of birth, death, and rebirth Carl B. Yoke identifies in "the literature of the remade world" (Yoke 2 ff.). They are typically found in post-apocalyptic literature, most prominently perhaps in Walter M. Miller's *A Canticle for Leibowitz*. Furthermore, cyclical concepts are also the basis of Giambattista Vico's *The New Science* which in turn was utilized by Joyce in *Finnegans Wake*. Post-apocalyptic writing is unthinkable without notions of an apocalypse that is survivable and repeatable. In *Beloved* there is the double cycle of Paul D.'s departures from Sethe and his returns, of Beloved's departures from and returns to Sethe. Most prominently, the second coming of "Whiteman" (262) recalls the coming of Schoolmaster (163). This time Sethe does not turn against her own children, but against the (innocent) white intruder and is stopped by Denver and the black community. History is here repeating itself—with a difference (see *Ulysses* 16.1525):

> At this moment, the cycle has rolled around to begin again. When the women take a step back to the beginning, they touch the eschaton, the boundary, and momentarily escape from the flux of time to the place where clear vision is possible. They remind us that apocalypse is not a synonym for disaster or cataclysm. Rather, it is linked to revelation. Seeing clearly into the past, the women can take hold again of what they had lost in forgetting. (Bowers 71)

In other words, a second incident of timelessness occurs. Whether there is hope in this—redemption and opening up of the future through the past, as Bowers thinks (69–70)—seems debatable. The revelation is—as usual in such cases—double-edged. On the one hand, the intervention of the community exorcises the ghost of the first apocalypse, but on the other hand Sethe sets out to kill again—thus revealing the potential for new cataclysms. This is particularly telling as the second incident is only a rather weak echo of the first. Bodwin hardly qualifies even as a single horseman of the apocalypse, he is not even on a horse (*Beloved* 259). Sethe's reaction to him is not justified by any factual threat; she is reacting to a phantom threat of her memory, and if that is enough to turn a loving mother into a mad murderer, attempting to kill the very man who is "the main one [who] kept Sethe from the gallows in the first place" (265), what hope is there?

Bowers nonetheless tries to identify hope and considers only the positive effects of memory and knowledge: "What *Beloved* suggests is that tomorrow is made possible by the knowledge of yesterday, a knowledge that for contemporary African-Americans can be gained from imagining what it was like to walk in the flesh of their slave ancestors" (74). The dilemma is deeper here. If the knowledge is preserved, if it becomes "rememory," there is the danger of forming a response pattern of the type Sethe shows in her attack on Bodwin. History would then be repeating itself. But forgetting is no solution either, as this would simply imply that one cannot learn.

Memory and knowledge recorded in *Beloved* are extremely painful and the novel also suggests that they are dangerous for that very reason. In a cruel paradox, they have to be recovered, remembered, and told as part of (personal) history, while they must be forgotten so that one may live in peace with oneself and with one's neighbours—regardless of race and/or colour. It seems doubtful whether "the experiencing of suffering and guilt can begin to be transformed into knowledge" (Bowers 74) on either of these levels. On the first level the experience is "resolved" in the telling, while on the second it is inscribed into the landscape, both physically and mentally. Only on a third level, at which the story "was/is not a story to pass on" has, on the final page, paradoxically just been passed on (*Beloved* 275). At this level—and only here, outside the story and the novel, and in an act of aesthetic distancing—is a transformation into an aesthetic knowledge possible. The unbearably painful experience is presented as a work of art.

The conflict of forgetting and remembering within Sethe is reflected in the novel's structure, "the text of *Beloved* moves through a series of narrative starts and stops that are complicated by Sethe's desire to forget or 'disremember' the past. . . . Thus, the early sections of the novel reveal the complex ways in which memories of the past disrupt Sethe's concerted attempt to forget" (Mobley 194). We cannot ask a work of art to solve the problem; what we can ask of it is recording the dilemma as clearly as possible. The fragmentation of the text throughout *Beloved* keeps its readers aware of the conflict, involves them in a story that victimizes them in its own way, as Morrison points out: "The reader is snatched, yanked, thrown into an environment completely foreign. . . . Snatched just as the slaves were from one place to another, from any place to another, without preparation and without defense" (1990, 228). This technique of pushing the readers into a situation in which they have to grope for meaning, where they are being displaced repeatedly, where they enter spheres of knowledge and experience completely alien to them, is typical for post-apocalyptic writing. In this way, post-apocalyptic writing "forcasts the common future as it colors the common experience of a society just at or beneath the threshold of awareness" (Gitlin 352). "Pre-apocalyptic" readers, in awe of and still oriented towards the (nuclear or racist) apocalypse will gain a perspective on the future. Indeed, many post-apocalyptic novels are set in a future. *Beloved*, and Paul Auster's *In the Country of Last Things*, for example, may bring us to the threshold of the awareness that this future has already arrived; it is here already, and we are part of it (cf. Auster 1992, 306). Thus, it can hardly be surprising that anxiety is at work in the edgy debates about postmodernism (Gitlin 347).

Like many post-apocalyptic novels, *Beloved* is beyond the boundaries of the traditions it is rooted in. Although clearly a slave narrative, it does not quite fit into this category either: "while the slave narrative characteristically moves in a chronological, linear narrative fashion, *Beloved* meanders through ime, sometimes circling back, other times moving vertically, spirally out of ime and down into space" (Mobley 192). The post-apocalyptic dynamics of *3eloved* break through conventions of chronology, narration, language, eader's expectations, circle and spiral through time and space, almost leaving vriting behind. Throughout the text readers are subjected to all kinds of lelays, flashbacks. There are chapters in which the fragmentation enters anguage itself, disrupting the narrative and syntactic flow with gaps of vhiteness (e.g., 210–13). The page can barely contain the cacophony of oices. Ordinary language cannot relate the horrors and pain of apocalypse: 'unspeakable words unspoken" (199) seem to vanish into and break out of he whiteness, before the memories can be "recollected" and reorganized, ınd the narration turns into poetic chanting (215–17). Although a written ext, *Beloved* assaults the tradition of writing, aiming at something beyond, as Mobley points out, "the fragments constitute voices which speak to and omment on one another, the text illustrates the call and response pattern of he African-American oral tradition" (193). These traditions are not exclusively African-American; even Modernism—e.g., Dada—has taken up oral raditions, although one of the more prominent "oral" texts is, perhaps, oyce's *Finnegans Wake*, a post-apocalyptic text "pleasing to the ear," as Joyce out it (Ellmann 702).

Another post-apocalyptic text drawing on this tradition—perhaps in a nore radical way than *Beloved*—is Russell Hoban's *Riddley Walker*, a text lerived from an oral culture on the threshold of literacy. Or, a literate culture n the verge of orality, closing the circle, faced with apocalyptic experiences hat push a literary text back to the beginning, knowing full well that "In the eginning there were no words. In the beginning there was the sound" *Beloved* 259). It is this "sound that [breaks] the back of words" generating "a vave of sound wide enough to sound deep water" (*Beloved* 261), pushing a iterary text beyond itself, where it, in Walter Pater's words, "*constantly aspires towards the condition of music*" (86): "And the sound of the novel, sometimes cacophonous, sometimes harmonious, must be an inner ear sound or a sound just beyond hearing, infusing the text with a musical emphasis that words can do sometimes even better than music can" (Morrison 1990, 228).

Musicality expressed in words is the highest development of post-apocalyptic writing in *Beloved* as in *Finnegans Wake* or *Riddley Walker*. It is a modern mode of finding structures, words, and forms which suffice when a post-apocalyptic work of art is to encompass haunting and horrifying apocalyptic experiences and truths.

"Something postmodern has happened," Gitlin writes, and he is right—although no-one seems to know what it is (347). Perhaps also, because no-one really *wants* to know what it is and this touches a fundamental problem of post-apocalyptic literature. Writing about traumatic experiences is all but easy. Bringing half-repressed, half-forgotten, painful memories to the surface again is disturbing. Realizing this, Morrison "expected *Beloved* to be the least read of all her books because 'it is about something that the characters don't want to remember, I don't want to remember, black people don't want to remember, white people don't want to remember. I mean it's national amnesia'" (Bowers 74). Although no-one wants to remember, these memories are important; denying their existence will not make them disappear, for they will then surface violently elsewhere, as Beloved does in the novel.

These memories are of a post-apocalyptic quality. For Sethe they have become "my rememory" (36), a memory that is more acute, "a thought picture" which stays "not just in my rememory, but out there, in the world" (36). Her memory has taken on a universal timeless photographic quality in which nothing is lost, and in which what has happened once will happen again. A memory that cycles and re-cycles; a memory that reaches back through the apocalypse and has (potential) access to all horrors of history. A rememory speaking in impressions, pictures and sounds is notoriously hard to capture in words. Rememory: "mememormee!" (*Finnegans Wake* 628.14), flowing into the next cycle, which begins at the end of the *Wake* and at the end of *Beloved*.

Attempts to classify *Beloved* as a historical novel in the tradition of the slave narrative—see, for instance, Samuels and Hudson-Weems (95–96)—lead us astray. As Mobley has shown, *Beloved* clearly subverts this tradition (192). Despite its factual core, *Beloved* insists on its artificiality and so does Toni Morrison (1990, 228–30). She does not pretend to relate a "true" story:

> I did research about a lot of things in this book . . . but I did not do much research on Margaret Garner other than the obvious stuff, because I wanted to invent her life, which is a way of saying I wanted to be accessible to anything the characters had to say about it. Recording the life as lived would not make me available to anything that might be pertinent. (Qtd. in Samuels and Hudson-Weems 95)

Although based on fact, *Beloved* presents a fictional view. Objective facts, a mother becoming a killer, murdering her own child, are there, but the reality of the fiction takes us beyond those facts, makes us partake in her struggles to come to grips with her deed and her attempts at finding a *modus vivendi* in the post-apocalypse. They metamorphose her tragedy and suffering into a post-apocalyptic work of art which takes us beyond itself into a realm of timeless being where Beloved, killed, dead, and buried, comes alive as a rememory all readers share, alive forever in their minds, calling them to contemplation, removing them—particularly in its final pages—from reality, its political pressures for aportioning blame and calls for action, thus allowing them to let the rememory get to them where they might be repressing it or otherwise looking elsewhere, enabling them to acknowledge what has happened, to share the experience from the inside.

The baby is dead and nothing can change this. The apocalypse has happened and cannot be reversed, but Beloved remains, turned into *Beloved*, i.e., aesthetic knowledge, into a rememory which, though painful, will never be forgotten. She has become music, a symphony in words, our thought picture, rendering this fictional reality intensely ours. The aesthetic knowledge recorded here is beyond delivering simple messages of hope or doom; as post-apocalyptic art it makes us partake in a complex vision.

The breaking down of boundaries, the striving for an openness characteristic of modern works of art—as Eco defines it (27–59)—is also reflected in the closure of *Beloved*. The "climax" for which the novel seems to be heading—the second coming (261–62)—is not its end: "*Beloved* does not conclude with a climactic moment" (Bowers 73). This ending is rejected when Denver stops Sethe's attack on Bodwin. *Beloved* has a happy ending, in which Paul D. joins Sethe in her reclamation of self: "'Me? Me?'" (273), and again the book could have ended there. It does not, as it represents an ongoing post-apocalyptic work of art that is larger than Sethe's or Paul D.'s stories. The novel's central "character" never dies (*Beloved* 36). As *BELOVED* she is present before the novel begins, engraved on the novel's cover; as "Beloved" she remains imprinted outside the story as the novel's final word (275).

Beloved has no end and the memory of Beloved cannot be exorcized. Her disembodied voice appears again in the post-narration on the final pages full of paradox: "Disremembered and unaccounted for, she cannot be lost because no-one is looking for her," yet she finally asserts herself in print (274–75). Thus, here is the essence of *Beloved*: Forget and remember; the necessity of forgetting all too painful "rememory"; the painful impossibility to forget; the necessity to remember in order to build up a fund of knowledge to improve on the reaction to threats to one's life;

and the potential uselessness of this knowledge in different, if similar, situations.

"There is no hope in this," as Paul Auster pointed out in a different context, "but neither is there despair" (1992, 176). "Postmodernism [as] an art of erosion" has post-apocalyptically eroded both (Gitlin 360). Although post-apocalypse suggests no hope left, no paradise or perfect state to look forward to, there is more in it than total despair. After all, if you have survived one apocalypse, at least you know there is a chance of survival: "it will remember itself from every sides" (*Finnegans Wake* 614: 20). Thus the rest is definitely not silence, but—as the novel has it on its concluding page: "weather" (275). Everything is moving, everything is changing; and small butterflies may cause (unpredictably) large effects, cycling and recycling (cf. Gleick 9–31 and *passim*). To exorcise Beloved would be attempting to erase her completely, thus remembering by trying to forget. In whatever shape or form, she will always be part of the system (like any impulse remains in the weather system). No matter how minute the power of that memory will be, under the "right" circumstances effects may again be devastating. "Power was everywhere," but one never knows what input will produce which effect—and on what scale—in this highly complex system called humanity (Gitlin 358). A system, indeed, which is failed time and again by attempts at subjecting it to linear descriptions and systems. Once a deed is done, nothing can ever erase it, effects of apocalypses will never go away. The fact that in a very profound sense there is no end (*Beloved* 36) is aesthetically reflected in the closure of Morrison's novel, keeping "disorderly life in its flux against orderly death in its finality" (Gitlin 359). *Beloved* closes its own cycle, composing a work of "beauty out of discord," resting self-content (Gitlin 349). If "a ***knowing*** blankness results" (Gitlin 353; my emphasis), that is something, after all.

CAROLINE RODY

Toni Morrison's Beloved: *History, "Rememory," and a "Clamor for a Kiss"*

i am accused of tending to the past
as if i made it,
as if i sculpted it
with my own hands. i did not.
the past was waiting for me
when i came,
a monstrous unnamed baby,
and i with my mother's itch
took it to breast
and named it
History.
she is more human now,
learning language everyday,
remembering faces, names and dates.
when she is strong enough to travel
on her own, beware, she will.

Lucille Clifton, "i am accused of tending to the past. . . ."

momma
help me
turn the face of history
to your face.

June Jordan, "Getting Down to Get Over"

You came right on back like a good girl,
like a daughter. . . .

Toni Morrison, *Beloved*

From *American Literary History* 7:1 (Spring 1995).

On the back of the New American Library edition of Toni Morrison's *Beloved*, reviewer John Leonard proclaims, "I can't imagine American literature without it." Evidently intended as consummate praise, this remark would seem to congratulate Morrison for having written into the incomplete canon of American literature the very chapter of American history it had long lacked: the story of the African Americans who survived slavery. In an important sense, *Beloved* is manifestly about the filling of historical gaps. "Sixty million and more," reads Morrison's dedication, simply, suggesting at once the numerous ancestors the novel attempts to memorialize and a vast absence its words could never fill.

Yet how odd it is that we should now be unable to "imagine American literature" without the strange, idiosyncratic imaginative world of *Beloved*. A reading of the novel as a recuperation of unrepresented history does not begin to account for its cultivation of the bizarre and uncanny; its revival of gothic conventions—the haunted house, the bloody secret, the sexually alluring ghost; its obsessive, claustrophobic plot focus; and an emotional climate that changes from pained repression to volcanic fury to a suspended lovers' swoon. All of this seems somehow excessive to the requirements of a historical novel that would recuperate the story of African-American slavery and survival.

Beloved is, however, a historical novel; Morrison rewrites the life of the historical figure Margaret Garner, who killed her child to prevent her recapture into slavery, and sets this story as the focus of an epic-scale recreation of African-American life under slavery and in its aftermath. What are we to make of the shape of this "history"? Why focus on an astonishing act of violence committed not *upon* but *by* a slave woman? Why should this slave story be central for Morrison, and why should we be brought to reimagine this chapter of American history through the prism of a haunting, passionate, violent, and ultimately unresolved relationship between a mother and daughter?

The peculiarity of this "history" suggests a design different from those described by most theories of the historical novel. Certainly Morrison's slavery novel achieves the realist portrayal of great "social trends and historical forces" that Georg Lukacs endorses, in the classic historical novels, as offering a "prehistory of the present" (34, 337). The plot of the ghost girl can also be seen to draw upon the modes of historical romance and supernatural tale, which have traditionally served to "[transform] black history into mythic fiction" (Campbell xvii). *Beloved* further suggests the influence on African-American historical fiction of magic realism, read in recent Latin American and third world fictional "histories" as a revisionary postcolonial narrative mode, mediating the cultural and epistemological clashes of colonial history (Slemon 20–21). Yet while we can read revisionary mythification in Morrison's history, we still have not accounted for its interest in a murderous mother and ghostly daughter.

Poststructuralist critics of African-American historical fiction would have us read *Beloved* as less a mimetic or mythic recreation of the real than an entrant into ongoing historiographic discourse, inescapably about the problem of writing history in the complicated moment in which we tell the past (see Gates xi; McDowell, "Negotiating" 144–47). Though touched by the prevailing postmodern irony toward questions of truth and representation, fiction and history, *Beloved* and most contemporary novels of slavery are not "historiographic metafictions" denying the possibility of historical "Truth" (Hutcheon 109, 113). For these novels, much as for abolitionist slave narratives, the burden of communicating an authentic truth remains, and the inherited conviction of slavery's evil renders the word of fictional slaves true in a sense not solely epistemological or even political but moral. Postmodern fictions with battles still to fight, today's African-American slave "histories," though they may center upon questions of memory, knowledge, and identity, share with many ethnic, feminist, and postcolonial texts the impulse "to create an authoritative voice, not to undermine an already existing one" (Zimmerman 176). Thus Morrison calls on writers to deemphasize the institution of slavery and put the "authority back into the hands of the slave" (qtd. in McDowell, "Negotiating" 160).

But this remark gathers irony when we return to the difficulty of interpreting *Beloved* as historical text: namely, the awesome authority Morrison puts into the hands of her slave-heroine. Surely we can read *Beloved* as a historiographic intervention, a strategic recentering of American history in the lives of the historically dispossessed. But by what logic does the plot of child murder serve any late twentieth-century ideological interest? In what sense does this plot assert the historiographic authority of an African-American woman's hands? If these theoretical approaches do not greatly illuminate the historicity of the ghost story without which our literature was incomplete, it may be because they view historical writing solely in terms of ideologies of representation, without considering the affective aspect of history writing, insofar as the historiographic project enacts a relationship of desire, an emotional implication of present and past. While *Beloved* is evidently a politically engaged novel, it is also a novel of extraordinary psychological reach. I suggest that to account for *Beloved* we integrate an ideological reading of historical fiction with a reading of the inscribed psychological project of reimagining an inherited past.

I

In contemporary black "histories," we may, indeed, have difficulty separating the political, the psychological, and the ethnic. Discussing the recent "flood" of African-American novels about slavery, Deborah McDowell muses, "Why the compulsion to repeat the massive story of slavery in the contemporary Afro-American novel? . . ." ("Negotiating" 144). This hint at a collective psychological source of the trend, if dropped somewhat playfully, probably confirms our vague sense that larger processes in African-American history and culture are at work here, that the slavery novels of our moment mark the arrival of African-American literature at a juncture of particularly profound cultural reckoning.

For the group of black writers who have attained unprecedented literary authority and audience in an era of intensifying social crisis for the African-American community, the return to the subject of slavery would seem to articulate an ironic coming-of-age. Time and success have brought black literature to a place where the vista seems to be all of memory and return. When Hazel Carby asked in the late 1980s why relatively few African-American novels had focused on slavery, it seems she merely spoke too soon (125). By 1993 the roster of such texts has grown long, and we are looking at a genre in full swing, exhibiting an astonishing diversity and range. Today's most celebrated black writers, engaged in the profound mythopoetic enterprise of identification with slave ancestors, return African-American literary culture to its "roots," reviving with new dignity the foundational genre of this literature: the slave narrative (Gates xxxiii).

Following Margaret Walker's epic *Jubilee* (1966) and gaining greatest popular notice with the phenomenon of Alex Haley's *Roots* (1976), African-American writers have undertaken a collective return to the story of slavery unimaginable in preceding decades. The reasons for the long deferral of this project are complex, but the return itself has a resonance that is unmistakable (see Campbell xiv, 112, 158; Christian 326, 330–32, 334–38; Carby 125–27). In the surge of African-American cultural production that followed the civil rights era, amidst an overriding concern with new articulations of racial identity, a moment arrived when it became possible—and, apparently, crucial—for writers to take on the fictional persona of a slave. As nations when they rise, for good or ill, look back and reexplain to the world the past that produced their emergence in strength, so Afro-America in the 1970s, '80s, and '90s has returned to the scriptural endeavor of rewriting the texts of its own genesis. Having attained a certain measure of power, perhaps a certain measure of safety, of distance from the slave past sufficient to risk intimacy, along with increased access to publication and a growing mainstream audience, black writers began to speak with the tongue of the ancestor, claiming their place in American culture and letters upon the same ground—in history's spiral—as that upon which the slave's voice first emerged. They thus invoke a heritage not only of suffering and resistance but also of self-definition in the face of racist ideologies of literary authority.

A devotee of slave narratives, Morrison long anticipated their literary resurgence. As a Random House editor in 1976, Morrison told an interviewer:

> You know . . . just for sustenance, I read those slave narratives—there are sometimes three or four sentences or half a page, each one of which could be developed in an art form, marvelous. Just to figure out how to—you mean to tell me she beat the dogs and the man and pulled a stump out of the ground? Who is she, you know? Who is she? It's just incredible. And all of that will surface, it *will surface*, and my *huge* joy is thinking that I am in some way part of that when I sit here in this office. . . . ("Intimate" 229)

In this remark the gender of slave narrators who most fascinate Morrison ("Who is she? . . . Who is she?") is explicit and somewhat remarkable, given that fewer than 12 percent of published slave narratives were written by women (Blassingame 83) and that the popular image of the slave has been male from abolition days to the present (see McDowell, "In the First Place"). Recent feminist scholarship on female slaves has been revising the gendering of this genre, and the large proportion of today's fictional "neoslave narratives" (Bell 289) to reimagine slavery from a black female point of view constitutes a collective symbolic reauthorization of the voice of the female slave, part of the recuperation of "herstory" ongoing in the post-1960s black women's literary "renaissance."

Though the rise in historical novels by black writers testifies to a sociopolitical rise to the authority and the desire to represent the genesis of their people, this aura of ascent should not obscure the psychological descent, the paradoxical willingness to hit psychic bottom that distinguishes today's African-American literary triumphs. The stories these novels recuperate are, after all, about deprivation and suffering often literally unspeakable. Morrison notes that slave narrators, "shaping the experience to make it palatable" for white readers, dropped a "veil" over "their interior life" ("Site" 110). Whether we view her attempt to unveil that "interior" in a novel as homage or audacity, the "anxiety of influence" operative in her retelling is shaped by a distinctive sense of inferiority, an "ethnic," "familial" relationship to an inherited, traumatic story. For an African-American writer, slavery is a story known in the bones and yet not at all. "How could she bear witness to what she never lived?" asks Gayl Jones's *Corregidora* (103), crystallizing the paradox of contemporary black rewritings of slavery. Writing that bears witness to an inherited tragedy approaches the past with an interest much more urgent than historical curiosity or even political revisionism. Inserting authorial consciousness into the very processes of history that accomplished the racial "othering" of the self, novels of slavery make their claims to knowledge and power face-to-face with destruction. We might think of such fictions as structures of historiographic desire, attempts to span a vast gap of time, loss, and ignorance to achieve an intimate bond, a bridge of restitution or healing, between the authorial present and the ancestral past.

Years before *Beloved* Morrison spoke of her fiction in terms of the transmission of cultural inheritance: because black people no longer live in places where parents "sit around and tell their children those . . . archetypal stories," the novel must take up the traditional "healing" function of African-American folk music and tales ("Rootedness" 340). The culture-bearing impulse generates in Morrison's novels characters of mythic stature, with tale-telling names and marked bodies, along with the voice of a communal chorus and a narrative voice of an "oral quality" ("An Interview" 409) modeled on "a black preacher [who] requires his congregation to . . . join him in the sermon"; "not the separate, isolated ivory tower voice of a very different kind of person but an implied 'we' in narration" ("Rootedness" 341–43). Aspiring to a voice that sounds like "we," Morrison attempts a communal textuality: "If anything I do, in the way of writing novels . . . isn't about the village or the community or about you, then it is not about anything" ("Rootedness" 344). Upon finishing a book, she has said, "I feel a little lonely, as though I've lost touch . . . with some collective memory" ("Toni Morrison" 131). Writing that contacts collective memory conflates the personal and the communal, works to open the "interior life" of the individual into the "anterior life" of the people (Clemons 75), what Morrison has referred to as "the life of that organism to which I belong which is black people in this country" ("Interview" 413).

In writing *Beloved* Morrison's Whitmanesque will to communal subjectivity confronts its antithesis and perhaps its deepest source—the catastrophic destruction of community under slavery. With a capacity for pain and a sustained focus on the dead unprecedented in the African-American novel, *Beloved* includes in the storytelling "we" numberless lost forebears. More than a "history," *Beloved* serves for its author as a substitute:

> There is no place here where I can go, or where you can go, and think about, or not think about, or summon the presences of, or recollect the absences of—slaves. . . . Something that reminds us

> of the ones who made the journey, and those who did not make it. There is no suitable memorial—or plaque, or wreath, or wall, or park, or skyscraper lobby. There's no three hundred foot tower. . . . And because such a place doesn't exist that I know of, the book had to. (Lecture)

Reconceiving the historical novel as memorial, Morrison illuminates the psychological structure of ethnic historical fiction. Like all memorials, *Beloved* is not a "place" of the dead but a place where survivors can go to "summon" and "recollect," to look upon the sculpted shape of their own sorrow. *Beloved* cannot recover the "interior life" of slaves, but by dramatizing the psychological legacy of slavery, it portrays that "interior" place in the African-American psyche where a slave's face still haunts.

When first conceiving her rewriting of Margaret Garner's life, Morrison has said, "It was an era I didn't want to get into—going back into and through grief" ("It's OK" 45). This "grief" seems almost a palpable atmosphere; in the personal psychological return required to write *Beloved*, it was not history Morrison had to go "back into and through" but an intensity of hovering emotion attributed neither to the ancestors nor to herself but filling the space between them. Merging the psychological, the communal, and the historical, Morrison's novel goes "back into and through" time and pain together. Returning to the surface, it brings to the present an archetypal figure for the emotional labor of its own recuperative writing: the return of a dead ancestor. I read the haunting, resurrection, and exorcism of the beloved ghost as the inscription of the writer's haunted negotiations with her people's past. Setting a metahistorical struggle between mother and ghostly daughter at the center of an epic reimagining of an entire ancestry, Morrison's history centrally dramatizes the problem of imagining, writing, and publishing—"witnessing"—a story about her own daughterly heritage. And, as I shall argue, the ghost Beloved, who gives a body and face to that which is in excess of African-American history—the absences at that history's core—also functions, in a dramatic reversal, as a marvelous figure for the struggle of daughterly historiographic desire itself.

II

In the "village" of *Beloved*, the multigenerational, culture-bearing black community of Morrison's ideal appears in devastated form, in the persons of a few traumatized survivors, eking out an existence in the aftermath of slavery. Foregrounded in the novel, the telling of stories becomes memory's struggle with catastrophe and loss. For Morrison's characters, as for the novel in its contemporary moment, cultural transmission requires the retrieval of traumatic memories. This "history" thus acquires the function of communal "talking cure": its characters, author, and readers delve into the past, repeating painful stories to work toward the health of fuller awareness.

Beloved opens upon the haunted house where, shunned by the neighborhood, Morrison's heroine Sethe is raising her daughter Denver in an atmosphere of stagnant grief. Together they have come to accept what drove two sons away from home: the "spiteful" baby ghost (3) who makes herself known by clashings of pots and furniture, pools of red light by the doorway, tiny hand prints in the cake. Into this scene walks Paul D, that rare "kind of man who could walk into a house and make the women cry" (17). His arrival changes the climate of repression: he chases the invisible haunter from the house and sparks in Sethe "the temptation to trust and remember," "to go ahead and feel" (30), for the first time in years. His past, too, has required profound repression: he has a "tobacco tin buried in his chest where a red heart used to be. Its lid rusted shut" (72–73). Together, Sethe and Paul D begin a mutual talking cure that promises a mutual future. As their halting, gradual storytelling is taken up by other characters, the novel's present unfolds entwined in multiple strands of time, voice, incident, and perspective.

Storytelling becomes the text's self-conscious task; many scenes present a character narrating his or her life to a listener. The novel's distinctive tone arises from the very difficulty of telling for those recovering from the traumas of slavery—witnessing the murder, torture, or sale of family and friends; being whipped, chained, led with an iron bit in the mouth, and housed in an underground "box"; being examined and catalogued in terms of "human" and "animal" characteristics, or forcibly "nursed" by white boys when one's breasts held milk for a baby. These experiences fragment and block the memories of Morrison's ex-slaves, whose stories are revealed in bits, out of sequence, in a painful eking out and holding back often rendered in spare synecdoche: "Paul D had only begun . . . when her fingers on his knee, soft and reassuring, stopped him. . . . Saying more might push them both to a place they couldn't get back from. Sethe rubbed and rubbed. . . . She hoped it calmed him as it did her. Like kneading bread . . . working dough. Nothing better than that to start the day's serious work of beating back the past" (73).

As the narrative loops around events, dramatizing pain's effect on memory, it also suggests a hesitance to force the past out of characters whose memories stand in for the suffering of innumerable unknown people. Any recuperations are performed against a blank background of storylessness, symbolic of our historical knowledge of African Americans and of their representation in our literature. Morrison chooses just one family's haunted house to explicate, but as Grandma Baby Suggs says, "Not a house in the country ain't packed to the rafters with some dead Negro's grief" (5). Every American house is a haunted house. As *Beloved* revives the past in the modes of haunting, memory, and storytelling, it becomes an exercise in the poetics of absence.

Morrison's prose inventively represents the multiple shades of loss and absence known to slaves: "Anybody Baby Suggs knew, let alone loved, who hadn't run off or been hanged, got rented out, loaned out, bought up, brought back, stored up, mortgaged, won, stolen, or seized" (23). Characters tend to gather around them clusters of the lost. "Did Patty lose her lisp?" Baby Suggs wonders about the children sold from her; "what color did Famous' skin finally take?" (139). On his postwar trek north, Paul D saw "twelve dead blacks in the first eighteen miles," and "by the time he got to Mobile, he had seen more dead people than living ones" (269). A traveling man, Paul D brings to the text a voice of tribal griot-cum-historical eyewitness: "During, before, and after the war he had seen Negroes so stunned, or hungry, or tired or bereft it was a wonder they recalled or said anything. Who, like him, had hidden in caves and fought owls for food . . . stole from pigs . . . slept in trees in the day and walked by night. . . . Once he met a Negro about fourteen years old who lived by himself in the woods and said he couldn't remember living anywhere else. He saw a witless colored woman jailed and hanged for stealing ducks she believed were her own babies" (66). Passages like this bring to the novel cinematic visions of an entire struggling people, among whom Morrison names a precious few characters for detailed narration. The reader learns, like Ella as she aids escaping slaves, to listen "for the holes—the things the fugitives did not say, the questions they did not ask . . . the unnamed, unmentioned people left behind" (92). To demarcate the "holes" Morrison has characters repeat isolated remembered details, metonymies for unrecountable emotional experiences, the more poignant for their banality. Baby Suggs recalls, "My first-born. All I can remember of her is how she loved the burned bottom of bread. Can you beat that? Eight children and that's all I remember" (5).

"That's all you let yourself remember," Sethe replies. In this landscape of loss it is Morrison's pensive heroine, the "queenly woman" (12) with blood on her hands and a "tree" scarred into her back, who articulates the novel's theory of memory and repression in a distinctive, neologistic vocabulary. To the girl who arrives at the door from nowhere and claims to have no past, Sethe says, "You disremember everything? I never knew my mother neither, but I saw her a couple of times. Did you never see yours?" (118–19). The suggestive verb "disremember" is complemented in Sethe's usage by the idiosyncratic "rememory," which works as both noun and verb: "I don't 'spect you rememory this, but . . ." (160). The repetition of "rememory" underscores the text's preoccupation with the problematics of the mind in time. Sethe explains her experience of time and "rememory": "If a house burns down, it's gone, but the place—the picture of it—stays, and not just in my rememory, but out there, in the world. . . . Some day you be walking down the road and you hear something or see something going on. So clear. And you think it's you thinking it up. . . . But no. It's when you bump into a rememory that belongs to somebody else . . ." (35–36). For Sethe a "rememory" (an individual experience) hangs around as a "picture" that can enter another's "rememory" (the part of the brain that "rememories") and complicate consciousness and identity. "Rememory" as trope postulates the interconnectedness of minds, past and present, and thus neatly conjoins the novel's supernatural vision with its aspiration to communal epic, realizing the "collective memory" of which Morrison speaks. For while the prefix "re" (normally used for the act, not the property of consciousness) suggests that "rememory" is an active, creative mental function, Sethe's explanation describes a natural—or a supernatural—phenomenon. For Sethe as for her author, then, to "rememory" is to use one's imaginative power to realize a latent, abiding connection to the past.

"Rememory" thus functions in Morrison's "history" as a trope for the problem of reimagining one's heritage. The novel's entire poetics of memory, all of Sethe and Paul D's troubles with remembering, can be seen to figure the problem not of Morrison's own memory, of course, but of her imagination as it encounters her people's past. The characters who do not want to or can not remember their stories reverse the desire of the writer who wants to know and tell a communal history. She must work to "rememory" these ancestors who wish they could forget. In the absence of their particular faces, she must create the characters she wants to mourn. The elevation of memory to a supernatural power that connects all minds, making it possible to "bump into a rememory that belongs to somebody else," is generated by authorial desire to write like a "we" about unknown ancestors. "Rememory" transforms memory into a property of consciousness with the heightened imaginative power sufficient to the ethnic historical novel's claim to represent the past.

Along with this heightened notion of memory, the text's inscription of the psychological project of ethnic historical recuperation relies upon heightened tropes of naming and love. Morrison's epigraph, a passage from Romans 9.25, combines these: "I will call them my people, / which were not my people; / and her beloved, / which was not beloved." Suggesting that the naming function of the text be read as an offering of narrative love, the epigraph proposes a kind of history-telling that can turn estrangement into intimacy. "Beloved," Morrison names the lost past, and "Beloved" is the novel's final word. This implied function of narrative love seeks to repair the violation of love wreaked upon Morrison's characters by slavery, separation, and death. Considering newborn Denver's chances of survival, Ella tells Sethe, "If anybody was to ask me I'd say, 'Don't love nothing'" (92). Like memory, love must defend itself against history. For Paul D in the prison camp, survival meant "you protected yourself and loved small": "Picked the tiniest stars out of the sky to own. . . . Grass blades, salamanders. . . . Anything bigger wouldn't do. A woman, a child, a brother—a big love like that would split you wide open. . . . to get to a place where you could love anything you chose—not to need permission for desire—well now, *that* was freedom" (162). Equating "freedom"—a consummate signifier in African-American literature and culture—with the right to love as one chooses, Morrison's text exercises its freedom to cast "long-distance love" (95) backward in time and bestow names upon—thus "freeing"—some of the African Americans history forgot. In the dialectic between the lost past and the rememorying function of narrative love, *Beloved* reconceives the historical text as a transformative space: a space in which the present takes the past in a new and transforming embrace, constructed for mutual healing.

The transforming power of narrative is underscored in *Beloved* by the many inset scenes of storytelling; the familial or communal contexts of these story "exchanges," in Ross Chambers's terms (8), dramatize the power of cultural transmission to transform family relationships. For example, at the novel's mythological core is the story Sethe often tells Denver of her birth under horrid conditions while her mother ran from slavery. This story—a significant feminization of the archetypal slave escape narrative—is "exchanged" in the understanding that the hardships endured by the mother should contribute to the child's sense of self. Denver is the daughter who emerges from the storytelling a woman, embraces her community, learns to read and write, and even plans to go to college. This storytelling exchange is a model for the intergenerational transmission of African-American oral culture; it is Denver who actually retells the escape-childbirth story in the novel. Born in a canoe on the Ohio River, between slavery and freedom, Denver the survivor and story-inheritor becomes a proto-Morrison, bearer of the family exodus saga into literate American culture.

The storytelling transaction between Sethe and Paul D is different: the lovers engage in a mutual unburdening of the past in the hopes of a mutual healing and of a future together. "He wants to put his story next to hers," Morrison concludes their protracted and arduous romance (273). The reconciliation of the sexes resulting from this story exchange is a particularly notable transformation, given recent controversy about the representation of black men in black women's texts (see McDowell, "Reading"). Morrison, who has consistently written complex and nuanced black male characters (for example, Cholly Breedlove, Shadrack, Milkman Dead, Son, and Joe Trace), here creates a man whose entry into the house of fiction starts a rush not just of female tears but of female autobiography. A muse to the storytelling Sethe—or to Morrison—Paul D also offers hope of futurity at the telling's end: "Sethe," he says, "me and you, we got more yesterday than anybody. We need some kind of tomorrow" (273). The exchange between these two, developing from shared confessions to an actual romantic ending, gestures at a further transformation: the reconstitution of the black family after a time of devastation. When Paul D announces that the traumatic story has run its course and suggests its resolution in a vague futurity, his words manage the interface of this "history" and its crises with those of the present.

While most of the text's narrative exchanges can be read in terms of cultural transmission, the retrieval of stories to strengthen identity and community, this explanation cannot account for the tellings involving the ghost Beloved, which do not strengthen community but threaten Sethe's relationships and even her life. To understand the story transactions with Beloved—and the text's transactions with the past—we must examine the strange character at the novel's heart.

The mysterious, beautiful woman who emerges fully dressed from the stream behind Morrison's haunted house, remembering little besides crouching in the dark, longing for a certain woman's face, and crossing a bridge, turns out to be the resurrected baby Sethe murdered 18 years earlier. She wants her mother with all the intensity of an abandoned two-year-old. In this rememory of Margaret Garner and her daughter, however, the ghost comes to embody much "more," as Denver puts it (266). Morrison gives her the distinctive name everyone privately gives to their most beloved; it expresses at once the greatest anonymity and the dearest specificity. It is her name because she died still unnamed, and when Sethe heard the preacher speak the word *beloved* at her burial, she had it cut on her baby daughter's tombstone. But when the preacher said "Dearly Beloved," he must have been addressing the living assembled there and not, as the grieving Sethe thought, the dead child. "Beloved" names everyone, in the official, impersonal rhetoric of the church and names everyone who is intimately loved, but does not name the forgotten. Morrison has the name perform precisely this last function; the novel's defining conceit is to call the unnamed "beloved." Part of Beloved's strangeness derives, then, from the emotional burden she carries as a symbolic compression of innumerable forgotten people into one miraculously resurrected personality, the remembering of the "sixty million" in one youthful body. Another part is just the weirdness of a ghost: like all the ghosts in literature, she embodies a fearful claim of the past upon the present, the past's desire to be recognized by, and even possess, the living.

Yet to write history as a ghost story, to cast the past as longing for *us*, instead of the other way around, is to inscribe a reversal of desire that informs this text's structure—and the structure of all ghost tales—on a deep level. Indeed, in imagining the longing of the murdered child for the mother, Morrison reverses the usual direction of grief, in which the living mourn the dead; the child or descendent mourns the mother or ancestor. The novel's emblematic figure of the mourning baby girl, embodying this reversal of desire, can thus function to figure both the lost past and the mourning author—the "daughter" of this lost ancestry, desiring the face of the mother from whom time has separated her. This is to say that the historical project of the novel is in a profound sense a mother-quest, an African-American feminist "herstory" that posits a kind of "mother of history" and sends a surrogate, time-traveling daughter to enact its demonic errand of love or revenge: seeking to regain her, to heal historical separation, to know the story of the mother history forgot. Morrison spares no expense in articulating Beloved's primal, pre-Oedipal craving for her mother's face: "I am not separate from her . . . her face is my own and I want to be there in the place where her face is. . . . I want to be the two of us. I want the join . . ." (210–13). Embodying an insatiable, childish, jealous desire for the absent mother's face, to see and be seen, to commune and kiss and know and be known, Beloved is a marvelous figuration of the woman writer's struggle with and desire for the face of the absent past, for her matrilineage, for the lost mothers she would rewrite.

In the return of Beloved, Morrison's "rememory" of the murderer-mother thus demonstrates the psychological structure of a daughter's desire. "How could she do that?" Morrison wondered about Margaret Garner, and "because I could not answer that question," she has said, "I introduced into the book one who had the right to the answer, her dead daughter" ("African-Americans"). That the dead daughter of *Beloved* functions as a surrogate self becomes startlingly clear in Morrison's 1985 "Conversation" with Gloria Naylor on the evolution of her oeuvre. Discussing the imaginative project that impelled her first novel, *The Bluest Eye*, Morrison speaks of the recovery of a "dead girl" who was a lost aspect of herself: "I remembered being a person who did belong in this earth . . . [but] there was no me in this world. And I was looking for that dead girl and I thought I might talk about that dead girl . . ." ("Conversation" 198–99). Years later, developing the psychological world of *Beloved*, Morrison imaginatively conceived the "self" as a separate entity, like "a *twin* or a thirst or a friend or something that sits right next to you and watches you"; "I . . . just projected her out into the earth," she explains, "[as] the girl that Margaret Garner killed" (208). After years of sustained creative work, Morrison concludes, "[the girl] comes running when called—walks freely around the house. . . . She is here now, alive" (217). Thus personifying her developing oeuvre as a gradually resurrected girl-self, Morrison creates an emblematic figure for the contemporary black women's "renaissance."

Shaping that girl into the ghost Beloved, Morrison dramatizes the black literary daughter's imaginative return to maternal history. Though *Beloved* began as an inquiry into the motives of the mother, the energy of desire in the text is embodied in the phantom daughter, who returns through time to question the mother. And though the plot turns upon the loss of a child, this history-as-daughter's-rememory is pervaded with grief for lost mothers: Beloved's aching desire for Sethe; Sethe's mourning for Baby Suggs, the mother-in-law almost as present in memory after her death as is her ghostly granddaughter; and Sethe's loss of her own mother, remembered in excruciating fragments: a hat in the rice fields, a scar under her breast (61). This multiple mourning for mothers inscribes in our literature the tragic experience of African-American children and women under slavery, systematically denied mothers and denied the mother-right by the pitiless traffic in human labor and by enforced wet-nursing. Her mother sent to the fields, Sethe was suckled by the plantation nurse: "The little whitebabies got it first and I got what was left. Or none. There was no nursing milk to call my own. I know what it is to be without the milk that belongs to you . . ." (200). Echoing through this "history" is a cry for mother's milk, fusing a mass-scale historical deprivation with that of the thirsting self, the daughter deprived of her "disremembered" matrilineage.

The welling-up of mother-daughter longing reaches a climax at the moment when Sethe realizes Beloved is her daughter returned from death; in this moment of perfect restitution, though she holds a cup in her hand, "no milk spilled." A rush of mothers' voices is unleashed, recalling lost daughters or urging remembrance on them:

> From where she sat Sethe could not examine it, not the hairline, nor the eyebrows, the lips, nor . . .
> "All I remember," Baby Suggs had said, "is how she loved the burned bottom of bread. Her little hands I wouldn't know em if they slapped me."
> . . . the birthmark, nor the color of the gums, the shape of her ears, nor . . .
> "Here. Look here. This is your ma'am. If you can't tell me by my face, look here." (175)

Set amid the echoes of so many separations, the miraculous reunion of Beloved and Sethe gathers emotional force: one child restored, one grieving mother's wish come true.

The mother-daughter dialectic that shapes this "history" generates intensely relational forms of identity among female characters. Morrison's women are linked by a three-generation chain of scars, marking both bond and breach: Sethe's mother urges her daughter to recognize her body in death by the scar under her breast, and Sethe's resurrected daughter bears on her neck the mark of her mother's handsaw. Between them, Sethe has "a chokecherry tree" on her back, the scar of a brutal whipping. Schoolteacher's nephews whip Sethe for reporting their first act of violence against her—the one which looms much larger in her memory: forcibly "nursing" her breast milk. The tree is thus associated with Sethe's violated motherhood, the visible sign of the crime she repeatedly laments: "they took my milk!" (17). In this novel of mother-quest, Morrison replaces the prototypical white master's crime against black slave women—rape—with a virtual rape of Sethe's motherhood. The tree is a cruciform emblem of her suffering but also an emblem of her place in generation; as the second of three links—a "trunk" with roots and with "branches," "leaves," and "blossoms" (79)—Sethe carries the family tree on her back. As a child, she misunderstood the pain such scars record, and when her mother said, "you can know me by this mark," Sethe replied, "but how will you know me? . . . Mark the mark on me, too" (61). Though Sethe's mother slapped her, Morrison's portrayal of the lost mothers of African-American history inscribes, indelibly, the daughter's reckless willingness to bear the mark of the mother's pain.

The mother-daughter structure also surfaces in a surprising interchangeability of generational positions among female characters. This occurs not only in the ominous passage in which Beloved grows into the mother and Sethe shrinks into the child (250) but also in a curious play on the word "baby," most striking in the name of the matriarch Baby Suggs. "Grandma Baby," as she is oxymoronically called in her old age, got her name from an affectionate husband; the "baby ghost" returns as an infantile young woman; and Denver too is called "baby" at the moment in her eighteenth year when she leaves her mother's house and enters the community to seek work and food for her family: "'Oh baby,' said Mrs. Jones. 'Oh, baby,'" and Denver "did not know it then, but it was the word 'baby,' said softly and with such kindness, that inaugurated her life in the world as a woman" (248). The circulation of female identity through the positions "baby," "daughter," "woman," "mother," and "grandmother" links Morrison's female characters in an imaginative fusion that reflects the daughter-mother psychic dialectic of this "history," a time-transcending structure in which the novel of history meets the poetics of motherlove: "Grown don't mean nothing to a mother," Sethe says; "they get bigger, older, but grown? . . . In my heart it don't mean a thing" (45). Thinking back like a mother, to misquote Virginia Woolf, Morrison's history adds motherlove to its repertoire of tropes for the conquest of time.

If the ghostly daughter can figure both the return of the past and the desire of the past-questing writer, the obsessive mother-daughter dialectics of *Beloved* also make sense as a structure of literary inheritance. The search for the lost "mother" of history might be read as an agonistic struggle—or better, an ambivalent "female affiliation complex" (Gilbert and Gubar 168–71)—with the literary foremothers whose influence and whose loss to history Morrison feels so intensely ("Who is she? . . . Who is she?"): the writers of the slave narratives. Vital and impressive in their escape tales, these earliest African-American women writers represent for Morrison a culturally originary moment and a rich, barely tapped literary inheritance. Yet though their existence is foundational to Morrison's sense of authorship, as chosen antecedents they elude authorial desire, veiling in their near-anonymity much more than they reveal. These foremothers can be glimpsed today, usually, only in brief texts published under names recorded nowhere else, collected in volumes holding myriad variations on the same protean plot. In their day the slave narrators had much less literary authority than does the bestselling Morrison and even today the truth-status of their tales is debated. Still, the historical value of the narratives far surpasses that of a belated "neoslave narrative" that reimagines historical truth. Though it is Morrison's "*huge* joy" to help slave authors to "surface" in contemporary writing ("Intimate" 229), it is also her lot to view them from across a great divide and see in them the dim faces of origin she will never fully capture. In the jealous longing of the abandoned daughter, the novel figures its relationship to the unknown ancestress-muse of the African-American women's literary renaissance.

Just as the ghost daughter's return to the mother can be read as a reversal of authorial historiographic desire, the daughter also reverses the structure of narrative seduction identified by Chambers: rather than seduce a listener, Beloved seduces Sethe into telling her story. Coming from the place of the dead, this ghost begs to have history told to her. The novel's normative story-exchange between mother and child, carried out by Sethe and Denver in the daylight realm of the present, transacts the inheritance of a real daughter and promises real-world continuity; the exchange between Sethe and Beloved, however, is symbolic of the deep workings of the psyche in struggle with the past, involving guilt, longing, and fury, threatening disintegration and death. From the moment she arrives her strange appeal works on Sethe, who accepts her into the household, accepts her increasing physical intimacy, and finally recognizes her as her lost daughter. All the while, Beloved coaxes information from Sethe, stories she had never wanted to tell before but which now flow out of her. Toward the novel's emotional climax, Denver is excluded from the central drama, and Beloved has Sethe all to herself. The relationship intensifies to a frenzy; standing outside the house the old man Stamp Paid hears "a conflagration of hasty voices," among which "all he could make out was the word *mine*" (172): "[H]e kept on through the voices, and tried once more to knock on the door of 124. This time, although he couldn't cipher but one word, he believed he knew who spoke them. The people of the broken necks, of fire-cooked blood and black girls who had lost their ribbons. What a roaring" (181).

In this mother-daughter struggle Stamp hears the concentrated agony of the entire people. The reunion of Sethe and Beloved crystallizes the vast problem of facing and reclaiming African-American history in a terrible mother-daughter seduction-struggle for the story. Morrison's desire to represent Margaret Garner and her generation and to write a story that could lie "next to hers," so to speak, generates the bodily form of a ghostly child who floats through time, finds the mother for whom she longs, wins her embrace, and nearly strangles her to death. The mother's murder of her daughter, the daughter's resurrection, and all the novel's gothic horror seem excessive to history in the sense of an objective "prehistory of the present" because they illustrate quite a different sense of history: the subjective, ethnic possession of history understood as the prehistory of the self. Encountering the story of Margaret Garner, Morrison could not get it out of her mind, and her return to embrace this impossible mother-figure in fiction suggests the impossibility and the urgency of embracing one's inheritance of such a history, one's living relationship to so much death. In a moment when a black woman writer at last possesses the authority to take her history into her own hands, Morrison risks—and confirms—that authority with the figure of a fearsome foremother, thereby revealing a daughter's vulnerability to her history, its haunting, violent grip on the mind, the dangerous pull of love that draws her back. If our literature was incomplete without *Beloved*, it was because we had not been told the story of slavery by a writer willing to undertake the life-and-death story of the surviving self.

III

We can read in the obsessive relationship at the center of this text the figuration of authorial desire/grief for a lost mother-of-history, the active principle in Morrison's reimagining of her ancestral community. Our account is incomplete, however, without attention to the implications of the gendering and sexuality of the ghost: Beloved's haunting is a metaphoric return of the past in the form of an excess of female desire. Figuring the disremembered past as "the girl who waited to be loved" (274), Morrison conflates the problematics of time, loss, and representation with a drama of inconsumable female desire. Calling the past "Beloved" and re-membering it in a female body, the text gives one name to the lost of history and buried female desire, and it stages the simultaneous resurrection of both.

When the lost past returns in *Beloved*, it demonstrates a startling sexuality. Susan Willis has argued that Morrison tends to figure history, particularly "the loss of history and culture" resulting from the African-American northern and urban migrations in "sexual terms"; sexuality erupts in her novels to evoke earlier, more vital modes of black life (35). When the bourgeois black women in *The Bluest Eye* maintain vigilance against "eruptions of funk" (68), Willis claims, "funk" signifies "the intrusion of the past in the present" (41). The "funk" in Morrison's earlier novels suggests, then, a distinctively black female sexuality inseparable from a sense of historical continuity. Yet the ghost Beloved is an eruption of powerful, physical female desire that radically threatens the distinction between past and present as well as the household and the throats of the living. The disruptive sexuality of a murdered girl returned from the dead is a funky nightmare, an agony of limitless sexual desire expressive of the lot of the disremembered in time.

Strikingly, this ghostly longing does not restrict its objects by gender. Beloved seduces Paul D but cannot "take her eyes off Sethe": "Stooping to shake the damper, or snapping sticks for kindlin, Sethe was licked, tasted, eaten by Beloved's eyes. . . . she felt Beloved touch her. A touch no heavier than a feather but loaded . . . with desire. Sethe stirred and looked . . . into her eyes. The longing she saw there was bottomless" (57–58). When one day Beloved's massaging strokes turn to "lips that kept on kissing," Sethe startles, saying, "You too old for that" (97–98). If this moment can be explained as just the cognitive clash produced by the returned baby-ghost plot, a central section of the book is even more substantially homoerotic in content and structure.

When Sethe discovers Beloved's identity, she interprets her reappearance as a sign of forgiveness, and in immense relief she turns her back on the world and devotes herself to loving Beloved. The novel then embarks upon 18 pages of "unspeakable thoughts, unspoken" (199) by Sethe and her two daughters, now an isolated and passionate trio, who, having locked the door, enter a communion of love, outside time. Echoing the *Song of Songs*, each speaks a monologue in turn: "Beloved, she my daughter. She mine"; "Beloved is my sister"; "I am Beloved and she is mine" (200–10). Their voices then join in a fugue of woman-woman love: "You are my sister / You are my daughter / You are my face; you are me"; "I have your milk / I have your smile / I will take care of you"; "You are mine / You are mine / You are mine" (216–17).

In this fantasy of fulfilled female desire, the text seems to find its heart. When Beloved's "lesbian" desire first disrupts Sethe's household, it is one with the volcanic return of the repressed past she brings with her, out of the closet, as it were, and into the house of the present. But when Sethe locks her house against the world—in particular the male world of Stamp Paid and Paul D—lesbian desire is no longer disturbing; rather, the *jouissant* communion that ensues seems a momentary utopian resolution of the war between present and past. If the fluctuations of sexuality in Morrison can be seen to encode historical process, this "lesbian" section of *Beloved* might constitute a momentary "separatist" resolution of historical tensions, in a realm "free at last," as Morrison suggestively puts it (199), of male interpretation or authority—free, in fact, of history. But if, as I have argued, Beloved figures both the lost past and the desiring present, her desire for Sethe suggests a "matrisexual" narrative desire. The seduction of the ancestress for her story, which Beloved undertakes for Morrison, here rests in an ahistorical, pre-Oedipal fantasy that unites "mother" and "child" as lovers. As the form joins their separate voices in ritualized call and response, female historiographic agon is, for a moment, perfectly resolved.

The perfect, timeless moment passes, however; Sethe has left her job, and when the food runs out, Denver goes into the world to find some and begins to bring her haunted family back into its community and into time. At home the love-feast has passed the satiation point; Beloved demands more and more from Sethe, while accusing her of desertion. Slowly she begins to grow bigger, while Sethe diminishes, so that it seems to Denver that "the thing was done": "Beloved bending over Sethe looked the mother, Sethe the teething child. . . . Beloved ate up her life, took it, swelled up with it. . . . And the older woman yielded it up without a murmur" (250). The murdered baby turned lesbian ghost has become a vampire. A difficult emotional crossing is made when the text acknowledges that the murdered innocent, the forgotten past, can become, if allowed to return and take over our present-day households, a killer. When the women of the town hear that Sethe's murdered baby has returned, they overcome their longtime disgust and decide that "nobody got that coming" (256). Thirty-strong, they march to the house and perform a collective exorcism; Beloved vanishes. Paul D then returns to bring Sethe out of a traumatic withdrawal, and into "some kind of tomorrow."

Having shaken the fictional present of Sethe's life free of the burden of its past, Morrison ends her story. She then closes the text with a two-page coda that leaves Sethe's living family behind and meditates only on Beloved and her meaning for our present moment. There is a recognition here that, like the ghost-vampire of Sethe's past, writing, too, can feed on the historical mother, grow larger than her, potentially kill her, and "when you kill the ancestor," Morrison has said, "you kill yourself" ("Rootedness" 344). Taking leave of history, the novel leaves the slave mother to her own moment, to herself—whoever she was. When she reads a slave woman's narrative, Morrison wonders, "Who is she? . . . Who is she?" But at her slave novel's end, she lets the foremother question herself: "Me? Me?" Sethe asks, her story's final words and her reply when Paul D tells her "You your best thing, Sethe" (273). Beloved ultimately leaves the mother of history to possess herself, stops haunting her with the losses of the past or with our present longing.

Yet the text does not give up Beloved. She is a possession rescued from the past, a mirror-image of the daughter who searches backwards in time. In the final two pages Morrison diminishes Beloved's body once again to a haunting, carrying the losses of history as "a loneliness" that we banish from thought as we banish denied desire (274). Having told history as the painful re-membering of the forgotten, *Beloved* ends by "witnessing" the process of dis(re)memberment, as "the girl who waited to be loved and cry shame erupts into her separate parts, to make it easy for the chewing laughter to swallow her all away" (274). The coda depicts human collusion with passing time—the general hunger to reabsorb and repress loss that afflicts the storytelling village: "Disremembered and unaccounted for, she cannot be lost because no one is looking for her. . . . They forgot her like a bad dream. . . . Sometimes the photograph of a close friend or relative—looked at too long—shifts, and something more familiar than the dear face itself moves there. They can touch it if they like, but don't . . ." (274–75).

The meditations of this prose-poem, "transfiguring and disseminating the haunting" (Lecture), bring history to an unclosed closure and the haunt to our own houses. Morrison seems to unravel the illusion of historical mimesis created in the preceding fiction and to describe the text's history-telling as the inverse of cultural transmission, the shadowy underside of family inheritance, a romance with the painfully reanimated body of loss. The text repeats three times in closing that this is "not a story to pass on," a statement best read not as a warning against repetition but as a description by negation. *Beloved* is not a story of presence and continuity but one that delineates the place of absence: "By and by all trace is gone. . . . The rest is weather. Not the breath of the disremembered and unaccounted for, but wind in the eaves, or spring ice thawing too quickly. Just weather. Certainly no clamor for a kiss. Beloved" (275). Speaking in negatives, Morrison makes absence exquisitely tangible; the lost past is "not the breath of the disremembered and unaccounted for" but "just weather"; the lovely nonsubstance "just weather" rolls away before the stunning silence, "certainly no clamor for a kiss." For us of course, closing the book, there is nothing but weather. The past does not exist unless we choose to hear its clamor. Morrison stages an encounter with the past in a drama of such clamorous desire that she does make us seem to hear loss clamor back. And in ending, having once again hushed the obscure absences and denied desires that her fiction aroused, she seals our relationship to the lost past with the offering of a name: "Beloved." Thus her history achieves its embrace.

JAMES BERGER

Ghosts of Liberalism: Morrison's Beloved *and the Moynihan Report*

This essay places Toni Morrison's 1989 novel *Beloved* in particular discursive contexts of the 1980s, reading the text as an intervention in two ongoing debates about American race relations. *Beloved* opposes neoconservative and Reaganist denials of race as a continuing, traumatic, and structural problem in contemporary America but also questions positions on the left that tend to deny the traumatic effect of violence within African American communities. In emphasizing the African American family as a site of violence—emanating both from a racist society and from within the family—*Beloved* takes up debates that emerged and then were stifled in the wake of the Moynihan report of 1965.

Daniel Patrick Moynihan's *The Negro Family: The Case for National Action*, the last major statement of liberal ideology and policy on race and, in effect, the close of the first phase of the civil rights movement, was a pivotal moment in American racial discourse. The report was vehemently criticized by black nationalists and the New Left when it was published. Later, in the 1980s, some of its more emotionally charged arguments regarding African American family structures were appropriated (or misappropriated) by neoconservatives. After the report's disastrous reception, discussion of race became less open, giving way to evasions and euphemisms—to talk of "crime" and "welfare" on one side of the political spectrum and to overly broad characterizations of racism on the other. In my reading, *Beloved* returns to an essentially liberal concern with the traumatic effects of institutional racism and thus revives the tradition of liberal sociology that culminated in the Moynihan report. But Morrison, by emphasizing African American and feminist perspectives, corrects the most damaging liberal errors—the denial of African American culture and agency and the slighting of African American women that characterized liberal thought from E. Franklin Frazier to Moynihan.

The political terms I use in this essay—*liberal, conservative, Reaganist, New Left, black nationalist*—have mobile and fluid meanings that represent conjunctures of complementary and contradictory discursive traditions. Gary Gerstle writes of "the protean character" of twentieth-century liberalism and describes how it coalesced out of certain elements of Progressivism and shifted emphases as a result of the two world wars, the depression, and the social crises of the 1960s. The "liberal" has been sometimes a populist, moralist, or technocrat, sometimes a cold warrior, civil rights activist, or labor activist who deemphasized racial issues. Likewise, conservatism, and its renaissance as Reaganism, is a convergence of disparate movements. Reagan, as Thomas Byrne Edsall observes, was able to "bridge divisions between the country club and the fundamentalist church, between the executives of the Fortune 500 and the membership of the National Rifle Association" (270). In this essay, however, I am concerned with the consensus of attitudes and policies toward race among liberals from the 1930s through the early 1960s that Walter Jackson calls a "liberal orthodoxy." This consensus regarded African American culture as damaged by the legacies of slavery but believed that government interventions in employment, education, housing, and health care could integrate African Americans into mainstream (that is, for these liberals, white) American culture. While the liberal consensus on race was never a national consensus or even a consensus within the Democratic party (and perhaps existed more concretely in the writings of sociologists than in legislative agendas), it exerted significant influence on public policy, particularly on Lyndon Johnson's Great Society programs. In the mid-1960s, however, under the pressures of the Vietnam War, of the white backlash that followed urban rioting, and of activists' resentment of the slowness and ambivalence with which the federal government fulfilled civil rights commitments, the consensus shattered. This essay tells part of the story of the growth and disintegration of the liberal discourses on race, especially those on the African American family.

In reading *Beloved* as an intervention in these discourses, I begin by viewing Sethe's infanticide as an act that is traumatic in the lasting, symptomatic effects of its overwhelming horror and revelatory in its demonstration that the source of the trauma lies in both institutional and familial violence. I then trace the emergence of the liberal consensus on race from the 1930s through the 1960s, describing the importance of theories of the African American family, and show how the fragmentation of the consensus in the mid-1960s, in part because of the Moynihan report, helped produce the discursive context in which Morrison wrote *Beloved*. Finally, I discuss several influential interpretations of *Beloved* that neglect or misinterpret Morrison's portrayal of family violence, particularly the infanticide and the reenactment of it in Sethe's attack on the abolitionist Bodwin.

History and Apocalypse: Locating the Site of Trauma

Beloved is a historical novel. It is based on a documented event—an act of infanticide by the fugitive slave Margaret Garner, who murdered her daughter to prevent the child from being sent back into slavery. Described in a newspaper report Morrison discovered while working on *The Black Book* for Random House, Garner's action becomes the model for Sethe's infanticide. The accounts in the novel of life at Sweet Home and of Sethe's and Paul D's escapes from slavery lead unswervingly toward Beloved's death; likewise, the events that follow the murder remain charged with its horror and cannot be interpreted apart from it. *Beloved*'s narrative spirals around, is ordered by, a traumatic event whose model is historical.

Morrison frames this event, however, in the language of apocalypse. "When the four horsemen came . . . ," the beginning of the chapter in which the infanticide occurs, signals the approach of a world-ending catastrophe. The reference to the book of Revelation makes the slave hunters' entrance into Baby Suggs's yard a sign and portent that transcends history, rends it apart, restructures its movement, and perhaps brings it to an end. The apocalyptic event constitutes a pivotal moment that separates what came before from what comes after. The apocalypse determines the form and direction of everything that follows, and it rewrites all previous history as premonitory.

The apocalyptic event, then, generates new meanings and new historical narratives, as it obliterates old ones. It is a definitive catastrophe, not so much in its finality as in its power to delineate what was implicit all along. As the etymology of *apocalypse* suggests, the event is a revelation, an unveiling. Struggling to kill her children, Sethe "collected every bit of life she had made, all the parts of her that were precious and fine and beautiful, and carried, pushed, dragged them through the veil, out away, over there where no one could hurt them. Over there" (163). The apocalyptic scene, as Morrison presents it, is both catastrophic and revelatory.

In African American intellectual history, a reference to "the veil" evokes W. E. B. Du Bois's *The Souls of Black Folk*, in which the veil is a figure for both American racial separation and African American double consciousness. Du Bois maintains the etymological link between the veil and revelation, as he writes that the American Negro, "born with a veil, and gifted with second-sight in this American world," can achieve "no true self-consciousness" but can only "see himself through the revelation of the other [i.e., white] world" (3). Morrison's characterization of Beloved's death as a forced journey through the veil parallels Du Bois's account of the death of his infant as an escape from the veil: "All that day and all that night there sat an awful gladness in my heart,—nay, blame me not if I see the world thus darkly through the Veil,—and my soul whispers ever to me, saying, 'Not dead, not dead, but escaped; not bond, but free.'" For Du Bois, as for Morrison, release from the veil has apocalyptic significance. "Surely," he writes, "there shall yet dawn some mighty morning to lift the Veil and set the prisoned free" (213). In *Beloved*, however, the apocalyptic unveiling is not deferred to an uncertain future but has taken place and continues to take place within history.

But if this scene of maternal violence is apocalyptic, what exactly does the scene reveal? Four horsemen enter; Sethe pushes Beloved through the veil: a sign, a catastrophe, a revelation. What is revealed? First, that these horsemen are not the cosmic forces of war, drought, pestilence, and famine; they represent, rather, an alliance of political forces, who commit acts of political and racial violence and transgression. In a perfect Foucauldian constellation, the schoolteacher joins with the sheriff—knowledge with power, legal ownership with legal coercion—to enter the property of a free black woman in a free state. For Baby Suggs, the revelation or unveiling in this scene is that "they came in my yard" (179). This trespass means that no African American, slave or free, can genuinely own property or live as a subject in a society that gives overriding value to property rights. Even in a free state and after slavery, the former owners, under the auspices of law and science, can still regard the African American as object, property, and specimen. Morrison reinforces this point in many ways throughout *Beloved*. The first revelation coming under the sign of the four horsemen is of a continuing series of transgressions, violations, and dispossessions. The scene reveals a political and social history whose entire duration—which has not ended—is traumatic and apocalyptic.

The second revelation—Sethe's pushing Beloved through the veil—occurs at the moment when Schoolteacher and the others come into the yard. In the context of white societal, institutional violence against blacks, Morrison describes an act of unspeakable violence between blacks, within an African American family. The catastrophes of continuing white racism and of

African American self-destruction are the twin themes of Morrison's work. Racial violence shapes the social and political space of her novels, while in the foreground—in *The Bluest Eye*, *Sula*, *Song of Solomon*, and *Beloved*—are forms of individual and collective suicide.

Morrison's use of apocalypse to figure trauma is a method for engaging politics and history, not avoiding them. Trauma—the apocalypse of the psychoanalytic narrative, a formative and revelatory catastrophe—obliterates (removes from memory) old modes of life and understanding at the same time that it generates new ones. After the trauma, everything is changed, even as the trauma itself has been forgotten. And yet, the impact of the trauma is continually felt in the form of compulsive repetitions and somatic symptoms. The attempt to work through these effects and remember the traumatic event gives shape to a new narrative, a new history. And, as Morrison recognizes, trauma and symptom, remembering and forgetting, are not merely personal but also social and historical phenomena. Her representation of the familial and political forms taken by the forgetting and remembering of infanticide recalls Cathy Caruth's observations on the role of trauma in the construction of historical narratives. "History can be grasped," Caruth writes, "only in the very inaccessibility of its occurrence." And yet, "history, like trauma, is never simply one's own. . . . [H]istory is precisely the way we are implicated in each other's traumas" ("Unclaimed Experience" 187, 192).

The Moynihan Report, the Critique of Liberalism, and the Denial of Historical Trauma

Because of *Beloved*'s concern with violence committed both against and within African American communities, the novel can be read as an intervention in two distinct but related debates on American histories of race. The neoconservative and Reaganist polemics of the 1980s attributed the poverty and violence of urban ghettos to individual moral deficiencies, as well as to the liberal policies of the War on Poverty. The common factor in these arguments, as Michael Katz writes, was "the attempt to classify poor people by moral worth" (*Undeserving Poor* 140), which culminated in various theories of the "underclass," a group virtually without socialization and composed of single mothers on welfare, drug addicts, and gang members. Writers like George Gilder, Charles Murray, and Lawrence Mead claimed that since the elimination of legal discrimination against racial minorities in the mid-1960s, racial injustice had ceased to have any role in social problems. The few negative reviews of *Beloved* emerged from the conservative position and condemned the novel for setting Sethe's infanticide in the context of general social injustice. Martha Bayles wrote in the *New Criterion*:

> [A] slave commits a crime, but it's not really a crime because it was committed by a slave. The system, and not the slave, stands unjustly condemned for a deed that would possess another meaning if committed in freedom. . . . In Morrison's mind there seems to be only one crime, that of slavery itself, and no person who lives under it has to answer for anything. (36)

Likewise, in the *New Republic*, Stanley Crouch declared that Morrison

> explains black behavior in terms of social conditioning, as if listing atrocities solves the mystery of human motive and behavior. It is designed to placate sentimental feminist ideology and to make sure that the vision of black woman as the most scorned and rebuked of the victims doesn't weaken. (39)

Morrison's emphasis in *Beloved* on the systemic, structural effects of racism opposes the conservative view. The political and psychological links between the good slave owner (Garner), the bad slave owner (Schoolteacher), and the abolitionist (Bodwin) expose a pervasive racism that mere legislation cannot eradicate. The repeated returns of the murdered child's ghost in the North during Reconstruction suggest that racial violence will inevitably return at any time and in any place as long as the systemic nature of racism is not addressed. Morrison responds to the conservative polemics of the Reaganist 1980s by showing that the violence within the African American community cannot be understood without the recognition that law and science, power and official knowledge continue to violate African American lives.

By depicting the most alarming violence within African American communities, however, *Beloved* joins another debate, about the status and representation of the black family. Sethe is a single mother working at a low-paying job. She suffers a mental breakdown and loses her job, and the community must support her. Her sons leave home, never to be seen again. One of her daughters is incapable of leaving home, and Sethe murders the other one. Sethe's family is certainly dysfunctional, if not (to use a loaded term from the Moynihan report) pathological. Since the family has occupied a central and problematic place in discussions of race from the 1960s to the present, reading *Beloved* in the context of the Moynihan report and the debates that followed its publication can help historicize more concretely this novel and Morrison's work, which address African American families so powerfully and painfully.

In June 1965 at Howard University, in a speech cowritten by Daniel Patrick Moynihan (then an assistant secretary of labor), Lyndon Johnson described changes he envisioned in civil rights policies. Congress had passed legislation in 1964 effectively ending legal discrimination against racial minorities, but Johnson argued that legal equality was not enough. "You do not wipe away the scars of centuries by saying: Now you are free to go where you want, do as you desire, and choose the leaders you please." Emphasizing employment, housing, and health care, Johnson sought "not just equality as a right and a theory but equality as a fact and as a result" (126). He announced a conference to be held in the fall of 1965 to discuss the economic problems of black America and to frame policies to address them. In the context of the 1980s, when Morrison wrote *Beloved*, Johnson's speech is an extraordinary document. Johnson spoke of scars, the continuing effects of historical wounds; he acknowledged the history of race as a glaring, traumatic failure in American history. And he spoke of the need for major economic reform, for an equality of result with regard to race.

Needless to say, the massive reforms that Johnson called for did not take place. Neither did the idea of American racial history as traumatic remain on the surface of political discourse; American racial trauma, rather, became submerged, appearing in disguised forms in discussions of crime, welfare, and the underclass. This suppression was due partly to the Vietnam War, which diverted Johnson's attention and the country's resources, and to the white backlash that followed urban racial violence, most immediately the Watts riots, two months after Johnson's speech. And the diminishing of the dialogue on race was due also to major shifts in the thinking and practices of civil rights activists, who in the middle and late 1960s increasingly came to reject the policies of white liberals.

Johnson's speech relied largely on the then unreleased report Moynihan had prepared for the Department of Labor's Office of Policy Planning and Research. A subsidiary but important point of the speech came to be the major topic of contention in the Moynihan report—the view that a breakdown in African American family structures was a major factor in the continuation of black poverty. Borrowing a phrase from Kenneth Clark, Moynihan described black urban life as a "tangle of pathology" at the center of which was "the weakness of the family structure" (76). Moynihan was particularly critical of what he saw as the matriarchal organization of black families. His implication that black women were usurpers and black men emasculated aroused enormous resentment among African American readers. Bayard Rustin, for example, criticized the report for concentrating "almost solely upon what is negative in Negro life" and for neglecting "the degree to which the 'abnormality' of some of the ghetto mores . . . represents a desperate, but intelligent attempt on the part of a jobless Negro to adapt to a social pathology" (422). James Farmer, the director of the Congress of Racial Equality, blamed the report for providing "a massive academic cop-out for the white conscience" (410). Responding to the report's particular animus against "matriarchy," Dorothy Height, the president of the National Council of Negro Women, wrote, "You need recognition of the fact that women have saved the family in the crises of three hundred years, and there would be no family at all without what they have done. There are strengths in the family which should have been brought out by Moynihan" (Rainwater and Yancey 186).

Moynihan's strong endorsement of major investments in employment, housing, and health care programs was forgotten in the controversies surrounding his perceived attacks on black manhood and womanhood, indeed on black culture as a whole. The report, then, furthered the severing of ties between liberal policy makers and African American activists and thinkers, who increasingly turned toward black nationalism and separatism in the late 1960s. As a missed opportunity for changing social policy, as a symptom of liberal insensitivities and of black feelings of militance and vulnerability, as a register of shifts in attitudes about race, the debate over the Moynihan report represents a pivotal moment in American racial discourse.

The report is also, however, the culmination of a line of liberal thinking—a "liberal orthodoxy," as Walter Jackson calls it—on race and the black family that goes back to radical black social scientists like E. Franklin Frazier and Ralph Bunche in the 1930s. They were important sources for Gunnar Myrdal's widely influential book *An American Dilemma: The Negro Problem and Modern Democracy* and for the work of subsequent liberal thinkers and policy makers, including Moynihan. This tradition focuses on the traumatization of African American culture under slavery and on the continuing of racial oppression later. In *The Negro Family in the United States* (1939), Frazier described the history of black family life as a series of wrenching dislocations, the first of which was the nearly total removal from African culture: "Probably never before in history has a people been so nearly completely stripped of its social heritage as the Negroes who were brought to America" (15). Lacking a culture, the slaves were forced to adopt, or at least adapt to, the culture imposed by their masters. After this adjustment, emancipation arrived as a second apocalyptic cultural break—"a crisis in the life of the Negro that tended to destroy all his traditional ways of thinking and acting. To some slaves who saw the old order collapse and heard the announcement that they were free men, emancipation appeared 'like notin' but de judgement day'" (73). The third major disruption in black cultural life came with the great migrations to northern cities, in which rural blacks, "uprooted from the soil," lost their "roots in a communal life and [broke] all social ties" (224). For Frazier, these overarching cultural traumas had specific results destructive to black family life—illegitimate births, the abandonment of families by men, households headed by single women, and thus a family structure Frazier classified as matriarchy. Frazier's book now appears naive in its confident assessments of social and sexual mores. Nevertheless, it argued against the powerful current of "scientific" racism by focusing attention on historical and social determinants of African American family life and denying the possibility of intrinsic or biological racial characteristics of the sort that Schoolteacher in *Beloved* seeks to bolster his racism. Strikingly, however, Frazier's account attributed no agency to African Americans. The African American community was the community traumatized beyond culture.

In *An American Dilemma* (1944), a book that became the major reference for liberal policy makers from the Roosevelt through the early Johnson era, the Swedish sociologist Gunnar Myrdal and his colleagues drew largely on Frazier's description of African Americans, as well as on the work of Ralph Bunche and St. Clair Drake. Yet Myrdal ignored other directions of research, by Melville Herskovits, Carter Woodson, and W. E. B. Du Bois, all of whom stressed the autonomy of African American culture, its continuities with African cultures, and its influences on American society. According to Walter Jackson, Myrdal regarded black history, the discipline being pioneered by Woodson, "as a 'waste field' . . . and he failed to investigate carefully the growing literature that examined black institutions and portrayed Afro-Americans as historical actors rather than as the objects of white action" (112). As Myrdal wrote in *An American Dilemma*, "In practically all its divergences, American Negro culture is not something independent of general American culture. It is a distorted development, or a pathological condition, of the general American culture" (928–29). Like Frazier before him and Moynihan after, Myrdal recommended massive political and economic reforms to create an environment for black social equality. The "American dilemma," however, was to be resolved by white Americans. African Americans, as he depicted them, were too severely damaged by oppression to take an active role in their own redemption.

By the end of 1965, after the Watts riots and the Moynihan controversy, this line of liberal thinking and its implied practices and policies were largely discredited. Civil rights activists stressed the need for African American communities to organize and mobilize themselves rather than rely on policy makers in Washington, and scholarship on African American social structures spoke more of strengths and adaptiveness and less of deficiencies or pathologies. In *Black Power: The Politics of Liberation in America* (1967), Stokely Carmichael and Charles Hamilton declared, "There is no 'American dilemma,' no moral hang-up, and black people should not base decisions on the assumption that a dilemma exists" (77). They rejected the premise that African American culture was merely a shattered distortion of a homogenous white American culture and attacked racial integration as a policy "based on the assumption that there is nothing of value in the black community and that little of value could be created among black people" (53). Carmichael and Hamilton called for African Americans to "win [their] freedom while preserving [their] cultural integrity" (55).

Paralleling these shifts in civil rights theory and strategy were changes in the writing of history and social science. Eugene Genovese and Herbert Gutman challenged liberal assumptions that slavery and racism had overwhelmingly traumatic effects on African American social and family structures. In *Roll, Jordan, Roll: The World the Slaves Made* (1976), Genovese, a Marxist historian, acknowledged that slavery exerted "extraordinary" pressures on black families and "took a terrible toll," but he wrote nevertheless that "the slaves created impressive norms of family life, including as much of a nuclear family norm as conditions permitted, and . . . they entered the postwar social system with a remarkably stable base" (451–52). Considering family life, work, religion, and the open and subtle resistance to slavery, Genovese rejected in particular Stanley Elkins's view that the slaves were passive and infantilized. Gutman's *The Black Family in Slavery and Freedom, 1750–1925* (1976) aimed to show how blacks "adapted to enslavement by developing distinctive domestic arrangements and kin networks that nurtured a new Afro-American culture, and how these, in turn, formed the social basis of developing Afro-American communities" (3). Genovese and Gutman viewed their work as direct responses to Frazier, Myrdal, and Moynihan. Genovese began his chapter "The Myth of the Absent Family" with a reference to "the ill-fated Moynihan Report" and its reliance on Frazier's work, which inaugurated "the conventional wisdom according to which slavery had emasculated black men, created a matriarchy, and prevented the emergence of a strong sense of family" (450). Gutman criticized Frazier for underestimating "the adaptive capacities of slaves and ex-slaves" (10) and devoted much of his afterword to a critical review of the Moynihan report.

The sociologist Carol Stack set out to demonstrate the effectiveness of African American kinship in a housing project in Chicago in the early 1970s. Her *All Our Kin: Strategies for Survival in a Black Community* (1974) was highly influential as contemporary confirmation of Genovese's and Gutman's historical arguments for African American adaptiveness and as a powerful alternative to Moynihan's view. Stack concluded that

> highly adaptive structural features of urban black families comprise a resilient response to the social-economic conditions of poverty. . . . [T]he distinctively negative features attributed to poor families, that they are fatherless, matrifocal, unstable, and disorganized, are not general characteristics of black families living substantially below economic subsistence in urban America. The black urban family, embedded in cooperative domestic exchange, proves to be an organized, tenacious, active, lifelong network. (124)

Thus, by the mid-1970s, in the emerging New Left and black-nationalist analyses, African American culture in general and its family structures in particular were regarded as functioning, adaptive, resistant, and fundamentally healthy. At the same time, since national economic growth declined through the 1970s and the early 1980s and the massive economic and social reforms promised by Lyndon Johnson at Howard University were never accomplished, conditions for urban blacks deteriorated. In response, the New Left and black-nationalist analysts, who denied that there were social problems intrinsic to black urban communities, could offer only generalized descriptions of racism. In embracing Reagan, the American electorate chose conservative positions that revived the old liberal notions of ghetto pathology but that ignored the liberal social policies intended to cure the problems. These parameters define the debate on poverty in the 1980s, in which the right used the term underclass to describe a range of cultural and family pathologies and behaviors, while the left tended to reject the term and its implications altogether. William Julius Wilson relates this debate to the Moynihan report: "The controversy surrounding the Moynihan Report had the effect of curtailing serious research on minority problems in the inner city for over a decade, as liberal scholars shied away from researching behavior construed as unflattering or stigmatizing to particular racial minorities" (4). The discourse of race in the 1980s, then, was constrained by a double denial: Reaganist conservatives denied American racism, and descendants of the New Left denied any dysfunction within African American communities.

Toni Morrison's novels oppose both forms of denials. *Beloved* is a challenge to all American racial discourse of the 1980s—to Reaganist conservatism and to the New Left and black nationalism. The novel revives the liberal position of Frazier, Myrdal, and Moynihan, placing historical trauma—the continuing apocalypse within history—at the center of American race relations. But *Beloved* revises traditional liberalism by insisting on African American personal and cultural agency and on a powerful role for women.

Whereas the right and the left deny trauma in history, *Beloved* insists that a traumatic presence in excess of any discourse is a key factor in historical transmission. The novel should be read as the attempt to describe the "passing on" of "unspeakable thoughts"—and unspeakable actions—"unspoken" (199). Morrison introduces historical trauma into the narrative primarily through the figure of the returning and embodied ghost. There is not space here to discuss in the necessary detail the ghost's status as symptom of the traumas suppressed in the debates I have outlined—how Beloved's returns, her existence in a physical body, her ambivalent, often destructive, connections to symbolic and social structures conflate all the social, personal, and familial traumas of American race relations, which persist to this day. Instead, I turn to the end of the novel, to Beloved's exorcism and the novel's puzzling final chapter, and attempt again to evaluate *Beloved* in terms of American discourses on race. Finally, I relate Morrison's treatment of Bodwin, the abolitionist, to critiques of liberalism and of the Moynihan report.

Bodwin and Moynihan: The Abolitionist as Liberal?

At the end of *Beloved*, the symptomatic ghost disappears, exorcised by the community, at the same moment when Sethe attacks Bodwin, mistaking his appearance for the return of Schoolteacher. Beloved's exorcism and the subsequent dispersal of her memory mark the novel's final repressions of her traumatic signature, after the tombstone inscription that Sethe purchases with her body and Paul D's initial exorcism of the baby ghost. Denver, Sethe's living daughter, is often rightly viewed as a locus of optimism at the novel's conclusion. But we should also recall her participation in the repressing of Beloved's memory when she cuts off her conversation with Paul D. Discussing who or what Beloved was, Paul D begins, "Well, if you want my opinion—." "I don't," replies Denver; "I have my own" (267). While this response is evidence of Denver's new maturity and independence, her maturity also has the effect of ending the discussion. Presumably, as the novel's enigmatic final chapter suggests, Denver and Paul D will never mention Beloved again:

> They forgot her like a bad dream. After they made up their tales, shaped and decorated them, those that saw her that day on the

> porch quickly and deliberately forgot her. It took longer for those who had spoken to her, lived with her, fallen in love with her. . . . So, in the end, they forgot her too. Remembering seemed unwise. . . . [B]y and by all trace is gone. (274)

Thus Beloved is gone, deliberately forgotten, utterly effaced. And yet the Freudian logic of trauma and symptom, which seems to inform this novel, insists that nothing is forgotten. Traumatic memories that are repressed or denied return. Only if traumas are remembered can they lose, gradually but never entirely, their traumatic effects. The narrator of the final chapter can claim that the world at last contains "just weather," that the wind is simply wind and "not the breath of the disremembered and unaccounted for" (275)—that the world is no longer a landscape of symptoms, no longer haunted. But the final word of the novel, "Beloved," shatters this claim. Even if the story is not passed on, the ghost will return to inhabit each succeeding present until the crimes that repeat themselves are worked through in every organ of the body politic. The ending of *Beloved* reminds us of Theodor Adorno's judgment: "We will not have come to terms with the past until the causes of what happened then are no longer active. Only because these causes live on does the spell of the past remain, to this very day, unbroken" (129).

Events in the United States today make it difficult to agree with readers who claim that the exorcism of Beloved represents a successful working through of America's racial traumas. Indeed, in my view, such optimistic interpretations of *Beloved* participate in the repressions and denials of trauma that the novel opposes. For instance, Ashraf Rushdy holds as exemplary Sethe's friend Ella's repressive attitude toward the past, arguing that by "exorcising Beloved, by not allowing the past to consume the present, [Ella] offers Sethe the opportunity to reclaim herself" (584). Rushdy's statement that "the novel both remembers the victimization of the ex-slaves who are its protagonists and asserts the healing and wholeness that those protagonists carry with them in their communal lives" (575) seems particularly suspect in view of the destructive divisions Morrison portrays in the African American community after Baby Suggs's feast. The community comes together under Ella's leadership to expel the naked, pregnant, and beautiful figure of Beloved, who has perhaps finally become the "flesh" that Baby Suggs urged her congregation to love. While the community, led by Ella, overcomes its divisions and readmits Sethe and Denver, the absent space where Beloved stood is another scar in the symbolic order, sutured by repression. The ritual that can put Beloved to rest must instead resemble Baby Suggs's ceremony in the forest, involving laughing, dancing, and crying. Beloved must, first of all, be mourned.

Some readings render not only the exorcism but even the infanticide unproblematic. Bernard Bell describes *Beloved* as a "retelling of the chilling historical account of a compassionate yet resolute self-emancipated mother's tough love." This bizarre formulation relates Sethe's act to "the historical rape of black American women and [to] the resilient spirit of blacks in surviving as a people" (9); both connections are correct, but Bell's interpretation evades what Morrison takes pains not to evade: the traumatic violence within African American communities and the damage to the resilient spirit Bell speaks of.

Bell and Rushdy would agree with Mae Henderson that "the story of oppression becomes a story of liberation; a story of inhumanity has been overwritten as a story of higher humanity" (79). What these and similar interpretations miss, in my view, is that Beloved's story is not over, that the child will return—indeed, has returned. Henderson rightly regards Sethe's attack on Bodwin during the exorcism as a repetition of the apocalyptic (or, as she puts it, "primal") scene of infanticide. However, Henderson sees Sethe's violence against the white abolitionist as part of a successful working through of the trauma of the infanticide, since Sethe, taking Bodwin for Schoolteacher, believes that she attacks the slave owner and not her daughter. "Thus, by revising her actions,' Henderson writes, "Sethe is able to preserve the community, and the community, in turn, is able to protect one of its own" (81).

Bodwin, however, contrary to Henderson's suggestion, is not Schoolteacher. Bodwin is a lifelong and active abolitionist, not an owner of slaves. Sethe, in a state of delusion, mistakes him for Schoolteacher. She sees Bodwin's entrance as portending a reenactment of the apocalyptic scene—that condensation of a multitude of historical traumas—in which her borders were violated by white institutional power and she pushed her daughter through the veil. Henderson's argument raises the question whether there is in fact a hidden connection, recognized by Sethe, between the white abolitionist and the white slave owner. Placing *Beloved* in the context of racial discourses of the 1980s extends the question. Is Sethe's attack on Bodwin an attack also on white liberals? Does Morrison's presentation of Bodwin suggest that, as Kenneth Clark argued in 1964, the white-liberal position on race is a "more insidious" form of racism?

The most prominent evidence for regarding Bodwin as racist is a statuette near the back door of his house of a kneeling black boy, who has an enormous mouth filled with coins for tradesmen and rests on a pedestal bearing the words "At Yo Service" (255). While Bodwin despises slavery, he still regards blacks as subservient and has, apparently, no comprehension of African American culture apart from stereotypes. Moreover, during his ride toward his unexpected encounter with Sethe, Morrison shows Bodwin as a vain and self-absorbed man whose chief interest in abolitionism may have been the feelings of moral elevation and political excitement he derived from the movement personally. And Morrison, I believe, links Bodwin here with a view of 1960s liberalism seen from the 1980s. As Bodwin looks back from *twenty years later* to the time of his greatest political and moral achievements, he muses, "Nothing since was as stimulating as the old days of letters, petitions, meetings, debates, recruitment, quarrels, rescue and downright sedition." For Bodwin, as for liberals and leftists in the age of Reaganism, "those heady days were gone now; what remained was the sludge of ill will; dashed hopes and difficulties beyond repair. A tranquil republic? Well, not in this lifetime" (260). Bodwin (like the liberals) senses that his greatest victory, the abolitionist movement (like the civil rights movement), was only a minor triumph in a larger story of defeat. And in both his self-congratulation and his despair, he remains blind to the interests and culture of African Americans, as his facile memory of the murder of Beloved suggests. He recalls "a runaway slavewoman [who] lived in his homestead with her mother-in-law and got herself into a world of trouble. The Society managed to turn infanticide and the cry of savagery around, and build a further case for abolishing slavery. Good years, they were, full of spit and conviction" (260). Good years, that is, for feelings of moral rectitude; terrible years in their content of racial injustice and suffering.

Bodwin shares with twentieth-century liberals the features that led the civil rights movement of the late 1960s to reject the Moynihan report and the tradition of Frazier and Myrdal. Sethe's attack, like Henderson's interpretation, rejects white liberalism as hypocritical, blind to African American culture, and implicitly critical of (or at least condescending to) the victims of racial oppression. For Morrison, however, these aspects of Bodwin, and of liberalism, are not the whole story. Bodwin is a man with his own history and concerns, which are not congruent with those of African Americans. At the same time, he provides jobs and housing for the African American community, exactly what civil rights activists have demanded since they repudiated the Moynihan report. For all the liberals' spiritual failings, jobs and housing have always been at the center of their agenda—including its embodiment in the Moynihan report and in Lyndon Johnson's original prescriptions for the War on Poverty. Morrison insists that we recognize Bodwin's contribution and therefore realize that Sethe's attack on him is delusional; immersed in the symptom of trauma, she mistakes him for someone else. Sethe is not the only one to make this mistake, as we see in the history of attacks on liberalism from the left and in Henderson's interpretation of Sethe's attack as a successful therapy. Stamp Paid's judgment of Bodwin seems accurate: "He's somebody never turned us down. Steady as a rock. I tell you something, if she had got to him, it'd be the worst thing in the world for us" (265).

This analysis has suggested a kind of detachment for Bodwin. He helps with jobs and housing but remains absorbed in his own concerns. Morrison's portrayal does not allow us to grant Bodwin this detachment. Although the fact barely enters his consciousness, Bodwin is intimately and irrevocably connected to the black community. With his white hair and black mustache, he is a kind of hybrid—a "bleached nigger" to the racists (260). Moreover, the house he is visiting—where Baby Suggs, Sethe, and Beloved lived, the site of apocalyptic and historical trauma—is also the house where he was born. Going to his violent meeting with Sethe, where Beloved was murdered, Bodwin goes to the place of his origin. Neither he nor Sethe knows it, but their histories are entwined.

Bodwin's self-absorption, his privacy, is as delusional in its way as Sethe's attack on him. These qualities, further, define the American—and, in particular, Reaganist—delusions of the 1980s: beliefs that the private, unregulated pursuit of wealth can eliminate poverty, that the poor and the rich, whites and blacks live in separate nations. Like the African American characters in the novel and like most Americans in the 1980s, Bodwin lives under the weight of an enormous repression of personal and historical memory. After all, he returns to 124 not only to pick up Denver for her new job but also to locate things he had buried there as a child. Among these things is a box of tin soldiers, perhaps like the box of tobacco that Paul D uses to hold his unwanted memories. Bodwin wants to "recall exactly where his treasure lay" (261), a recollection that would also reveal, as Jesus says in Matthew, the location of his heart. Bodwin, like Sethe and Paul D, is trying to uncover his heart, which, like theirs, like ours, is buried at a site of historical trauma.

PAMELA E. BARNETT

Figurations of Rape and the Supernatural in Beloved

Toni Morrison's *Beloved* is haunted by history, memory, and a specter that embodies both; yet it would be accurate to say that *Beloved* is haunted by the history and memory of rape specifically. While Morrison depicts myriad abuses of slavery like brutal beatings and lynchings, the depictions of and allusions to rape are of primary importance; each in some way helps explain the infanticide that marks the beginnings of Sethe's story as a free woman. Sethe kills her child so that no white man will ever "dirty" her, so that no young man with "mossy teeth" will ever hold the child down and suck her breasts (251, 70). Of all the memories that haunt Morrison's characters, those that involve sexual abuse and exploitation hold particular power: rape is the trauma that forces Paul D to lock his many painful memories in a "tobacco tin" heart (113), that Sethe remembers more vividly than the beating that leaves a tree of scars on her back, that destroys Halle's mind, and against which Ella measures all evil.

I say that the book is haunted by rape not to pun idly on the ghostly presence that names the book but to establish the link between haunting and rape that invigorates the novel's dominant trope: the succubus figure. The character Beloved is not just the ghost of Sethe's dead child; she is a succubus, a female demon and nightmare figure that sexually assaults male sleepers and drains them of semen. The succubus figure, which is related to the vampire,

From *PMLA* 112:3 (May 1997).

another sexualized figure that drains a vital fluid, was incorporated into African American folklore in the form of shapeshifting witches who "ride" their terrified victims in the night (Puckett 568), and Beloved embodies the qualities of that figure as well. In separate assaults, Beloved drains Paul D of semen and Sethe of vitality; symptomatically, Beloved's body swells as she also feeds off her victims' horrible memories of and recurring nightmares about sexual violations that occurred in their enslaved past. But Beloved functions as more than the receptacle of remembered stories; she reenacts sexual violation and thus figures the persistent nightmares common to survivors of trauma. Her insistent manifestation constitutes a challenge for the characters who have survived rapes inflicted while they were enslaved: directly, and finally communally, to confront a past they cannot forget. Indeed, it is apparent forgetting that subjects them to traumatic return; confrontation requires a direct attempt at remembering.

Morrison uses the succubus figure to represent the effects of institutionalized rape under slavery. When the enslaved persons' bodies were violated, their reproductive potential was commodified. The succubus, who rapes and steals semen, is metaphorically linked to such rapes and to the exploitation of African Americans' reproduction. Just as rape was used to dehumanize enslaved persons, the succubus or vampire's assault robs victims of vitality, both physical and psychological. By representing a female rapist figure and a male rape victim, Morrison foregrounds race, rather than gender, as the category determining domination or subjection to rape.

History and Collective Memory: "The Serious Work of Beating Back the Past"

Two memories of rape that figure prominently in the novel echo the succubus's particular form of sexual assault. The narrator refers several times to the incident in which two "mossy-toothed" boys (70) hold Sethe down and suck her breast milk (6, 16–17, 31, 68–70, 200, 228). No less important, Paul D works on a chain gang in Alfred, Georgia, where prisoners are forced to fellate white guards every morning (107–09, 229). In addition, Ella is locked up and repeatedly raped by a father and son she calls "the lowest yet" (119, 256), and Stamp Paid's wife, Vashti, is forced into sex by her enslaver (184, 232). Baby Suggs is compelled to have sex with a straw boss who later breaks his coercive promise not to sell her child (23) and again with an overseer (144). Sethe's mother is "taken up many times by the crew" during the Middle Passage (62), as are many other enslaved women (180). And three women in the novel—Sethe's mother, Baby Suggs, and Ella—refuse to nurse babies conceived through rape. Other allusions to sexual violation include the Sweet Home men's dreams of rape (10, 11), Sethe's explanation for adopting the mysterious Beloved—her fears that white men will "jump on" a homeless, wandering black girl (68)—and the neighborhood suspicion that Beloved is the black girl rumored to have been imprisoned and sexually enslaved by a local white man who has recently died (119, 235). There are also acts of desperate prostitution that are akin to rape: Sethe's exchange of sex for the engraving on her baby's tombstone (4–5, 184) and the Saturday girls' work at the slaughterhouse (203).

These incidents of rape frame Sethe's explanation for killing her baby daughter. Sethe tries to tell the furious Beloved that death actually protected the baby from the deep despair that killed Baby Suggs, from "what Ella knew, what Stamp saw and what made Paul D tremble" (251): horrific experiences and memories of rape. Whites do "not just work, kill, or maim you, but dirty you," Sethe tells Beloved, "Dirty you so bad you [can't] like yourself anymore." Sethe passionately insists that she protected her beloved daughter and also herself from "undreamable dreams" in which "a gang of whites invaded her daughter's private parts, soiled her daughter's thighs and threw her daughter out of the wagon" (251). For Sethe, being brutally overworked, maimed, or killed is subordinate to the overarching horror of being raped and "dirtied" by whites; even dying at the hands of one's mother is subordinate to rape.

Sethe is haunted by the ghost of the child she has killed; Beloved's return to life corresponds to the return of many of Sethe's painful repressed memories of her enslaved past. Memory is figured as a menacing force in Sethe's life—it seems to stalk her—and she works hard to avoid it. She sees her future as "a matter of keeping the past at bay" and begins each day with the "serious work of beating back the past" (42, 73). As Freud observes in *Beyond the Pleasure Principle*, "[P]atients suffering from traumatic neurosis" are not "much occupied in their waking lives with memories. . . . Perhaps they are more concerned with *not* thinking of it [the traumatic event]" (Caruth 61). Cathy Caruth, in a reading of Freud, argues that such unsuccessful effort is at the center of traumatic experience. Trauma is the event survived, but it is also defined by "the literal return of the event against the will of the one it inhabits" (59), often in the form of hallucinations and nightmares. Traumatic nightmares make the painful event available to a consciousness that could not initially assimilate or "know" it (4). Sethe is traumatized both by the past and by the present task of surviving it. For Caruth, the core of trauma stories is the "oscillation between *a crisis of death* and the correlative *crisis of life*: between the story of the unbearable nature of an event and the story of the unbearable nature of its survival" (7). Sethe's infanticide manifests that correlative crisis as certainly as any story of trauma can: she has survived what she prevents her daughter from surviving.

Beloved, like the repressed, returns against Sethe's will, and when she arrives, she is hungry for more than her mother's love and attention. She has an insatiable appetite, a "thirst for hearing" the "rememoried" stories that animate her ghostly frame, a hunger for the voicing of the unspeakable. As Sethe discloses, "everything" in her past life is "painful or lost," and she and Baby Suggs have tacitly agreed "that it [is] unspeakable" (58). Sethe has never told these stories to Denver or Paul D, but she willingly shares them with Beloved, who feeds on a diet of Sethe's past and serves as the materialization of Sethe's memory.

Beloved also acts as a catalyst for Paul D's recollection of his past. Although she has no particular knowledge of his past, his contact with her brings unpleasant memories to the surface of his consciousness. As Paul D says, Beloved "reminds me of something; something, look like, I'm supposed to remember" (234). Despite the characters' efforts to diffuse the power of the past, the ghost baby, like the traumatic nightmare, intrudes on the present, forcing Sethe and Paul D to remember what they have tried unsuccessfully to forget.

Beloved represents African American history or collective memory as much as she does Sethe's or Paul's individual memory. The narrative merges Beloved's memories of death with the histories of women who endured the Middle Passage, where the institutionalized rape of enslaved women began. Both Sethe's mother and her mother's friend Nan are violated en route to North American slavery. Beloved remembers and recounts their horror: "dead men lay on top of her. . . . [S]he had nothing to eat. Ghosts without skin stuck their fingers in her and said beloved in the dark and bitch in the light" (241).

Morrison has explained in an interview that Beloved speaks "the language of both experiences, death and the Middle Passage" in this section and that the language "is the same" for both ("Realm" 6). But Beloved is also speaking a revised language of rape structured by the historical narratives of rape in slavery. In Beloved's language *white* and *black* are nouns rather than modifiers. Largely about men and women, the available idiom of rape in American culture has obfuscated the centrality of race. For instance, there is no widely recognizable story of white men's rape of black women, and narratives of homosexual rape are even less visible when the victim is black. The only recognizable narrative of interracial rape is what Angela Davis has called "the myth of the black rapist" (172).

Morrison powerfully narrates the rape of black women and of black men by white enslavers. As Morrison has commented, slave narratives are often silent about "proceedings too terrible to relate" (Henderson 63). Harriet Jacobs's *Incidents in the Life of a Slave Girl* is notable for taking sexual exploitation as its explicit subject, and Morrison gestures toward Jacobs's text by violently articulating the history Jacobs delicately describes (Keenan 56). Morrison revises the conventional slave narrative by insisting on the primacy of sexual assault over other experiences of brutality.

Beloved embodies the recurrent experience of a past that the community of women in the novel wants to forget. The women take responsibility for exorcizing Beloved, but Ella, whose life has been irrevocably marked by "the lowest yet," is the most determined to eradicate the violation Beloved represents. Ella has refused to nurse a baby conceived through rape; that child represents a monstrous sign of past horror, and Ella staunchly maintains that such horrors must not intrude on the community's present. Yet through Beloved the women also confront their memories and wounded histories. This attempt to know the incomprehensible trauma done to them is a step toward healing. I say "a step" because Beloved never definitively leaves, not even at the end of the novel. Characters continue to encounter traces of her—footprints that "come and go," the sound of skirts rustling, and the sensation of "knuckles brushing [their] cheek[s]" as they wake from sleep (275). The insistent crisis of trauma is "truly gone. Disappeared, some say, exploded right before their eyes." But Beloved is more than her manifestation. What she represents is always there to be survived. Significantly, "Ella is not so sure" that Beloved is not "waiting for another chance" (263).

"Like a Bad Dream": Beloved and Supernatural Assault

At the end of the novel, Beloved seems to disappear, and the townspeople forget her "like an unpleasant dream during a troubling sleep" (275)—indeed, like a nightmare. In *On the Nightmare* Ernest Jones outlines the derivation of the word *nightmare* from the Anglo-Saxon word for "succubus" or "incubus," *mara*. Jones notes that "from the earliest times the oppressing agency experienced during sleep was personified" (243). Before the community forgets Beloved "like a bad dream," Paul D and Sethe experience her as a sexually menacing nightmare figure (274). After Paul D is forced out of Sethe's bed and from room to room, Beloved visits him in the cold house. He tries to resists her sexual coercion, and he is frightened when she lifts her skirts and pronounces, "You have to touch me. On the inside part." He silently lists the things he must not do if he is to be safe (117). When Paul D does reach the inside part, the act is described as occurring against his will. He finds himself "fucking her when he [is] convinced he [doesn't] want to"

(126). He says there is "nothing he [is] able to do about it" though "he trie[s]" (126). He imagines telling Sethe, "[I]t ain't a weakness, the kind of weakness I can fight 'cause something is happening to me, that girl is doing it . . . she is doing it to me. Fixing me. Sethe, she's fixed me and I can't break it" (127). Near the end of the novel, Paul D remembers this nightmarish experience, but in "daylight he can't imagine it. . . . Nor the desire that drowned him there and forced him to struggle up, up into that girl like she was the clear air at the top of the sea. . . . It was more like a brainless urge to stay alive." He had "no more control over it than over his lungs" (264). The visitation scene ends with Paul D crying out so that he wakes Denver and then himself (117). He survives, and he wakes from his sexual assault as if from a nightmare.

Beloved attacks her mother, Sethe, in a form that more closely resembles that of a vampire. "The Vampire superstition," Jones writes, "is evidently closely allied to that of the Incubus and Succubus. . . . Just as Incubi suck out vital fluids and thus exhaust the victim . . . so do Vampires often lie on the breast and induce suffocation" (125). The vampire is "a blood-sucking ghost or re-animated body of a dead person; a soul or re-animated body of a dead person believed to come from the grave and wander about by night sucking the blood of persons asleep, causing their death" (98). Beloved is the reanimated body of Sethe's murdered baby, and she metaphorically drains Sethe's vitality.

Within moments of being discovered at 124 by Sethe, Paul D, and Denver, Beloved drinks glass after glass of water as water correspondingly gushes from Sethe in a supernatural birthing. The connection between Sethe's body and Beloved's is also evident at the novel's end—Beloved ingests while Sethe is drained. Like the "mossy-toothed" boys who assault Sethe in the barn, Beloved also sucks Sethe dry. Although Sethe is initially thrilled to realize that Beloved is her dead daughter returned, she and Beloved soon enter into a struggle for survival, "rationing their strength to fight each other" (239)—a struggle that Beloved seems to win. As Sethe grows so thin that the flesh between her forefinger and thumb fades, Beloved eats all the best food and grows a "basket-fat" stomach (243). Beloved animates her ghostly flesh with food but also with Sethe's life: "Beloved [eats] up [Sethe's] life, [takes] it, swell[s] up with it, gr[ows] taller on it" (250).

Like the succubus, the vampire drains its victims of fluid in an attack with sexual resonances. H. Freimark writes, "Though it is not an absolute rule, still it can be observed that in most cases women are constantly visited by male Vampires, and men by female ones. . . . The sexual features characterize the Vampire belief as another form of the Incubus-Succubus belief—it is true, a more dangerous one" (Jones 125). The vampire trope is usually played out in the heterosexual paradigm of the earlier nightmare figures, but the vampire figure in *Beloved* enacts an incestuous, homosexual desire. Paul D remarks that Beloved is constantly aroused, but he knows she is not "shining" for him. Rather, her appetite is for Sethe, who is "licked, tasted, eaten by Beloved's eyes" (57). Beloved tells Paul D, "You can go but she is the one I have to have" (76). Sethe experiences Beloved's attentions as a night visitation: Sethe is "sliding into sleep when she [feels] Beloved touch her. A touch no heavier than a feather but loaded, nevertheless, with desire" (58). When Beloved kisses Sethe's neck in the clearing, Sethe is transfixed but suddenly becomes aware that the act is inappropriate. Perhaps she also senses the danger of a kiss on the neck as a prefiguration of a vampiric attack. This haunting is marked by an infantile sexual desire for the mother, as Sethe's reprimand suggests: "You too old for that" (98).

As Beloved drains Paul D and Sethe, her animated ghostly frame becomes an embodiment of the traumatic past and the embodied threat of that past's intrusion on the future. By the end of the novel, Beloved has "taken the shape of a pregnant woman" (261), a manifestation that derives from the medieval belief that "a succubus, or demon masquerading as a voluptuous woman, molested men, while an incubus, a demon masquerading as a man, molested women." It was thought that the two could work in tandem to impregnate sleeping women: "Though sterile, the incubi were said to be able to impregnate women with semen collected from the nocturnal emissions of men" (Guiley 92). In Reginald Scot's *The Discoverie of Witchcraft* (1584), "The divell plaieth *Succubus* to the man and carrieth from him the seed of generation, which he delivereth as *Incubus* to the woman" (*OED*, s.v. *succubus*). Beloved, who plays succubus and incubus, collects sperm from Paul D to impregnate herself, then uses the life force of her mother's body to sustain her spawn. When Ella and the neighborhood women come to drive out the "devil-child," they notice her "belly protruding like a winning watermelon" (250). An effect of heterosexual assault on Paul D, Beloved's pregnancy is a figure for one function of rape in slavery: multiplying human beings as property. But the pregnancy also means that the past of rape threatens to intrude on the future. Beloved's child would represent for the community of women something they wish to exorcize, something they will not tolerate in the future—the memory of children forced on their bodies in the past.

"Mossy Teeth, an Appetite": Sexual Violence, Sucking, and Sustenance

Like Beloved, the other rapists in Morrison's novel attempt to annihilate their victims—sexual violence is figured as eating one's victim up. Beloved embodies the particular violations Sethe and Paul D have suffered, violations characterized by sucking (being sucked or being forced to suck). Through this trope of eating, which links sexual violence with vampirism, a human being becomes the source of another's sustenance. The link to the institution of slavery is clear.

The first assault in the novel, which Sethe tries to forget, appears as a "picture of the men coming to nurse her" (6). The boys cruelly mock the maternal associations of nursing by treating Sethe as an animal to be milked. They enact an assault of the kind perpetrated by alps, the German nightmare figures that suck milk rather than semen or blood (Jones 119). In recollection, Sethe expresses the horror of this violence, which, as the loss of a life-sustaining fluid, prefigures and even structures Beloved's vampiric attack. In other references to rape, Sethe often speaks of appetite. When the white girl Amy finds her lying in the wild onion field and approaches her, Sethe believes she is about to be discovered by another white boy with "mossy teeth, an appetite" (31). And when Sethe has sex with the engraver to pay for the name on her baby's gravestone, the engraver's son looks on, "the anger in his face so old; the appetite in it quite new" (5).

The eating imagery associated with Sethe's rape reappears in the morning ritual of Alfred, Georgia, where prisoners are forced to fellate prison guards. After the prisoners line up, they must kneel and wait "for the whim of a guard, or two, or three. Or maybe all of them wanted it" (107). That whim is announced with taunts such as "Breakfast? Want some breakfast nigger?" and "Hungry, nigger?" which deflect the guards' appetite onto the prisoners and force the prisoners to name it as their own in their reply: "Yes sir" (107, 108). Lee Edelman argues in *Homographesis* that by forcing the prisoners to express homosexual desire, the guards symbolically "castrate" them. This violence is both racist and homophobic: "white racists (literally) *castrate others* while homosexuals (figuratively) *are castrated themselves*" (56). Edelman argues that this scene, where the prisoners are marked with homosexuality, figures the "violent disappropriation of masculine authority that underlies the paranoid relation of black and white in our modern, 'racially' polarized, patriarchal social formation" (54).

In racist American culture the black man signifies the "hole," the "absence of all that constitutes manhood," and thus social domination of black men is often figured as sexual domination of black men by white men (53). This conflation of sexual and racial domination is a product of a prevailing definition of black masculinity as interchangeable with black male sexuality. When black masculinity is not called on to signify excessive virility, it paradoxically often suggests emasculation or social impotence. This discursive formation partly dictates the form of the prisoners' violation.

Symptomatically, the prisoners are emasculated by passive homosexuality—they are forced to "go down" (54), to express their social subordination as desire for penetration, and to assume the "faggot" identity (56). The degradation of being forced to voice desire for one's own rape echoes in Paul D's terrible experience of Beloved. He says he is humiliated by her power to move him from Sethe's bed and by his own uncontrollable "appetite" for her (126).

In Morrison's novel, even a satisfied appetite has negative connotations. When Paul tells Sethe about Halle's breakdown, she likens contemplating painful information to gorging:

> I just ate and can't hold another bite[.] I am full God damn it of two boys with mossy teeth, one sucking on my breast the other holding me down. . . . I am still full of that, God damn it, I can't go back and add more. (70)

Fullness is dangerous for Sethe. During the beating she bites her tongue and fears that she may "eat [herself] up," finishing the job that the boys have started (202). When she imagines that she is about to be discovered by a "hungry" white boy, she thinks of biting him, eating him violently: "I was hungry . . . just as hungry as I could be for his eyes. I couldn't wait. . . . [S]o I thought . . . , I'm gonna eat his feet off. . . . I was hungry to do it. Like a snake. All jaws and hungry" (31). Sethe links appetite with the desire to annihilate, figuring the attack she plans and her own violation in the same terms.

"The Last of the Sweet Home Men": Manhood and Naming

When Paul D realizes the sexual punishment he will suffer on the chain gang, he vomits. Earlier, after an aborted escape attempt, he has endured the horror of being forced to suck an iron bit. These experiences are two of the horrible contents sealed in the tobacco tin Paul D substitutes for his heart. He does not want anyone to get a "whiff of [the tin's] contents" because such a disclosure would "shame him" (73). Thus he places his painful memories "one by one, into the tobacco tin lodged in his chest. By the time he [gets] to 124 nothing in this world [can] pry it open" (113).

But Beloved is not of "this world," and she has the power to force the box open by traumatizing Paul D. Valerie Smith argues that "the act of intercourse with Beloved restores Paul D to himself, restores his heart to him" (348). Late in the novel Paul does express a bewildered and confused gratitude, but what Smith calls a "bodily cure" (348) I view as rape. And yet without this nightmare experience, Paul D would not be able to overcome his numbing defense mechanisms or perform the necessary exorcism. Beloved forces Paul D to reexperience sexual violation; ironically, he might heal if he can assimilate the previously unknowable trauma. Because of the humiliation of succumbing to Beloved, Paul D confronts the pain that he has locked away. As he nears climax, the tobacco tin bursts open and he cries out, "Red heart. Red heart. Red heart" (117). As much as it hurts to feel his heart again, he needs it if he is to love. Unfortunately, Paul D's attempted "incorporation of trauma into a meaningful (and thus sensible) story" does not promote healing.

The subordination Paul D experiences at Beloved's hands, at Sweet Home, and on the chain gang tests his conviction of his own masculinity. He is the only principal character who must deal with two forced sexual encounters, and these encounters are central to his constant meditation on the meaning of his manhood. Paul D is introduced as "the last of the Sweet Home men" (6). Garner, the master of Sweet Home, brags about his "men," but the term seems to be a self-fulfilling designation for the men's productivity. Thus encouraged by Garner, they work hard to make the plantation more productive and thus to make him more prosperous. With the exception of Sixo, the Sweet Home men take pride in their name until they learn, after Garner's death, that they are "only Sweet Home men at Sweet Home" (125). Though free, Paul D continues to ask, "Is that where the manhood lay? In the naming done by a whiteman who was supposed to know?" and to wonder whether Garner was "naming what he saw or creating what he did not" (125, 220). Paul D is certain that Sixo and Halle are men regardless of Garner, but "concerning his own manhood, he [can] not satisfy himself on that point" (220).

Paul D believes that he cannot stop Beloved's assault because he is not "man enough to break out." He needs Sethe even though "it shame[s] him to have to ask the woman he want[s] to protect to help him" (127). But the shame is too great, and rather than ask for help he reverts to anxious assertions of his masculinity. Instead of explaining, "I am not a man," he tells Sethe he wants her pregnant with his child: "suddenly it was a solution: a way to hold onto her, document his manhood and break out of the girl's spell" (128). The connection is clear—he must "document his manhood" because he is a victim of a supernatural rape that he feels has emasculated him just as the guards in Alfred, Georgia, have.

Paul D and his fellow prisoners must choose between saying "yes sir" and death, but they articulate the choice as a choice between manhood and impotence. Stamp Paid says that he "hand[s] over" his wife, Vashti, "in the sense that he did not kill anybody, thereby himself, because his wife demanded that he stay alive" (184–85). But in fact he had no power to offer or deny her body to the white man who enslaved them both. Halle, who sees the attack on Sethe from the loft, is in a similar quandary. He does not fight the attackers, because he hopes to escape with his family. Like Paul D and Stamp, Halle is rendered powerless and ostensibly passive, and Paul D and Stamp both view that position as emasculating. Because the conceptual categories and language Paul D and Stamp know for masculinity cannot account for men oppressed by slavery, both consider their powerlessness a sign of their failure as men. Furthermore, Paul D has been raped, and he cannot speak of that experience in a language that does not account for the sexually victimized male body or that casts that body as feminized. Though he is victimized as a black man in a racist system, he articulates his sexually subordinate position in terms of gender. Thus he struggles alone in the church basement with painful feelings and memories, but he will never be able to confront them publicly or with the help of the community because his shame as a male rape victim is too great. He cannot join the community of women that finally challenges and exorcizes Beloved and what she represents, and his violation remains unspeakable or incomprehensible.

Notably, critics who do refer to Paul D's experience of rape are also confounded by the "unspeakability" of his story, and many write of his violation euphemistically if at all. Although Paul D is distressed by Beloved and unwilling to have sex with her, the incident, because of its supernatural quality, is not easily recognizable as rape, a term bound by legal definitions. But critics treat even Paul D's experience on the chain gang as unrelatable. Valerie Smith describes Paul D as having "endured the hardships of the chain gang" (346); Marilyn Sanders Mobley refers to the "atrocities such as working on the chain gang" (193); Sally Keenan mentions the "story of the prison farm" as something Paul D cannot speak aloud (68). Mae Henderson acknowledges that the boys' assault on Sethe is her primary violation but equates the assault with Paul D's experience of wearing the horse's bit in his mouth, neglecting to mention the final trauma to his hurting heart—"breakfast" in Alfred, Georgia.

Paul D's experience is unrelatable because it exceeds American understandings of rape and gender, but it is also unspeakable because it is dehumanizing. Morrison challenges Paul D's and Stamp's conceptions by emphasizing that Halle's destruction goes beyond his destruction as a man. Halle is reduced to utter madness. When Paul D sees him for the last time, Halle is sitting at the churn, his face smeared with butter—a substance associated with his wife's stolen milk and indicating Halle's relational identification with his family. Halle is primarily a human being who loves, not specifically a man. When Paul D recounts being shackled with a bit in his mouth, he tries to explain to Sethe that the greatest humiliation of all was "walking past the roosters looking at them look at me" (71). Paul D believes that the cock, which, significantly, is named Mister, has smiled at him. This episode makes Paul D feel that he is "something else" and that "that something [is] less than a chicken sitting in the sun on a tub" (72). Because Paul D recognizes Mister as nothing more than a chicken, the scene is unequivocally one of dehumanization rather than of emasculation. Moreover, Paul D understands that the guards in Alfred, Georgia, are "not even embarrassed by the knowledge that without gunshot fox would laugh at them" (162). Morrison suggests that both rapist and victim are dehumanized—the victim left feeling reduced as a human being, the rapist aligned with the animal.

Reinventing the Discourse of Gender and Rape

Beloved explodes the dichotomies not only, as Valerie Smith argues, "between life and afterlife, living and dead, oral and written, self and other, and so on" (350) but also between male and female, rapist and victim. Morrison challenges the idea that sexually subjected bodies fall within clear gender and heterosexual parameters. In reworking Harriet Jacobs's text, Morrison suggests that sexual exploitation is not only the black woman's story of slavery. The gendered discourse of rape, as well as feminist literary criticism that has sought to recover women's lost texts and stories, has unwittingly veiled Paul D's brutalization. Moreover, it seems inconceivable for Beloved to figure as a female rapist because twentieth-century notions of women and rapists exclude the assaultive agency of the succubus (see Elliot). Morrison foregrounds the variability and historicism of the gendered discourse of rape and thus the mutability of seemingly entrenched conceptualizations.

Beloved serves as a powerful reminder that rape was and often still is a racial issue, that it is not, as Susan Brownmiller has asserted, "a process of intimidation by which *all men* keep *all women* in a state of fear" (15). While *male* and *female* do not formulaically describe rapist and victim in the novel, *white* and *black* almost always do. Beloved is a black perpetrator, but she embodies memories of whites' assaults on blacks. Morrison depicts rape as a process by which some white men keep some black women and even some black men in a state of fear. In this way, she constructs a discourse for the rape of black women and men that has been largely absent in twentieth-century America and thus asserts the complex and various powers that structure rape."

In the novel, free African American men and women have survived rape and slavery, but they are not free of the recurrent experience of trauma. They can neither contain nor repress their memories, and hence survival is, as

Caruth says, a kind of crisis. However, the novel suggests that the community might survive at least a gradually mitigating crisis. Once Beloved emerges from the darkness of private dreams and becomes a communal memory, only traces of her remain. Indeed, the last paragraph of the novel claims that "by and by all trace is gone." Yet the closing sentences carry those denied traces. Morrison writes that "the rest is weather. Not the breath of the disremembered and unaccounted for . . . certainly no clamor for a kiss." These deliberate negations are mobilized against a persisting presence. Similarly, the narration repeatedly insists, "[T]hey forgot her," the repetition signaling that the memories can never be "disremembered and unaccounted for" (275). Ella warns that Beloved "[c]ould be hiding in the trees waiting for another chance" (263), and the novel's conclusion suggests that Beloved will get that chance should the community fail to realize that forgetting, not communal memory, is the condition of traumatic return.

Chronology

1931	Toni Morrison born Chloe Anthony Wofford on February 18 in Lorain, Ohio, the second child of George Wofford and Ramah Willis Wofford.
1953	Graduates with B.A. in English from Howard University; changes name to Toni during years at Howard.
1955	Receives M.A. in English from Cornell University for thesis on the theme of suicide in William Faulkner and Virginia Woolf.
1955–57	Instructor in English at Texas Southern University.
1957–64	Instructor in English at Howard University.
1958	Marries Harold Morrison, a Jamaican architect.
1964	Divorces Morrison and returns with her two sons to Lorain.
1965	Becomes editor for a textbook subsidiary of Random House in Syracuse, New York.
1970	Morrison's first novel, *The Bluest Eye* published; takes editorial position at Random House in New York, eventually becoming a senior editor.

1971–71 Associate Professor of English at the State University of New York at Purchase.

1974 *Sula* published and an edition of Middleton Harris's *The Black Book.*

1975 *Sula* nominated for National Book Award.

1976–77 Visiting Lecturer at Yale University.

1977 *Song of Solomon* published, receives the National Book Critics Circle Award and the American Academy and Institute of Arts and Letters Award.

1981 *Tar Baby* published.

1984–89 Schweitzer Professor of the Humanities at the State University of New York at Albany.

1986 Receives the New York State Governor's Art Award.

1986–88 Visiting Lecturer at Bard College.

1987 *Beloved* published and is nominated for the National Book Award and the National Book Critics Award.

1988 *Beloved* awarded Pulitzer Prize in fiction and the Robert F. Kennedy Award.

Since 1989 Toni Morrison has been Robert F. Goheen Professor of the Humanities at Princeton University.

Contributors

HAROLD BLOOM is Sterling Professor of Humanities at Yale University and Professor of English at New York University. His works include *Shelley's Mythmaking* (1959), *The Visionary Company* (1961), *The Anxiety of Influence* (1973), *Agon: Towards a Theory of Revisionism* (1982), *The Book of J* (1990), *The American Religion* (1992), and *The Western Canon* (1994). His forthcoming books are a study of Shakespeare and *Freud, Transference and Authority*, which considers all of Freud's major writings. A MacArthur Prize Fellow, Professor Bloom is the editor of more than thirty anthologies and general editor of five series of literary criticism published by Chelsea House.

MARGARET ATWOOD is one of Canada's most distinguished novelists, poets, and literary critics. Her critical works include *Survival: A Thematic Guide to Canadian Literature* (1972) and *Second Words: Selected Critical Prose* (1982). Among her many novels are *The Handmaiden's Tale* (1986), *Cat's Eye* (1989), *The Robber Bride* (1993), and *Alias Grace* (1996).

ROGER SALE teaches in the Department of English at the University of Washington, Seattle. His works include *Modern Heroism: Essays on D.H. Lawrence, William Empson, and J.R.R. Tolkien* (1973), *Literary Inheritance* (1984), and *Closer to Home: Writers and Places in England, 1780–1830* (1986).

MARILYN SANDERS MOBLEY is Assistant Professor of English at George Mason University. She has written essays on Morrison, Sarah Orne Jewett, Ann Petty, and Zora Neale Hurston. She is currently at work on a study of narrative poetics in Morrison's novels.

SUSAN BOWERS is co-editor of *Gender, Culture, and the Arts: Women, the Arts, and Society* (1993), *Politics, Gender, and the Arts* (1992), and *Sexuality, the Female Gaze, and the Arts* (1992).

BERNARD W. BELL is Professor of English at Pennsylvania State University. His most recent volume of criticism is *The Afro-American Novel and Its Tradition* (1987).

STEPHANIE A. DEMETRAKOPOULOS teaches at Western Michigan University and has written extensively on the interrelationship of psychology and spirituality in literature. She is co-editor of *New Dimensions of Spirituality: A Biracial and Bicultural Reading of the Novels of Toni Morrison* (1987) and author of *Listening to Our Bodies: The Rebirth of Feminine Wisdom* (1983).

LINDA KRUMHOLZ has recently taught American literature as a Visiting Assistant Professor at Oberlin College.

ELIZABETH FOX-GENOVESE is Eleonore Raoul Professor of the Humanities and Professor of History at Emory University. Among her published works are *Feminism Without Illusions: A Critique of Individualism* (1991), *Within the Plantation Household: Black and White Women of the Old South* (1988), and, with Eugene Genovese, *Fruits of Merchant Capital: Slavery and Bourgeois Property in the Rise and Expansion of Capitalism* (1983).

ASHRAF H.A. RUSHDY is author of *The Empty Garden: The Subject of Late Milton* (1992).

JAMES BERGER is assistant professor of English at Hofstra University. He is the author of *After the End: Representations of Post-Apocalypse* (University of Minnesota Press, 1999), from which the essay in this volume is adapted.

PAMELA E. BARNETT is assistant professor at the University of South Carolina. Her articles have appeared in *Women's Studies* and *Signs*; the essay published in this volume is part of her current, book-length project, *The Language of Rape: Sexual Violence and Late-Twentieth-Century American Narrative*.

Bibliography

Crouch, Stanley. "Aunt Medea," *New Republic* (October 19, 1987): 38–43.

Davis, Cynthia. "Self, Society and Myth in Toni Morrison's Fiction," *Contemporary Literature* 23:3 (1982): 323–42.

Goldman, Anne E. " 'I Made Ink': (Literary) Production and Reproduction in *Dessa Rose* and *Beloved*," *Feminist Studies* 16 (1990): 324.

Henderson, Mae G. "Toni Morrison's *Beloved*: Re-membering the Body as Historical Text," *Comparative American Identities: Race, Sex, and Nationality in the Modern Text*. Hortense J. Spillers, ed. New York: Routledge, 1991. 62–86.

Horvitz, Deborah. Nameless Ghosts: Possession and Dispossession in *Beloved*," *Studies in American Fiction* 17 (1989): 157–67.

Keenan, Sally. " 'Four Hundred Years of Silence': Myth, History, and Motherhood in Toni Morrison's *Beloved*," *Recasting the World: Writing after Colonialism*. Jonathan White, ed. Baltimore: Johns Hopkins University Press, 1993. 45–81.

Kubitschek, Missy Dehn. *Claiming the Heritage: African-American Women Novelists and History*. Jackson: University Press of Mississippi, 1991. 174, 177.

Morrison, Toni. *Paradise*. New York: Knopf, 1998.

———. *Beloved*. New York: Knopf, 1987.

———. *Tar Baby*. New York: Knopf, 1981.

———. *Song of Solomon*. New York: Knopf, 1977.

———. *Sula*. New York: New York: Knopf, 1973.

———. *The Bluest Eye*. New York: Holt, Rinehart, & Winston, 1970.

———. "The Pain of Being Black: an Interview with Toni Morrison," with Bonnie Angelo. *Conversations with Toni Morrison*. Danielle Taylor-Guthrie, ed. Jackson: University Press of Mississippi, 1994. 255–61.

———. "In the Realm of Responsibility: A Conversation with Toni Morrison," With Marsha Jean Darling, *Women's Review of Books* (March 1988): 5–6.

———. "Unspeakable Things Unspoken: The Afro-American Presence in American Literature," *Michigan Quarterly Review* 28 (1989): 32.

Otten, Terry. *The Crime of Innocence in the Fiction of Toni Morrison*. Columbia: University of Missouri Press, 1989. 82–83.

Page, Philip. "Circularity in Toni Morrison's *Beloved*," *African American Review* 26:1 (Spring 1992): 31–40.

Sale, Maggie. "Call and Response as Critical Method: African-American Oral Traditions and *Beloved*," *African American Review* 26:1 (Spring 1992): 41–50.

Samuels, Wilfred D., and Clenora Hudson-Weems. " 'Ripping the Veil': Meaning through Rememory in *Beloved*," *Toni Morrison*. Boston: Twayne, 1990. 94–138.

Sitter, Deborah Ayer. "The Making of a Man: Dialogic Meaning in *Beloved*," *African American Review* 26:1 (Spring 1992): 17–30.

Smith, Valerie. " 'Circling the Subject': History and Narrative in *Beloved*," *Toni Morrison: Critical Perspectives Past and Present*. K.A. Appiah and Henry Louis Gates, Jr., eds. New York: Amistad, 1993. 340–54.

Valade, Roger M. III, "Post Aesthetic Movement," *The Essential Black Literature Guide*. New York: Visible Ink Press, 1996. 299.

Acknowledgments

"Haunted by Their Nightmares" by Margaret Atwood from *The New York Times Book Review* (September 13, 1987): 49–50. Copyright © 1987 by The New York Times.

"Morrison's *Beloved*" (originally "American Novels, 1988") by Roger Sale from *Massachusetts Review* 29:1 (Spring 1988): 81–86. Copyright 1988 by the Massachusetts Review.

"A Different Remembering: Memory, History and Meaning in Toni Morrison's *Beloved*" by Marilyn Sanders Mobley from *Modern Critical Views: Toni Morrison*, edited by Harold Bloom. Copyright © 1988 by Marilyn Sanders Mobley.

"*Beloved* and the New Apocalypse" by Susan Bowers from *The Journal of Ethnic Studies* 18:1 (Spring 1990): 59–75. Copyright © 1990 by The Journal of Ethnic Studies.

"Fleshly Ghosts and Ghostly Flesh: The Word and the Body in *Beloved*" by David Lawrence from *Studies in American Fiction* 19: 2 (Autumn 1991): 189–201. Copyright © 1991 by Northeastern University.

"*Beloved*: A Womanist Neo-Slave Narrative; or Multivocal Remembrances of Things Past" by Bernard W. Bell from *African American Review* 26:1 (Spring 1992): 7–15. Copyright © 1992 by Bernard W. Bell.

"Maternal Bonds as Devourers of Women's Individuation in Toni Morrison's *Beloved*" by Stephanie A. Demetrakopoulos from *African American Review* 26:1 (Spring 1992): 51–59. Copyright © 1992 by Stephanie A. Demetrakopoulos.

"The Ghosts of Slavery: Historical Recovery in Toni Morrison's *Beloved*" by Linda Krumholz from *African American Review* 26:3 (Fall 1992): 395–407. Copyright © 1992 by Linda Krumholz.

"Unspeakable Things Unspoken: Ghosts and Memories in *Beloved*" by Elizabeth Fox-Genovese published as "Unspeakable Things Unspoken: Ghosts and Memories in the Narratives of African-American Women" from *The 1992 Elsa Goveia Memorial Lecture presented at The University of the West Indies, Mona, Jamaica, 26 March 1992*. Copyright © 1993 by the Department of History, The University of the West Indies.

"Daughters Signifyin(g) History: The Example of Toni Morrison's *Beloved*" by Ashraf H.A. Rushdy from *American Literature* 64:3 (September 1992): 567–97. Copyright ©1992 by Duke University Press.

"*Beloved*: Toni Morrison's Post-Apocalyptic Novel" by Josef Pesch from *Canadian Review of Comparative Literature* 20:3–4 (September-December 1993): 395–408. Copyright © 1993 by the Canadian Comparative Literature Association.

"Toni Morrison's *Beloved*: History, "Rememory," and a "Clamor for a Kiss" by Caroline Rody from *American Literary History* 7:1 (Spring 1995): 92–117. Copyright © 1995 by Oxford University Press.

"Ghosts of Liberalism: Morrison's *Beloved* and the Moynihan Report" by James Berger from *PMLA* 111:3 (May 1996): 408–19. Copyright © 1996 by The Modern Language Association of America.

"Figurations of Rape and the Supernatural in *Beloved*" by Pamela E. Barnett from *PMLA* 112:3 (May 1997): 418–27. Copyright © 1997 by The Modern Language Association of America.

Index

VIVA Modern Critical Interpretations

Available Titles in the Series

Viva

Alice's Adventures in Wonderland

9788130906362 Rs. 145

Animal Farm

9788130906355 In Print

As You Like It

9788130918723 Rs. 195

The Adventures of Huckleberry Finn

9788130907390 Rs. 165

Beowulf

9788130907406 In Print

Beloved

9788130918884 Rs. 195

Black Boy

9788130906737 Rs. 125

Brave New World

9788130906348 In Print

Cat on a Hot Tin Roof

9788130906393 Rs. 99

VIVA Modern Critical Interpretations

Available Titles in the Series

Crime and Punishment

9788130906409 Rs. 175

The Chronicles of Narnia

9788130907468 Rs. 145

The Crucible

9788130906416 Rs. 125

Darkness at Noon

9788130906423 Rs. 145

David Copperfield

9788130918730 Rs. 145

The Death of Artemio Cruz

9788130907475 Rs. 145

Death of a Salesman

9788130906744 Rs. 125

The Divine Comedy

9788130918846 Rs. 175

Don Quixote

9788130904658 Rs. 125

VIVA Modern Critical Interpretations

Available Titles in the Series

Viva

Dracula

9788130906430 Rs. 195

Emerson's Essays

9788130906577 Rs. 175

Emma

9788130918839 Rs. 165

A Farewell to Arms

9788130918754 Rs. 175

Frankenstein

9788130907413 Rs. 145

The General Prologue to the Canterbury Tales

9788130918747 Rs. 175

The Glass Menagerie

9788130907482 In Print

The Grapes of Wrath

9788130906751 Rs. 145

Great Expectations

9788130904597 Rs. 175

VIVA Modern Critical Interpretations

Available Titles in the Series

Viva

The Great Gatsby
9788130906454 Rs. 145

Gulliver's Travels
9788130906461 Rs. 195

Hamlet
9788130918877 Rs. 165

The Iliad
9788130907895 Rs. 145

Invisible Man
9788130906485 In Print

Heart of Darkness
9788130918815 Rs. 165

Jane Eyre
9788130918860 Rs. 195

Julius Caesar
9788130906492 Rs. 125

King Lear
9788130918853 Rs. 165

VIVA Modern Critical Interpretations

Available Titles in the Series

Viva

Moby-Dick

9788130906546 Rs. 165

Oedipus

9788130906768 Rs. 165

One Flew Over the Cuckoo's Nest

9788130907444 Rs. 125

One Hundred Years of Solitude

9788130907451 In Print

The Old Man and the Sea

9788130906553 Rs. 125

Othello

9788130918891 Rs. 165

Paradise Lost

9788130906560 In Print

The Pardoner's Tale

9788130904665 Rs. 125

A Passage to India

9788130906584 Rs. 145

VIVA Modern Critical Interpretations

Available Titles in the Series

Persuasion

9788130906591 Rs. 175

Pride and Prejudice

9788130906607 Rs. 195

The Red Badge of Courage

9788130906614 Rs. 145

Romeo and Juliet

9788130906621 In Print

The Rubaiyat of Omar Khayyam

9788130904641 Rs. 145

The Scarlet Letter

9788130907505 Rs. 175

Silas Marner

9788130906638 Rs. 125

Song of Solomon

9788130906645 Rs. 145

Sophie's Choice

9788130906652 Rs. 175

Modern Critical Interpretations

Available Titles in the Series

The Sound and The Fury

9788130906676 Rs. 195

A Streetcar Named Desire

9788130918716 Rs. 145

Sonnets

9788130918907 Rs. 165

A Tale of Two Cities

9788130906683 Rs. 145

The Tempest

9788130918822 Rs. 175

To Kill a Mockingbird

9788130906775 Rs. 125

Waiting for Godot

9788130906706 Rs. 99

Ulysses

9788130906690 Rs. 145

The Waste Land

9788130904689 Rs. 175

Wuthering Heights

9788130906713 Rs. 175

Young Goodman Brown

9788130906720 Rs. 125